MONACANS AND MINERS

Samuel R. Cook

MONACANS AND MINERS

Native American and Coal Mining Communities in Appalachia

University of
Nebraska Press
Lincoln & London

© 2000 by the University of Nebraska Press
Manufactured in the United States of America

Library of Congress Cataloging-in-Publication Data
Cook, Samuel R., 1965–
    Monacans and miners : Native American and coal mining com-
munities in Appalachia / Samuel R. Cook.
        p. cm.
    Includes bibliographical references and index.
    ISBN 0-8032-1505-3 (cloth : alk. paper) — ISBN 0-8032-6412-7
(pbk. : alk. paper)
    1. Monacan Indians—Virginia—Amherst County—History. 2.
Monacan Indians—Virginia—Amherst County—Social conditions.
3. Irish Americans—West Virginia—Wyoming County—History.
4. Irish Americans—West Virginia—Wyoming County—Social conditions. 5. Scottish Americans—West Virginia—Wyoming
County—History. 6. Scottish Americans—West Virginia—Wyoming County—Social conditions. 7. Coal mines and mining—West
Virginia—Wyoming County—History. 8. Amherst County (Va.)—
History. 9. Wyoming County (W. Va.)—History. I. Title.
E99.M85 C66 2000
975.4'45004973—dc21   00-036502

For the mountains of the Virginias.

The most forgiving landscape I know.

CONTENTS

ILLUSTRATIONS

PHOTOGRAPHS *following p. 134*

MAPS

TABLE

ACKNOWLEDGMENTS

It seems unjust to restrict my acknowledgements to the few pages allotted here, as there are too many people in this world who helped to make this book a reality. The obvious place to begin is with the editors of the University of Nebraska Press who were enthusiastic about my work from the outset.

This book evolved from my dissertation research. Therefore I owe an endless debt of gratitude to my Ph.D. committee members at the University of Arizona who convinced me of my potential, pushed me at just the right times, but always knew when to give me space to grow.

First and foremost, I thank Dr. David E. Wilkins who has been a friend and mentor since the first day I set foot on the University of Arizona campus. At times I thought David was pushing me beyond my limits when he actually saw a potential within me that needed to be honed. As David's student and research assistant I learned more about archival research in one semester than most people (including scholars) learn in a lifetime. I can honestly say that until David became my mentor, I did not realize what it meant to be a critical thinker. Academic mentoring aside, David was always there throughout my graduate career when I needed moral support. His wife Evelyn and children Sion, Niłtooli, and Nizhone, to whom I am

XII ACKNOWLEDGMENTS

also indebted, have welcomed me into their home and offered me their unconditional friendship. Thank you all.

The second of my mentors at Arizona was Dr. Tom Holm, who is still known for his open-door policy both in the office and at home. Tom has consistently provided me with a sea of constructive criticism, sage advice, and many good laughs. In acknowledging his generosity as a professor and as a friend, I must also thank his wife Ina and sons Garret and Mike for putting up with a constant flow of students in their home.

The third in my triumvirate of mentors at Arizona was Dr. Nancy Parezo, whose brutally practical advice and advocacy for me have only been surpassed by her friendship. Nancy's many noteworthy accomplishments pale in the wake of the inspiration she has provided for her students. It is no wonder that she is often seen at professional meetings with a formidable entourage of students, old and new, surrounding her. I cannot adequately express how much I appreciate her guidance over the years.

I am also thankful for the support of my other committee members who saw me through preliminary exams and ensured that my dissertation research was off to a good start. I am thankful to Dr. Barbara A. Babcock, who has been an inspiration to say the least, and who went above and beyond the call of duty to help me clear various obstacles during my graduate career. Likewise, I cannot forget Dr. Michelle Grijalva, who has the rare gift of making anyone see the value of their own knowledge. Endless thanks are also due to Shirley Dickey, Mary Staugaard, and Dawn Winsor-Hibble, the graduate administrative assistants in whose hands my academic fate rested at various points in my graduate career.

Considerable research and revising followed the completion of my dissertation, and certain individuals have had a profound bearing on the final product. My deepest debt goes out to the reviewers of the manuscript for this book. Dr. Paul Salstrom has been an inspiration to me since the publication of his first book, so it was an incredible honor to receive his constructive and meticulous comments on my manuscript. Likewise, Dr. Jeffrey Hantman's familiarity with the contemporary Monacan community has been invaluable to me, and his acute theoretical knowledge of ethnic politics and the construction of identity helped me to bring this study into perspective. It is with great humility that I say that the privilege of having such esteemed scholars review and endorse my work is an important milestone in my life.

Several of my esteemed colleagues deserve thanks for their support, comments, and patience prior to and during the writing of this book. At the University of Arizona, the late Robert K. "Uncle Bob" Thomas turned my attention back to the Southeast (to my knowledge, Uncle Bob was the only cultural anthropologist until now to have spent any significant length of time with the contemporary Monacans). I am also indebted to Jay Stauss, director of American Indian Studies, for providing support at vital points in my graduate career. I would also like to acknowledge Vine Deloria Jr., Carol Kramer, the late Daniel Nugent, Jane Hill, Robert A. Williams, and Ofelia Zeppeda for their lasting influence on my academic destiny. Cliff and Donna Boyd, Melinda Wagner, and Mary LaLone at Radford University offered consistent words of praise during my tenure in the anthropology department, both as an instructor and as a student ten years earlier. At Virginia Tech, Betty Fine, Anita Puckett, and my old friend Jeff Corntassel (whom I've known since graduate school) have provided moral and academic support and constructive feedback. Finally, it would be a grave injustice to deny my debt to my old friends and colleagues, Eric Lassiter and Cedric Woods for their knowledge and empathy.

My fieldwork would not have been possible if certain individuals had not opened doors and made my transition smooth. At Bear Mountain my endless gratitude goes out to George Whitewolf, who introduced me to his Nation. I am also indebted to Diane Johns Shields for her infinite generosity in its many forms, to her brother Johnny Johns for his friendship and ideas, to Karenne Wood for her advocacy and creative temperament, to Phyllis Hicks for her hospitality and courage, and to B. Lloyd for his many miles on the road and for knowing where everyone lives. In Wyoming County it would have taken me a long time to get to know people again had it not been for Wanda Lester in the southern part of the county, Paige Cline in Pineville, and Jack and Sarah Lou Frank in Mullens. I am also indebted to Jack Feller and William "Sarge" McGhee, respected local historians and sages.

Ethnohistorians are not excused from archival research, and thus I am obliged to acknowledge the importance of certain regional and local archives in the creation of this book. I would like to thank the good people at the Highlander Research and Education Center in New Market, Tennessee, for opening their library to me, both as a scholar and as an activist. I am also indebted to the Monacan Indian Nation for giving me free access to the archives in the Ancestral Museum, and for giving me permission to use numerous letters and photographs. I am especially indebted to the University of Virginia's Alderman Library Special Collections archivists for granting me access to photographs from the Jackson Davis Collection. Finally, I thank Stuart McGehee and the people at the Eastern Regional Coal Archives of the Craft Memorial Library, Bluefield, West Virginia, for allowing me to reprint vintage photographs from the Wyoming County coalfields.

Having acknowledged my professional debts, I am compelled to express my endless gratitude and love for a number of friends and relatives who have helped me all along my journey, and who have in some way influenced the outcome of this book. Without intending to rank friendships, I begin with those who have recently honored me in ways that I cannot begin to repay. Presley and Toni Hickman have been my loyal friends from almost the beginning of my tenure in Arizona, and they acknowledged the depth of that friendship when they asked me to carry the water at their traditional Navajo wedding. I am proud to call their son Nazhone my nephew. Likewise, Michael Keller and Leslie Shiel, who recently honored me beyond words when they asked me to be the godfather of their daughter Jordan, have consistently and sincerely followed my progress from the time this book was a vague idea. My old friends Frank and Kelli Huffman saw me through many intense times, good and bad, and offered their assistance when possible. So many others offered tremendous support which, as far as I am concerned, is woven into this book, including Thurman and Josephine Lester, Carl Cook, Jayne and Neal Penny, Gary Nichols, Concetto Arena, Eda Saynes-Vasquez, Terry Abrams, Charles England, Mariah Gover, Phyllis Eagletree, Tammie Curtis, Lucian Branham, Larry Gibson, Dovie Thomason and Mick Sickles, and Shirley Stewart. I wish I could devote a chapter to each of you for the various ways you have positively impacted my life.

Finally, but in no way least of all, I thank those closest to me beginning with my father, the late Thomas E. Cook, who left behind some shoes that I can never begin to fill, and who is still beside me when I need him most. My unconditional love and gratitude also goes to my mother, Mary A. Cook, whose sacrifices for my benefit I will never be able to repay. Where would I be without you? And although my parents have a longer track record of dealing with me, my undivided love, trust, and gratitude go to my partner, Susan Fleming, who I feel like I've known for thousands of years. You and your sons Ian and Morgan have been inspiring and patient on this final stretch. Finally, I thank the Creator, for everything.

* * *

The early stages of research for this book were made possible through a grant from the Graduate College of the University of Arizona. Small portions of chapters 6 and 7 were previously published in an article entitled "The Depression, Subsistence, and Views of Poverty in Wyoming County, West Virginia," in *The Journal of Appalachian Studies* 4, 2 (fall 1998).

MONACANS AND MINERS

INTRODUCTION

A Regional Comparison

"No one today is purely *one* thing," wrote cultural critic Edward Said in *Culture and Imperialism.* "Labels like Indian, or woman, or Muslim, or American are not more than starting points, which if followed into actual experience for only a moment are quickly left behind" (Said, 1993: p. 336). If this is the state of the world today, anthropology is in flux. We can no longer categorize or isolate cultures for any extent of time before we have to rethink what we have done. It is no longer possible to produce "original" ethnographic works in the tradition of Malinowski's *Argonauts of the Western Pacific* (1922) or Evans-Pritchard's *The Nuer* (1940). Not only have such cultures been studied and written about time and again, but it seems we have finally reached a stage in the development of the profession at which culture can no longer be isolated and treated as static for any practical purpose: "While such primordial phenomena as traditions, communities, and kinship systems continue to be documented," writes Marcus, "they can no longer in and of themselves serve as the grounding tropes . . . which organize ethnographic description and explanation" (1994: p. 44). In short, cultural *change* is virtually all that is left to study in anthropology.

With the arrival of Wallerstein's (1975) world-system theory in the mid-1970s, there emerged a collective understanding in the so-

1

cial sciences that no culture, society, or single political unit could exist autonomously or in absolute isolation. Hence, in his *Europe and the People without History* (1982), Eric Wolf engaged the world-systems approach, urging us to realize that virtually all cultures today can only be understood in relation to the expansion of capitalism. Some anthropologists have taken this approach a step further to argue that the technological advances accompanying capitalist expansion in the aftermath of the cold war have set in motion a global process of cultural homogenization. So profound is this process that certain cross-cultural contexts are marked by "a diffusion of cultural traits gone wild, far beyond that imagined by the Boasians" (Kearney, 1995: p. 557). Ironically, global homogenization does not always signal the end of "otherness," but often serves to solidify and widen age-old contradictions (such as differential cross-cultural perceptions of the reproductive rights of women [Ginsburg and Rapp, 1995]) and constraints (such as enduring colonial situations in Latin America [Gledhill, 1994]).

How do we cope with cultural change and globalization in anthropology? Given the contradictions historically embedded in the discipline, it is difficult. As Lewellen succinctly notes, "Anthropologists seek no less than an understanding of humankind, yet they are suspicious of any generalization at all. They idealize a holistic view, yet by the very complexity of the systems they confront, they are forced to isolate small subsystems. . . . In sum, anthropologists are torn between diametrically opposed demands" (1992: p. 5).

This book is an effort to address these contradictions in anthropology by confronting contradictions in global processes. I make no claim of overcoming these contradictions; instead I move *toward* a holistic perspective by comparing the similarities and differences of two complex communities within a broad region. I do this by consolidating various theoretical perspectives and crossing disciplinary lines, bearing in mind that "history matters" (Wolf, 1997: p. ix). This book is about two communities in a region that epitomizes the contradictions of capitalist expansion and global homogenization. Appalachia, the broad geographical focus of this study, is quite simply an enigma. While the vast and diverse natural resources of the region offer the potential for local economic prosperity, much of the region is characterized by widespread poverty. What is more perplexing is the lack of regionwide cultural, economic, and environmental homogeneity. Resources and industry vary widely from subregion to subregion; some communities seem to fare better than others. And yet the same symptoms of uneven development—unemployment, poor health and housing, outmigration, and so forth—seem to be common themes throughout Appalachia at this time.

According to physical geographers, the Appalachian mountain chain reaches from Ontario to eastern Texas (Guyot, 1974). However, as Batteau (1990) convincingly argues, the *concept* of Appalachia is a fluid social construction that emerged with the expansion of America—a formidable testing ground for "otherness"—that is defined according to the specific agendas of various policymakers, media representatives, and activists. As David Whisnant correctly notes, "Appalachia's boundaries have been drawn so many times that it is futile to look for a 'correct' definition of the region" (1994: p. 134).

One of the most consistently cited definitions of the region was articulated by the federal Appalachian Regional Commission (ARC) in the 1960s to guide development strategies in the mountains and contiguous areas. The ARC's Appalachia (one of the most expansive but arbitrary renderings) consists of 400 counties in thirteen states, including long-term pockets of poverty from New York to Mississippi (ARC, 1974). However, Campbell's (1921) "traditional" definition of the region, based on what he perceived as clusters of sociocultural homogeneity, appears still to reflect most popular and scholarly *cognitive* perceptions of the region (see Raitz and Ullack, 1984: p. 14). According to Campbell, Appalachia consists of 205 counties in nine states from Maryland southward (with Kentucky on the western edge, Alabama and Georgia on the south, Virginia and the Carolinas in the east, and West Virginia in the dead center). Included in this area are four distinct geophysical provinces: the Allegheny Plateau, an area of rugged V-shaped valleys in which Wyoming County, West Virginia, lies; the limestone rich Ridge and Valley province, which includes the vast Shenandoah and adjacent valleys; the Blue Ridge Mountains of Virginia, North Carolina, and Georgia; and the Piedmont, gently rolling hills at the base of the Blue Ridge (Campbell, 1921: p. 12; Raltz and Ullack, 1984: pp. 41–49). Amherst County, Virginia, straddles the latter two provinces.

Rather than articulating yet another definition of Appalachia, I will adopt Campbell's rendering and refer to it as Southern Appalachia. This is the portion of the region that has drawn most attention from scholars, policymakers, and activists from within and without the region and especially from mainstream America.

Appalachia has received no shortage of scholarly attention, but surprisingly little has come from anthropologists. Those who do write about the region are virtually obliged to focus on themes of exploitation (Lewis, 1970; Lewis, Johnson, and Askins, 1978; Anglin, 1992, 1993) and themes of rapid cultural change in the midst of capitalist integration (Beaver, 1986; Stewart, 1996). This is precisely why Appalachia warrants closer attention. Appalachia is a paradox. For years outsiders have circumscribed it as a homogeneous sociocultural entity, when it never was. Now, as more anthropologists and other social scientists are seriously exploring the region's heterogeneity, globalization has long been at work. Appalachia has served for years as America's own unique "other"; now perhaps it is in danger of becoming a measuring stick for the homogenizing capacity of the capitalist world-system.

At the heart of this book is a comparative analysis of variations in internal colonial processes and conditions of dependency in Appalachia. I posit that the internal colonial and dependency models are complementary approaches to understanding the political economy in specific contexts. I use these two primary theoretical approaches to compare two very different communities within the Appalachia region. First, I examine the colonial experiences of the Monacan Indians of Amherst County, Virginia, historically and ethnographically. The politics of race have figured prominently (and often pejoratively) in shaping their history, if not in shaping who the Mona-

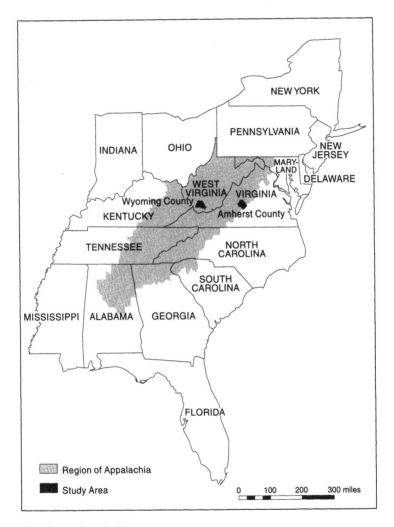

Southern Appalachia

cans are today. For contrast, I then examine the experiences of the residents of Wyoming County, West Virginia, a nonindigenous settler population now dominated by the coal industry. The basic premise of this study is that both communities were colonized by external forces at various points in time, and subsequently became integrated as subordinates in relationships of economic dependency.

This study uses one of anthropology's oldest methodological instruments—the controlled comparison—which necessarily implies that certain generalizations regarding social structure, economic organization, and so forth will be made. However, because I am also concerned with dynamic processes, I additionally draw on theoretical and methodological tools of other schools and disciplines. From history, for example, I have borrowed the "new rural history" approach (Mitchell, 1977; Salstrom, 1994: pp. 4, 45–50) for understanding the statistical implications of preindustrial commercial activity in the mountains. From comparative politics I have borrowed the "most different systems" method of binary analysis (Dogan and Pelassy, 1984: p. 144). Such an approach has allowed me to illuminate variables in the respective colonial processes and situations of dependency and this binary approach permits a "detailed confrontation" (Dogan and Pelassy, 1984: p. 127) that would have been less feasible had too many divergent cases been considered. Other theoretical and methodological perspectives—including neomarxian, world-systems, substantive exchange theory, ethnogenesis, and discourse analyses—have been drawn into this study at various stages. In sum, to navigate the breach between generalization and holism I have embraced the Foucaultian notion of theory as a "toolkit," which suggests that investigation "can only be carried out step by step on the basis of reflection (which will necessarily be historical in some of its aspects) on given situations" (Foucault, 1980: p. 145).

The esteemed legal scholar Felix S. Cohen (who literally wrote the book on American Indian law) once made the famous statement: "For us, the Indian tribe is the miner's canary and when it flutters and droops we know that the poison gasses of intolerance threaten all other minorities in our land. *And who of us is not a member of some minority?"* (1949: pp. 313–14). Although one of the groups involved in this study is a Native American community, this book is not exclusively about Native Americans. However, it might be suggested that the Monacan experience vis-à-vis regional and national political economies has implications for anyone who is less than equitably integrated into the world-system. The Monacans have endured over three hundred years of colonial domination, beginning with the British Crown and continuing through the epoch of the eugenics movement in Virginia, a movement for which the Monacans served as scapegoats. In spite (or perhaps, because) of it all, the Monacans have maintained a collective sense of ethnic "peoplehood" (in the sense that Barth [1969] and Spicer [1971] used the term). In fact, the past thirty years have seen dramatic changes in local and national political, social, and economic circumstances that have brought about favorable conditions for the tribe as a whole. For example, the Civil Rights movement coalesced with the decline of the orchard industry in Amherst County (a system that had exploited Monacan labor disproportionately and often without pay) at the same time miscegenation laws were ruled unconstitutional, the latter having been used to justify the exploitation of virtually free Monacan labor. Since then the tribe has gained official recognition from Virginia's state government and has reclaimed a small portion of its aboriginal land base. Yet the Monacans now find themselves at a precarious crossroads. They are currently petitioning the federal government for recognition as a sovereign Indian nation, and if denied may suffer a sobering blow to their collective esteem. At the same time, as tribal members are drawn more deeply into wage dependency in nearby metropolitan areas, indigenous modes of production are challenged and transformed more rapidly than ever (keeping in mind that they were never static) and the delicate sinew of community is being tested beyond its limit. Finally, whatever victories the Monacans can claim over colonial oppression, the specter of racism still rattles its chains in Amherst County.

Cohen's quote rings with particular irony when considered in light of the other community involved in this study. Wyoming

County, West Virginia, is populated primarily by the descendants of
Scotch-Irish settlers who arrived in the area at the end of the eighteenth century, and by a few descendants of later waves of industrial
migrant workers. Wyoming was one of the last West Virginia counties to be dominated by the coal industry; in fact, many residents
survived as relatively self-sufficient subsistence farmers into the
1930s. However, industrialization became complete in the wake of
the Great Depression, and relations of economic dependency between Wyoming County and the metropolitan areas are now firmly
entrenched (and seemingly irreversible). This structural relationship of dependency is held in place by a formidable (internal) colonial system that developed with the emergence of West Virginia as
an independent state. Since its inception, the state political system
has been dominated by and beholden to industrial capitalists. Tangible manifestations of this power structure are seen in Wyoming
County, where as much as 90 percent of the local land base is owned
by absentee industrialists (especially coal barons), who contribute
virtually nothing to the local tax base. Hence the political efficacy of
grassroots voices is extremely limited.

Thus, this book highlights a remarkable and rather anomalous
situation in which an *indigenous* (Native American) community has
actually managed to weaken the shackles of colonialism and dependency and seems to have become more equitably integrated into the
political economy than are certain *nonindigenous* communities in the
same broadly defined region. This calls into question the uniformity
of the assertion of certain scholars that Native Americans are the
most powerless people in America (e.g., Thomas, 1966/67; Jorgensen, 1971). It also suggests that power relations within the
world-system, especially relations of domination or dependency,
need not be viewed as permanent, but can change under certain circumstances.

The controlled comparison I propose is valuable for several reasons. First, while numerous scholars have pointed out that Appalachia is not a homogeneous region (e.g., Williams, 1972; Billings,
1974; Ergood, 1983; McCoy and Watkins, 1983; Whisnant, 1994),

scholars tend to focus on central Appalachian coal communities as the prototype for underdeveloped Appalachian communities. This particular comparison reveals the heterogeneity of Appalachia from a political, cultural, and demographic perspective. The Monacans represent a relatively homogeneous cultural and political entity that has remained enclaved in its ancestral homeland straddling the Virginia Blue Ridge Mountains and Piedmont. As a legal entity, the Monacan *tribe* also constitutes a *national* political entity by virtue of its indigenous status. In spite of over three hundred years of colonial relations with Euro-Americans, the Monacans continue to distinguish themselves—culturally and politically—from their non-Indian neighbors.

The coal communities in West Virginia, on the other hand, have experienced drastic population shifts, including major waves of in-migration and out-migration. This latter trend reduces the probability of homogeneity in any given coal community, though it does not render it impossible. Significant European settlement of Wyoming County began in the late eighteenth century with predominantly Scotch-Irish immigrants seeking land in the rugged valleys of the Allegheny Plateau. While their descendants still compose the majority of the population, more recent black and Italian immigrants now also inhabit the area. I have chosen the county as a unit of analysis for two reasons. First, a county is the most convenient geopolitical unit for considering the historical occurrence of cultural homogeneity in the area, as well as fluctuations therein. Second, while the recent admixture of disparate immigrant groups complicates the possibility of the county's population constituting a distinct national group in the political sense, my fieldwork suggests that these divergent minority groups often interact in a single community pattern. This evolving community configuration is important to this analysis, yielding insights about the degree to which grassroots political efficacy is linked to ethnic and/or cultural solidarity.

This analysis therefore presents a detailed comparison of homogeneity on both community and regional levels. Accordingly, it allows a deeper consideration of how cultural and political homogeneity relates to development trends in each community.

The second reason for the comparison is the paucity of detailed comparative analyses between Appalachian communities and American Indian communities. Comparative studies of colonialism in America should consider the original victims of such processes so that we may understand the historical development and longevity of colonial activities on this continent. Third, indigenous populations in Appalachia have attracted only modest scholarly attention (e.g., Finger, 1983, 1991; Neely, 1984, 1991; Hudson, 1976; Merrell, 1984; Kennedy, 1994). The Monacans represent a worthy example of a people who, although they have not lived in isolation, have preserved a collective sense of a unique political and ethnic identity. Finally, models of contemporary internal colonialism and dependency have been applied exclusively to federally recognized Indian tribes (Patterson, 1971; Lamphere, 1976; Anders, 1979; Jacobson, 1984; LaDuke and Churchill, 1985), while scholars have virtually ignored the possibility that such approaches might be applied to non–federally recognized tribes. When the federal government formally recognizes a tribe, it engages in a legal relationship with the latter that ideally recognizes the tribe's existence as a sovereign nation. This "trust relationship," however, has been variably interpreted by federal policy makers to designate a "guardian-ward" relationship, and many scholars have argued that this relationship is the hallmark of a colonial structure (e.g., Thomas, 1966/67: pp. a–b; Jorgensen, 1971).

I contend that nonrecognition must also be viewed as a mechanism of colonial power. The concept and process of federal recognition of Indian tribes is discussed in greater detail later in this study, but here I would point out that the legal and bureaucratic mechanisms through which nonrecognized tribes may become federally recognized entities (or conversely, denied such status) present the Indians in question with a double burden. Not only does the burden of proof for verifying their "Indianess" lie on the tribes in question but they face the contradictory threats of either being denied special legal protection of their sovereign rights, or being drawn into the excesses of federal largess if recognized.

These significant differences clearly illuminate the comparative value of the communities involved in this study. From a political economic perspective, the comparison is made even more intriguing by the peculiar history of Appalachia, and by scholarly debates concerning economic conditions therein. With the emergence of the New Left in the 1960s various scholars and activists eagerly embraced the internal colonial model to explain chronic poverty in the region (Caudill, 1963; Lewis, 1970; Lewis, Johnson, and Askins, 1978; Nyden, 1979; Gaventa, 1980). The problem with this paradigmatic trend was that it tended to characterize the whole of Appalachia as a colony, while usually focusing only on the experiences of communities in the central Appalachian coalfields. Here, I test the universal appropriateness of the internal colonial model by applying it to divergent communities.

Internal colonialism simply refers to a process of colonialism at work within the boundaries and under the auspices of a given nation-state. There have been numerous efforts to define colonialism (e.g., Casanova, 1965; Stavenhagen, 1965; Horvath, 1972; van den Bergne, 1978). The most flexible and succinct definition remains that of Blauner (1989), who describes colonialism as the political, economic, and cultural domination of one geopolitical unit by another. Such a process usually involves the establishment of special laws and agencies to rule the colonized territory, the colonizers' use of doctrines of racism or ethnocentrism to justify their domination, and their unilateral exploitation of human and natural resources in the colony.

The dependency model is arguably an offshoot of the colonial model with an emphasis on skewed economic relations. Dependency is not a single theory per se, but rather a broad field of analytical approaches within a common matrix. The hallmark of the dependency model is the concept of uneven economic relationships between *Metropolitan* or *Core* (developed) regions and *Satellite* or *Peripheral* (exploited) regions (see Baran, 1957; Frank, 1966; Love, 1990). Dos Santos's frequently-cited definition adds depth to this concept:

> By dependency we mean a situation in which the economy of certain countries is conditioned by the development and expansion of another economy to which the former is subjected. The relation of interdependence between two or more economies, and between these and world trade, assume the form of dependence when some countries (the dominant ones) can expand and can be self-sustaining, while other countries (the dependent ones) can do this only as a reflection of that expansion, which can have either a positive or negative effect on their immediate development. (1970: p. 251)

Approaches to dependency theory are as divergent as they are numerous, though most are articulated within the parameters of Dos Santos's (1970) definition. Although the dependency model initially used the *nation-state* as the standard unit of analysis, it has subsequently been modified to take into account how certain regions *within* nation-states are integrated into national economies less favorably than others (Salstrom, 1994).

One of the earliest applications of a dependency *related* model to Appalachia was David Walls's (1976) appropriation of world-system theory to discuss regional economic disparities. Walls adopted a rather materialist stance in criticizing proponents of the colonial model for suggesting that Appalachia had been excluded from the world capitalist system. He argued instead that the socioeconomic problems in the region were the result of the manner in which Appalachia has been integrated into the world-system. However, the proliferation of Walls's internal periphery model has had a polarizing effect on theoretical approaches to Appalachia's problems. At one extreme are economic analyses that emphasize Appalachia's integration into the capitalist economic system (Walls, 1976; Simon, 1980; 1981). Such approaches tend to treat economy and culture as mutually exclusive aspects of human life. At the other extreme are approaches that tend to overemphasize conflicting cultural systems as a focal point for Appalachian underdevelopment and exploitation by outside forces (Plaut, 1979; Batteau, 1990). Both approaches downplay the possible relationship between colonialism and capitalist integration, when in fact the two have historically been intimately related (Blaut, 1989). In this book, I attempt to move toward theoretical consolidation from the point of view of Arturo Escobar, who writes, "The economy is not only, or even principally, a material entity. It is above all a cultural production, a way of producing human subjects and social orders of a certain kind" (1994: p. 59).

I suggest a merging of hermeneutic and materialist ideas by using the internal colonial model to explicate one of many processes at work in Appalachia, and I suggest that integration into national and global economies is a manifestation of the colonial processes unfolding in the region. I use the internal colonial model to provide an initial framework for understanding uneven development in the region, and as a means of better considering the cultural conflicts that emerged with capitalist development.

Considering that Appalachia is neither economically nor culturally homogeneous, the colonial model could not be used as a definitive theoretical framework for this study. Colonial models tend to be presented more as a list of qualifying criteria describing a broad structure of oppression. Therefore, I also draw on dependency analysis to articulate a more thorough examination of underdevelopment. By way of comparative analysis, I use the dependency model to identify variables and degrees in the overall colonial process, as well as in the extent to which the particular communities in this study have been integrated into national and global economies.

Some *dependecistas* have applied such a rigid structural approach to their analyses that they ignore the possibility of degrees and variations of dependency in different regions. However, as Caporaso (1980) and Wilkins (1993) point out, it should be possible to consider such relationships in terms of "more" or "less" dependency. This is a key reason why the internal colonial and dependency models complement each other. While dependency theories are primarily concerned with the *historical* development of economic relationships vis-à-vis the world capitalist system, colonial models allow a consideration of other social, political, and cultural factors that have influenced the manner and extent to which a given region or society has been integrated into national and global economic systems.

By not confining its analysis to a single theoretical channel, this study affords the opportunity to construct a more holistic approach to examining patterns of capitalist integration, particularly in contexts specific to time and space. Taken together, the dependency and internal colonial models allow a look at a wider range of variables contributing to and resulting from uneven development in the region.

There is little scholarly consensus on precisely what qualifies a region or social group as an internal colony. One of the most viable models for making such determinations is Michael Hechter's (1975) in his classic work on the Celts. But Hechter notes that "there is no hard and fast line which can be drawn between the three multidimensional concepts colony, internal colony, and peripheral region" (pp. 348–49). Yet he suggests that a clearer articulation might be possible through the following model:

> These three concepts of peripherality may be tentatively sorted out by their relationship to five particular variables: (1) the degree of administrative integration [that is, the extent to which laws passed for the core apply to the periphery], (2) the extensiveness of citizenship in the periphery [with regard to civil, political, and social rights], (3) the prestige of the peripheral culture, (4) the existence of geographical contiguity, and (5) the length of association between the periphery and core. . . . If each of these variables is assigned a high or low rank, then a *colony* is a region generally ranked low on all five variables; an *internal colony* is given a high rank on (1), (2), and (4), and a medium rank on (5); and a *peripheral region* is ranked highly on all the variables. (Hector, 1975: p. 349)

This model comprises one of the analytical cornerstones in examining the two subregions under study. Although oppression is not a quantifiable phenomenon, I employ a counterintuitive approach in using this model to determine if the necessary preconditions for bal-

anced, meaningful development in each community are present, or if
certain conditions are deficient. I rank each of the five variables
stated above on a scale of one to five in order to explicate variations
in colonial patterns in each case. For example, although the Monacans were technically full-fledged citizens of the United States and
Virginia in the first half of this century, local officials frequently denied them the right to vote and the state implicitly endorsed such
actions through the articulation of miscegenation and Jim Crow
laws. In this case, I would assign the Monacans a rank no higher
than (3) in extensiveness of citizenship. The final chapter includes a
comparative articulation and detailed assessment of this model.

The above model provides a useful vantage point from which to
examine conditions of dependency, for it allows a consideration of
the historical relationships between various parties which facilitated
the emergence of conditions of dependency. In *The Roots of Dependency* (1983), Richard White provides an excellent analytical model
for gauging such historical interactions which, if combined with
Hechter's model, adds depth to this controlled comparison. In his
historical examination of three tribal entities—the Choctaws, Navajos, and Pawnees—White goes beyond conventional dependency approaches to show how economic, political, and cultural relations between the respective tribes and outside forces (primarily the federal
government) consolidated and worked to gradually deprive each
tribe of its political and economic autonomy, leaving each tribe politically subordinate to the federal government and economically dependent on the national economy. Significantly, White considers
how these relations contributed to the deterioration of each tribe's
physical environment that had traditionally been relied upon for
subsistence.

White begins, however, by noting that the "materialist emphasis of
dependency theory and the admittedly reductionist tendencies of
some work within the school" place certain limitations on the ability
of dependency analysis to explain conditions of dependency (1983: p.
xix). He does not address the possibility of degrees of dependency,
though his approach has the potential to explicate such variations

through comparison. In considering such possibilities, Walls's (1976, 1978) internal periphery model proves useful. Although Walls is a world-systems analyst in the tradition of Wallerstein (1974, 1975, 1983), it is important to bear in mind that world-systems analysis is arguably a corollary of the dependency school. Significantly, Walls suggests the possibility of differential levels of development in peripheral or dependent regions, which he bases on an adaptation of Wallerstein's (1974) concept of the *semiperipheral* country. According to Wallerstein, the existence of such countries prevents the acute polarization of the world into rich and poor countries (thereby diminishing the potential for an alliance of poor nations) and provides a channel for low-wage industrial capitalist investment from core countries. Thus, while semiperipheral countries are dependent on developed (core) countries, they are, relatively speaking less dependent and more developed than peripheral countries.

Walls argues that this three-way system may be applied to the study of uneven development within advanced capitalist countries, and that "the possibility of attaining semiperipheral status may preclude a strong alliance of one region with another worse off" (1976: p. 243). Moreover, he suggests that such a system may explain differential levels of development between subregions *within* Appalachia. Combined with White's broad, nuanced approach, Walls's internal periphery (or semiperiphery) model enables us to look at the historical development of differential degrees of dependency between the subregions examined herein.

This analysis begins with the understanding that dependency is "an evolutionary form of colonialism" (Pratt, 1979: p. 55). Thus, the guiding proposition of this study is that the groups described herein qualify as internal colonies, and that they are engaged as subordinates in a relationship of dependency. In the process of testing this proposition, I consider ten broad research questions:

1. What were the salient economic and cultural features of each group before the entry of colonial forces into their respective subregions, and how have these changed over time?

2. Who were the initial colonizers, and what were their initial responses to the people of the region? What was the initial impact on these groups following contact with colonial forces?

3. What resources—that is, natural, agricultural, human—did the prospective colonizers seek to exploit from each group and their respective regions?

4. To what degree did the colonizers' doctrines of racial or cultural superiority influence the process of exploitation in each case?

5. At what point did internal colonial structures emerge, and how have they endured and/or changed over time? Have the initial colonizers been supplanted or augmented by other colonial agents?

6. What roles did members of the colonized communities play in the process? Specifically, what patterns and forms (if any) of resistance emerged from within the colonized communities, and did certain natives facilitate the colonial process by cooperating with the colonizers?

7. At what point can a structural relationship of dependency be said to have emerged between the colonizer and colonized in each case? And once established, how entrenched did it become? That is, has the condition of dependency proven to be a permanent, immalleable structure?

8. Are local economies diversified, or do they rest primarily on the exploitation of a single resource? To what degree do fluctuations in the local economy hinge on fluctuations in the national and world capitalist economy? What is the precise relationship between the respective communities and metropolitan centers of commerce?

9. What is the relationship between each of the dependent colonized communities to national, state, and local governing entities? What is the role of these governments in facilitating, perpetuating, or attempting to alleviate the exploitation of and

conditions of dependency in the respective communities? Which, if any, of these seems most representative of the interests of each community?

10. Are there any identifiable internal cultural factors that facilitate relations of dependency? Are such factors actually cultural adaptations to relations of unequal distribution of wealth and power? What geographical or environmental features might serve to aggravate conditions of internal colonialism and dependency?

These research questions define the analytical parameters of this study, thus making a controlled comparison feasible and orderly. Each of the ensuing case studies is largely organized in accordance with these questions. In addition, these questions are used to draw more salient comparative conclusions in the final chapter. These questions delineate the methodological focus of this study.

The study examines the political economies of two disparate communities and the wider region in which they live from an ethnohistorical perspective. I utilize a wide range of data, both qualitative and quantitative, archival and ethnographic. The initial data collection phase took place from May 1996 to May 1997. Due to the breadth of this comparison, as well as financial and temporal constraints, I arranged to spend three months living in each community (for a total of six months of in-residence fieldwork). Before and after the extended field trips, I was centrally located in Blacksburg, Virginia, where there is a research-one university library, and where regional archives lie close by. I was also able to make frequent visits to each research community after the initial in-residence fieldwork, as Blacksburg lies roughly equidistant between the two. So I was fortunate to keep the field relationship intact when archival research raised new questions.

In collecting qualitative data, I used both conventional methods of participant observation, and semistructured interviews with collaborators in each community. In each of these capacities, the activities I engaged in, the questions I asked, and the things I looked for were circumscribed by the research questions guiding this study. As a participant-observer, I found myself visiting worksites of community members when feasible, sitting on porches, helping to clear fields, snapping pole beans, lounging at local gathering points, attending tribal meetings (in the case of the Monacans), attending church services, weddings, funerals, and a myriad of other activities. However, I was also concerned with locating objective signs of underdevelopment or relations of dependency in each community. For instance, I noticed that in Wyoming County (where the coal industry owns almost 90 percent of the local land base and is virtually exempt from taxation) there are two golf courses but not a single hospital. On a deeper level, I attempted to determine if certain attitudes among community members reflected a sense of uneven power relations. For reasons discussed in this book, many Wyoming County residents were quite cynical about state politics and the power of coal. On the other hand, many Monacans exhibited a positive outlook concerning their collective future and their efficacy as a local voting bloc.

My goal in this ethnographic project was aligned with Faiman-Silva's assertion that anthropologists should "develop collaborative, genuinely critically informed, praxis-oriented, and deconstructive texts that empower us, our subjects, and our audience" (1996: p. xx). Hence, an important component of my research is oral histories. I must admit to some predetermined interpretation even in this phase of my research, since oral histories were collected within the context of semistructured interviews (Bernard, 1994: ch. 10), which were based on the overall research plan. However, the epistemological base for this research was guided by the phenomenological methodology articulated by Schutz (1970) and Clifford (1988). Stated simply, instead of trying to impose an interpretation of meaning, I attempted to withhold my own interpretation of the respective participants' words (to the extent that that is possible), and to let community members convey the meanings they give reality through their own stories. Thus, my ultimate ethnographic objective was to present "a constructive negotiation involving at least two, and usually more, politically significant subjects" (Clifford, 1988: p. 41).

I selected participants so as to ensure a representative sample from each community on the basis of age and sex. The extensive interview material I collected has been integrated with the other data used in this analysis in an effort to bridge the many gaps in the written historical record. Oral testaments did not fill these gaps entirely but did serve to narrow them. Oral histories also confirmed specific patterns of uneven development as suggested by quantitative data, and I was able to use quantitative data to explicate the material scale of certain situations of oppression conveyed through oral accounts.

The reader will note that I often quote extensive passages from interviews. I do this for two main reasons. First, it empowers the reader by adding a dimension of humanness (and hence, accessibility) to the narrative. Secondly, I think it empowers the community members involved in this study by giving them a voice as ethnographic authorities. Although the sensitive nature of some of the interview material made it necessary to withhold names in most instances, I regard all those who provided oral histories as research collaborators. I found this phenomenological approach often led community members to new insights, as their collaborative role brought them to realize the validity of their own knowledge (Friere, 1970; Stull and Schensol, 1987; Ryan and Robinson, 1996; Medicine, 1998).

As mentioned, the qualitative data used herein has been supplemented by and integrated with other historical, archival, and statistical data. I drew this data from a variety of sources and repositories, including state historical societies, courthouses, local newspaper archives, and regional libraries. Although I have not engaged in rigorous statistical analyses, the quantitative data are revealing. Census data have provided insights into changing subsistence patterns, migration patterns during regional boom and bust cycles, and changing employment patterns. State and local government archives have provided information concerning land ownership and taxation patterns for determining the extent of absentee control of the economic base in each community. Such an analysis reveals patterns of economic helplessness on the part of many native residents (ALOTF, 1981).

Time did not allow a thorough compilation of ownership and taxation records in each county, but I made a listing of the major landowners, the amount of land they control, and their tax status in order to determine the extent to which local economies are externally dominated. The most current comprehensive compilation of such statistics for Wyoming County was made over twenty years ago, when it was found that 86 percent of the county's land base was absentee owned (Zimolzak, 1977). Current estimates suggest that that figure has risen and that fewer absentee owners hold more land. Due to inadequate census data on the Monacans, I found it more useful to conduct an informal survey among tribal members to determine how much land, if any, was owned and/or worked by each family.

In examining commercially related statistical data, I found the methodology of the "new rural history" school (e.g., Mitchell, 1977; Salstrom, 1994) quite useful, although I did not engage this methodology as thoroughly or rigorously as those historians who have developed this technique. For my purposes, this technique involved examining statistics concerning agriculture or other labor-intensive activities, and noting correlations between certain types of commercial activity, or certain exploitative practices (as the case often was). State and federal government documents, such as those of the Appalachian Regional Commission, federal and state agricultural agencies, and the United States Bureau of Mines, provided additional information on economic conditions and development strategies employed in the respective subregions. From these data I have been able to assess the success or failure of such strategies, and in some instances to determine just how representative certain government entities have been of the respective communities in this study. For example, Bureau of Mines statistics on mining accidents reveals that West Virginia mining laws prior to the 1940s were skewed in favor of mine operators, as most prosecutions thereunder indicted miners and not owners. Moreover, agricultural data reveals a strong correlation after the Civil War between the expanding orchard industry in Amherst County (which fed on the exploitation of Indian labor) and more elaborate miscegenation laws in the state of Virginia.

This research design presents a structured yet flexible matrix within which a localized political economy—such as that of Appalachia—can be examined on different levels. First, it allows a consideration of how local social, economic, environmental, and political conditions have historically affected development patterns in each community. Second, it provides a mechanism to gauge more generalizable development patterns throughout Appalachia and beyond. Finally, the theoretical framework and guiding research questions of this study present a viable means of considering how different segments of specific regions—in this case, Appalachia—have been integrated into the national and global political economies in different ways and degrees.

This book is divided into three sections. Chapters 1 through 3 concentrate on the Monacan tribe. Chapters 4 through 6 examine the cultural and political economic experiences of the Euro-American settlers of Wyoming County, West Virginia. The conclusion provides a hybrid analysis, summarizing the comparison in revealing ways, and critically assessing the theoretical framework.

At the bottom line, this is a study of power relations. It is not merely an examination of material inequities but of differential cultural confrontations within a set space. It is also a study of how power relations can *change*, and how human agency at *all* levels of the power structure can alter the entire configuration. I represent the Monacans and the residents of Wyoming County only as a concerned—albeit well-informed—outsider, and not as a definitive authority. At the same time, I hope to open the canon to an understanding of two underrepresented communities consisting of people whose stories should be told. Their stories are in some ways remarkably similar and in other ways are profoundly different.

"Capitalist expansion may or may not render particular cultures inoperative," writes Eric Wolf, "but its all-too-real spread does raise questions about just how the successive cohorts of peoples drawn into the capitalist orbit align and realign their understandings to respond to the opportunities and exigencies of their new conditions" (1997: p. xii). This study, then, is an effort to raise and to answer such questions. I attempt to answer the question of *how* two disparate communities have been integrated differentially into the regional political economy and into the larger capitalist system. "Seen from a local perspective," writes Escobar, "this means investigating how external forces—capital and modernity, generally speaking— are processed, expressed, and refashioned by local communities" (1994: p. 98). I have attempted to approach this comparison holistically by combining theoretical perspectives, particularly the internal colonial and dependency models. But in explaining the profound differences between these two communities in the wake of capitalist absorption, I have raised questions about *what* the nature of capitalist integration is. Globalization through capitalist integration, it seems, does not necessarily mean complete homogenization. In the long run, the only thing that is homogeneous is the process, not the results.

1 THE SEEDS OF COLONIALISM

The Monacan Alliance and Early European Contact

One of the pivotal elements of colonialism is the denigration of the culture and heritage of the colonized by the colonizer. The title of Eric Wolf's *Europe and the People without History* (1997 ed.) succinctly describes the attitude that the first Europeans on this continent and their progeny extended toward Native Americans. Most often, Native communities were treated as static and inferior societies that were incapable of attaining any meaningful history—a process that Hill refers to as "historicide" (1996: p. 16). Many Europeans perceived them as having failed to evolve from the original state of nature in which it was believed that all human groups once lived (Berkhoffer, 1978). Subsequently, these Eurocentric notions diffused into much of the scholarly treatment of Indians. From a traditional Western perspective, then, American Indian history commenced when the aboriginal societies of this continent began to be transformed by contact with non-Indians.

Of course, it is absurd to deem any human group as devoid of history, for history is first of all an attempt to chronicle human activity, whether in written or oral form. Yet for the Monacan Indians of Amherst County, Virginia, the legacy of colonialism did not merely mean that their colonizers ignored their history. Through the various cycles of the colonial process, they themselves were nearly robbed of their own history. This process came in the form of cultural genocide, economic oppression, and even periodic physical annihilation. Indeed, their collective experience vis-à-vis colonial forces bluntly illustrates the irony intended in the title of Wolf's book. However, as we shall see in subsequent chapters, the sustained colonial experiences of the Monacans ultimately worked to reinforce a group identity as a unique people while the general population overlooked, if not denied, their existence.

From a non-Indian perspective, the history of the Monacans has always been nebulous. When the first British explorers encountered them in 1608, they learned little more than the fact that the Monacans were enemies of the vast Powhatan alliance along the Virginia Tidewater. As Hantman (1990) aptly concludes, "Only briefly noted by fragmentary ethnohistoric texts, interpreted through European eyes, or those who chose to talk with Europeans, these people generically became the 'barbarians,' 'chichimecans,' or 'dead ones' of history" (p. 678). By the beginning of the nineteenth century, it was assumed that the Monacans and their confederates were long gone from Virginia, if not extinct. The Indians at the foot of the Blue Ridge, whom we now know as Monacans, were variously labeled as Cherokees, Seminoles, Portuguese, and "Negroes" well into the twentieth century (Houck, 1984: p. 18). No one suspected that they were, in fact, the remnant of a vast conglomeration of Siouan speaking peoples who once inhabited the southeastern United States.

The Monacans in Aboriginal Times

Prior to the arrival of Europeans in North America, the southeast was occupied by at least forty Siouan speaking tribes whose collective territory may have exceeded twenty thousand square miles (Mooney, 1894: p. 9). Euro-American contact with most of the eastern Siouan groups was at best infrequent in colonial times. We are thus left with little information to determine the origins and lifeways of these disparate groups. What does exist is a great deal of scholarly speculation based on rare colonial accounts of certain Siouan groups, and on an archaeological record only recently stud-

ied in depth. Even more difficult to surmise is the nature of tribal af-
filiations and associations or alliances between the various eastern
groups. Swanton (1943) suggests that there were two general divisions—the Virginia Siouans and the Carolina Siouans—and that
these respective divisions interacted only infrequently. The sharp
linguistic differences between these two divisions lend credence to
this argument, though there is no evidence of animosity between the
two divisions.

Among the Virginia Siouans were at least sixteen different tribes
or separately recorded groups. The only strong evidence to differen-
tiate these groups are the settlement patterns recorded by early explorers and investigated by archaeologists. It is not possible to determine the precise degree to which these groups identified with one
another, but it seems that three tentative alliances of tribes existed in
the Virginia Siouan territory. The Monacans, first encountered by
Captain John Smith in 1608, included tribes such as the Monacans
proper, Mahoc, and Nuntaly. The Tutelos included the closely affiliated Tutelos and Saponis, and the Occaneechis, among others. The
more northerly Manahoacs included the Manahoac proper, and possibly the Stegarake, and others (Mooney, 1894: Houck, 1984: p. 17).
There is evidence, however, that all of these tribes interacted freely
and may have formed frequent, albeit temporary alliances (Mouer,
1981, 1983).

In fact, there may have been less differentiation between these so-
called tribes than scholars have been willing to recognize. There is a
tendency in most of the spotty colonial records of the Siouan tribes
of Virginia and in subsequent scholarship to equate each village or
settlement recorded as a different tribal entity. But there is evidence
that the so-called Tutelo Confederacy was part of the Monacan alliance. One of the earliest documents relating to the Monacans is a
map made by Captain Smith in 1608 of the lands west of the falls of
the James River (near present-day Richmond). The map lists five
"Monacan" towns, one of which was named Monahassanugh. According to Mooney (1894: p. 30), this was possibly the same settlement visited by the explorer John Lederer in 1670, who referred to

the people there as "Nahyssen," otherwise known as Tutelos (Alvord and Bidgood, 1912: p. 143). While Mooney initially made this connection based on the similarities in the two recorded names, subsequent archaeological research has added strength to his argument (Bushnell, 1930). More recent archaeological surveys have yielded evidence of "a shared ideology and cultural continuity that underlay and defined the Monacan world. This unity included not only the Monacans east of the Blue Ridge Mountains, but also the relative (or ancestral) groups on the west side" (Hantman, 1990: p. 684).[1] Moreover, by 1714, most of the known Siouan tribes in Virginia (including the Manahoacs) were known to have been living together at Fort Christanna in Brunswick County (Byrd, 1866: v. 1, p. 188; Swanton, 1936: p. 375). The name Monacan itself, like many tribal names, is apparently indicative of a specific people, the land they occupy, and their lifestyle. Although Tooker (1895) argued that the name is derived from Algonquian appellatives for "diggers of earth" or "earth people" (probably in reference to the practice of digging for certain minerals and building earth lodges), Mooney held that many of these names were based on the Siouan prefix "ma," indicative of "earth" or "country" (1894: p. 27).[2]

Thus, if one considers the Monacans, Tutelos, and Manahoacs as being part of the same collective entity, their precolonial territory was significant. Some suggest that it began in the east along the fall line (roughly a straight line bisecting the falls of the James and Rappahannock Rivers), spanning as far north as the Potomac River and south to the Roanoke River, or roughly to the present-day Virginia–North Carolina border (Houck, 1984: p. 18; Feest, 1973). Brief accounts by European explorers in the mid-1600s mentioned a group called the Monetons—who may have been associated with the Monacans—far to the West along the Kanawha River (in present-day West Virginia) (Alvord and Bidgood, 1912: pp. 192, 224–27; Mooney, 1894: p. 36; Swanton, 1936: p. 373). However, recent comprehensive archaeological research suggests that "Monacan villages appear to have closely followed the major rivers of the [Virginia] piedmont, particularly the James and its tributary the Rivana, and the Rapahannock and its tributary the Rapidan (Hantman, 1994: p. 96). Moreover, many contemporary archaeologists agree that the Monacan territory extended across the Blue Ridge into the central part of the Shenandoah Valley (Hantman, 1990, 1994; Mouer, 1981, 1983). Recently, Hantman (1998) has presented convincing archaeo-political evidence that suggests that the Tutelos and Saponis of the Roanoke River basin might also have been included in the same cultural tradition as the "ancestral Monacans" (ca. AD 900–1700). In fact, Hantman argues that the Monacans, who seemed to disappear from the historical record after 1650, were probably "renamed by colonial powers as the Saponi and the Tutelo, among other names" (p. 4). This contemporary outline is based on solid material evidence of cultural homogeneity and therefore delineates precontact Monacan territory for the purposes of this study.

Unfortunately, the early explorers of the Monacan territory were not social scientists, and their records reveal little about aboriginal social and political organization within and among the various groups. The most informative (albeit vague) account was provided by the explorer John Lederer who visited various Siouan villages in 1670. Lederer described the Nahyssan (Tutelo) chief as an absolute monarch, warlike and rich (Alvord and Bidgood, 1912: p. 153) although he did not mention the criteria for leadership. This was probably a Eurocentric projection, as leaders in tribal or kin-based societies usually had to legitimate their positions by continually exhibiting wisdom, generosity, and equitability—in essence, as servants of the people (Deloria and Lytle, 1983: p. 89). It should be noted that John Fontaine, during his 1716 visit to Fort Christanna, said of the Saponis, "This nation hath no king at present, but are governed by twelve of their old men, which have power to act for the whole nation" (Alexander, 1972: p. 93). However, if Speck's (1942) account of the spirit adoption ceremony among Tutelo descendants in Canada in the 1930s is any indication of tribal practices in the seventeenth century, it would appear that there were also hereditary criteria determining who would hold positions of prestige. The

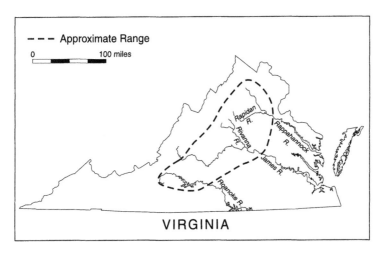

Aboriginal Monacan Territory, ca. 1900

spirit adoption ceremony entailed the adoption of a deceased chief's name (and hence, his essence) by a living descendant.

While existing data inhibits conclusions, Speck's (1942) work with the Tutelos would seem to indicate that many spiritual leaders derived their authority, at least in part, through paternal kinship ties. Moreover, while it is nearly impossible to ascertain what institutions may have been in place for governing social relations beyond the jurisdiction of spiritual leaders, it is likely that domestic relations were governed by families and whatever clan system may have existed. Lederer related, for example, that children were reared by persuasion, not command (Alvord and Bidgood, 1912: p. 144). Actually, in many aboriginal societies family and community social pressure were the primary means of maintaining internal domestic order for people of all ages (Deloria and Lytle, 1983: pp. 82–89).

Admittedly, most of the preceding generalizations are based on speculation. But certain conclusions can be drawn about intertribal relations. First, according to Smith's 1608 account, the village of Rassaweck was the principal town of all the Monacans, to which all other villages paid tribute (Smith, 1819). Smith obtained most of his information from a Monacan/Manahoac captive named Amoroleck, who spoke to Smith at the falls of the Rappahannock in 1608. Although Amoroleck spoke to Smith through a translator, and under considerable duress, the information he gave Smith might indicate that Rassaweck was an important economic, political, or ceremonial center. Considering that at least one of the five Monacan towns of Smith's account was possibly Tutelo, one can surmise that ties between the Tutelos and Monacans were intimate. There is strong evidence that the Tutelos and Saponis spoke slightly different dialects of the same language (Hale, 1883: p. 3).[3] Moreover, Mooney (1894) mentions that the history of the two groups was one and the same after 1700. Likewise, it is said that the Occaneechi language (spoken by the southernmost tribe of the Tutelo Confederacy, located at the confluence of the Dan and Staunton Rivers) was the common trade and religious language among many of the Siouan tribes of Virginia (Mooney, 1894: p. 33).

Needless to say, vague colonial records, coupled with a severely eroded archaeological record, leave us with very little information on the material culture and settlement patterns of the Monacans. In some respects their material culture was consistent with the broader woodlands culture of their Algonquian and Iroquoian neighbors. While the forests west of the fall line may have been more conducive to a hunting and gathering economy than those to the east, contemporary archaeological evidence suggests that a sedentary agricultural lifeway was as highly developed on the Piedmont prior to 1600 as it was on the Tidewater (e.g., Holland, Spieden, and Van Roijen, 1983). Indeed, archaeological data suggests that the villages of Mowhemicho and Monahassanugh had become extensive permanent settlements, home to perhaps hundreds of people by the time of Smith's arrival (Bushnell, 1930: pp. 9, 14; Hantman, 1990: p. 682).

While their southwesterly Iroquoian neighbors (e.g., the Cherokees) built more permanent structures of logs and clay, the Monacans—as well as their Algonquian neighbors on the coastal plain— evidently utilized easily collapsible bark structures. However, in contrast to the Cherokees and coastal Algonquians, there is no evidence that Monacan villages were ever palisaded for protection, as was common among neighboring tribes (Bushnell, 1930: pp. 9, 32). This may have reflected an itinerant lifeway. There was, however, a definite physical pattern of organization to some Monacan villages. Historical and archaeological records indicate a tendency of many Monacan villages to be organized in a circular pattern, with a central plaza often containing a stump or platform for orators. This pattern was recorded as late as 1716 when several Siouan tribes were conglomerated at Fort Christanna (Bushnell, 1930: pp. 28–31; Alexander, 1972: p. 96).

Various colonial records between 1607 and 1740 suggest that some of the Monacans and their confederates did move around considerably (Alvord and Bidgood, 1912: pp. 141–86; Lawson, 1880: p. 384: Alexander, 1972: pp. 90–97). This may have been attributable, to some degree, to their preference for a hunting and gathering economy. The rich forests west of the fall line provided ample breeding ground for a wide range of game including white-tail deer, rabbits, squirrels, turkey, a variety of grouse, and even elk. Perhaps one of the most important animals to these tribes was buffalo, which once existed in abundance in the East. A correlation exists between the vanishing of the buffalo in the East and the fading of most eastern Siouan groups from the historical record. John Lawson, the Surveyor General of North Carolina, reported in 1701 that there were buffalo "in great plenty" along the Cape Fear River, notably in a period when many of the Virginia Siouan peoples had moved into that area (Lawson, 1860: p. 384; Hale, 1883: p. 3). There is evidence that buffalo were bountiful in the Piedmont and Blue Ridge as late as 1730 (Alexander, 1972: p. 106), specifically in present-day Amherst County (Woods, 1901). Mooney says that buffalo were abundant in the Ohio Valley and Tennessee until the French and Indian War, and did not entirely vanish from the area until 1801 (1894: p. 11). However, while it is possible that the fluctuation of these herds influenced the movement (westward and northward in the case of the Tutelos) and dissipation of most of the Virginia Siouans, it cannot be considered the sole determinant of their destiny, as will be discussed.

Although hunting and gathering offered a more convenient mode of existence, the Monacans were engaged in some notable agricultural endeavors. The period of European contact, in fact, may have marked a transition for many Monacans toward greater reliance on agriculture. During Lederer's 1670 expedition into the Monacan territory, some of the people there told him that their predecessors were "savage" hunters who ate only raw meat, and that the present inhabitants taught them to plant corn (Alvord and Bidgood, 1912: p. 142). Although this statement leaves much to speculation, recent archaeological studies suggest that most of the Monacans were deeply entrenched in an agricultural economy by the time of European contact. Indeed, these surveys seem to indicate that contact period Monacans were highly dependent on corn as a dietary staple (Hantman, 1990: p. 682).[4]

Historical evidence also suggests that Monacan agricultural pursuits were not a novel introduction at the time of European contact.

According to accounts from Fort Christanna around 1716, women were responsible for growing and tending the cornfields (Alexander, 1972: p. 97). The implications of this account are twofold. First, it suggests that the Monacans, like their Iroquois neighbors, had a long-standing social tradition governing the means by which agricultural activities were to be carried out. But perhaps most significantly, it points to the possibility that women were held in high prestige in eastern Siouan societies, being charged (as in Iroquois and Cherokee society—see, for example, Rothberg, 1980; Perdue, 1998) with the care and control of a major element of subsistence.

In precolonial times, the Monacans had at their disposal a variety of oaks, chestnuts, hickory, poplar, and numerous other trees, which provided them with high carbohydrate nuts and very durable wood. Chestnut could be used to build permanent structures, as its grain was straight and the wood, once seasoned, was remarkably resistant to deterioration. Various species of birch, which once grew in great profusion, provided a strong, smooth bark that could support the siding necessary for bark housing. White oak splits provided an extremely malleable material for baskets, though vines such as honeysuckle were also used (Cook, 1996a). While most clothing was made from animal hides, the silky threads of milkweed were efficiently woven into certain textile products (Bushnell, 1930: p. 26).

In the 1920s, archaeologist David Bushnell (1930) found evidence that many Monacans mined significant quantities of minerals such as schist, sandstone, soapstone, steatite, and quartz. He suggested that the inclination toward extracting subterranean minerals apparently earned the Monacans a reputation among their Algonquian neighbors as "earth diggers," and possibly hastened the British desire to explore Monacan territory for precious metals. Bushnell's speculation had greater implications than he probably realized. Although the British may have been disappointed, the minerals extracted by the Monacans no doubt gave them a certain degree of leverage in trade relations with some neighboring tribes. Hantman suggests that the Monacans served as a vital conduit of the precolonial copper trade in Virginia (1990: p. 685; 1994). This metal, which was highly valued for trade within the Powhatan's chiefdom, had to be obtained in the mountains, and the coastal Algonquians would have had to go through Monacan territory to gain access to it.

In fact, the Monacans were apparently by the seventeenth century involved in a very complex and sophisticated intertribal trade network. While most of the Siouan tribes west of the fall line had minimal contact with Europeans until the eighteenth century, many were able to obtain European trade goods long before that period through their eastern neighbors, notably the Susquehannocks at the head of the Chesapeake Bay. Mooney suggested that the Susquehannocks had long been important trade intermediaries, and that their strength and strategic location allowed them to become the primary intermediaries between Europeans and many Virginia and Carolina tribes (1894: p. 32). By 1645, the Susquehannocks had gained possession of ample firearms from European traders, as evidenced by Maryland's prohibition that year against providing Indians with ammunition without a license. In 1670, John Lederer found that the Nahyssan (Tutelos) already had firearms despite their isolation from Europeans and it is most likely that these came from the Susquehannocks (Schaeffer, 1942: pp. viii–ix).

Interestingly, the Susquehannocks (an Iroquoian people) seem to have been close allies with the Occaneechis (Monacan confederates), whose island village at the confluence of the Dan and Staunton Rivers was itself an important trade center "for all Indians for at least 500 miles" (Mooney, 1894: p. 54). As previously noted, Occaneechi was the common trade language for many Siouan tribes. The Susquehannocks sought refuge with the Occaneechis during Bacon's Rebellion of 1676. As fate would have it, however, the wealth of animal furs passing through the Occaneechi settlement made it a prime target for Bacon's forces.

European Contact and Colonial Intrusions

For tribes such as the Occaneechis, Bacon's Rebellion marked an abrupt exposure to European peoples and their cultures. Like many inland Siouan tribes, direct contact with Europeans up to that time had been extremely limited, if it occurred at all. Yet the influence of Europe seems to have had an impact on many of these groups long before Bacon's fateful massacre. Tribes such as the Susquehannocks facilitated the influx of European trade goods into the Monacan hinterland, while other tribes to the north and east intermittently discouraged or excited European prospects for entering the territory east of the fall line. It might even be argued that the demise of the Monacans hinged largely on the manner in which European colonial forces affected relations between the Monacans and their tribal enemies.

With the exception of certain Iroquoian tribes in the south (the Nottoways and Meherins in Virginia, the Tuscaroras in the Carolinas), most of the Iroquoian peoples of the north—notably the powerful Five Nations Confederacy—had long been a military nemesis of many southern tribes. However, in the early seventeenth century the powerful Susquehannocks at the head of the Chesapeake Bay provided a formidable buffer for the tribes of Virginia against invasion by the Five Nations. It seems the greatest military foe for Virginia tribes was the Conestogas, who inhabited the southern portion of Pennsylvania (Mooney, 1894: p. 38; Schaeffer, 1942: p. vii). But although the Siouan and Algonquian tribes of Virginia may have had a mutual enemy in the Iroquois, they did not find sufficient grounds in this for intertribal solidarity. When Captain John Smith first entered the territory of the Powhatans near the falls of the James, Powhatan himself reportedly told Smith that the Indians to the west (Monacans) were his enemies (Barbour, 1968). Yet although the chief initially discouraged a European expedition west of the falls, his reference to the Monacans as "earth diggers" may have hastened the British pursuit of precious minerals in the Monacan territory (Bushnell, 1930; Hantman, 1990).

Smith's excursion marks the first known incident of European contact with the Monacans. Smith arrived at the falls of the James in 1607 and in 1608 sent Captain Christopher Newport with 120 men into the Monacan territory. Upon entering the territory, Newport seized a "petty king" of the Monacans to serve as a guide. En route, he visited the towns of Mowhemicho and Massanack, and produced a surprisingly accurate map recording three others: Rassaweck, Monasukapanough, and Monahassanugh. While Rassaweck (in present-day Fluvanna County, on the James River) was reported as the "capital" of the Monacans, Newport seems to have been more intrigued by Massanack (in present-day Powhatan County) as his pursuit of mineral wealth logically pointed him further inland. Evidently disappointed by the results of his survey, Newport turned back after traveling forty miles from the falls (Smith, 1819: v. 1, pp. 134, 195–97).

Smith's notes seem to have sparked a fleeting interest among certain British colonists in determining the mineral wealth of the Monacan region. A few years after Newport's expedition, William Strachey wrote of Newport's discovery of two "mynes" six miles west of the falls (not mentioned in Smith's notes), though he made no reference to what types of minerals were to be found (Strachey, 1849: p. 131). The extent to which the area was surveyed thereafter is unclear, but it is worth noting that after the Monacans had vacated Powhatan County, coal was later mined in the area (Mooney, 1894: p. 27).

There is scant evidence of contact between the Monacans and Europeans during the sixty years between Smith's arrival and Lederer's expedition in 1670. A 1669 colonial census of Virginia Indians accounted for only the Monacans proper—the easternmost Siouan people in Virginia—and none of their confederates. The census listed only 30 warriors among the tribe, with a total population of 100 to 120 members (Neill, 1886: p. 325). These numbers speak of a significantly diminished population in light of archaeological evidence of hundreds of people occupying these villages at one time (Hantman, 1990).

It is likely that the easternmost Monacans suffered losses at the hands of the colonial Virginia militia during its war against the Powhatans from 1625–45. During the same period, the Virginia Assembly enacted a proclamation calling for annual expeditions from the sea to river heads to exterminate Indians, and many Monacans must have felt the pressure of such endeavors (Mooney, 1894: p. 28). By 1643, however, tension seems to have diminished somewhat between Indians and colonists, for in that year the General Assembly authorized certain parties of whites to explore the lands west and south of the Appomattox River and to trade with the Indians there for a period of fourteen years (Alvord and Bidgood, 1912: pp. 101–5; Schaeffer, 1942: p. vi). Unfortunately, colonial records tell little of the exchanges these traders may have had with the Monacans.

Around 1654, tensions resurfaced between Indians and whites in Virginia when a party of six or seven hundred Indians appeared at the falls of the James, apparently intent on settling there. The records refer to the Indians as "Rechahecrians," though it is not known precisely who they were. While Mooney (1894) thought they were predominantly Cherokees, he also suggested that there may have been Monacans among them. This is supported by statements given to Lederer by certain "Mahacks and Nahyssans" (probably Monacans, Tutelos, and Saponis). The occupation of the falls hastened a colonial military alliance with the Powhatans, resulting in a battle in which the colonial forces were defeated and the Pamunkey chief Totopotamoy was killed. Lederer's informants indicated that they had taken part in this struggle (Alvord and Bidgood, 1912: p. 146). The bulk of the Indians at the falls may, in fact, have been a conglomeration of Manahoacs and Monacans who had been displaced by an increasing number of Connestoga raids from the northwest (Swanton, 1943: p. 55).

More coercive colonial laws toward Virginia Indians followed the confrontation at the falls. In 1665, the General Assembly passed laws prohibiting Indians from selecting their own chiefs and requiring them to accept chiefs appointed by the governor (Neill, 1886; Mooney, 1894: p. 29). Also in this period, the General Assembly began to issue stamped metal badges to Indians based on their particular tribal insignia. Such insignias were traditionally tattooed on the bodies of warriors among many Virginia tribes, the different tribes of the Monacan alliance being represented by various configurations of three arrows.[5] With the Virginia Assembly's appropriation of this practice, it was to be assumed that any Indians not bearing recognizable badges were hostile, and they were to be executed (Beverly, 1722: pp. 157, 181–82; Mooney, 1894: p. 31).

In 1670, the governor of Virginia commissioned German traveler John Lederer to explore the country west of the James Falls and southward into Carolina. However vague, Lederer's account is one of the best descriptions available on the Virginia Siouans of the period. Twenty days from the falls, Lederer came upon "Monacan Town," or the Mowhemicho of Smith's day. For the purposes of this study, the most important information contained in his account concerns European trade items. As Lederer entered Monacan Town, a volley of firearms greeted him, perhaps indicating that European traders had made at least indirect contact with the Monacans. Granted, the village marked the easternmost portion of Monacan territory at that time, and it is possible that these weapons came to them via their Susquehannock trade allies. Yet Lederer made certain remarks that suggest that many of the Indians he encountered had had minimal contact with whites. Notably, he advised traders traveling west of the falls to carry to those tribes *closest* to the frontier implements such as trade cloth, awls, hoes, scissors, and edged tools. For more remote tribes, however, he recommended simpler items, such as small mirrors, trinkets, beads, bracelets, pictures, and knives (Alvord and Bidgood, 1912: pp. 169–70).

One year later, Thomas Batts set out on a journey 120 miles west of Appomattee Village (present-day Bermuda Hundred, near Petersburg). Along the Otter River, he encountered a Saponi settlement, probably in Campbell County, near present-day Lynchburg. Further west, he encountered "Totera" (Tutelo) settlements probably in the vicinity of the present-day city of Salem and Patrick County, Virginia, the latter nestled deep in the Blue Ridge (Alvord and Bidgood, 1912: pp. 185–86; Mooney, 1894: pp. 34–35). Interestingly, Lederer had encountered both groups a year earlier in the locations charted by Newport in 1608. Indeed, some archaeological evidence suggests that the Saponi inhabitants of Monasukapanough (near present-day Charlottesville) were in the process of leaving the village around

1670, though a few may have remained into the early 1700s (Bush-nell, 1930: pp. 13, 19, 22).

These accounts evoke the question as to why the Tutelos and Saponis in particular seem to have moved about so suddenly. It is possible that the westerly settlements had existed for some time, though as previously noted, there is evidence that the Tutelo and Saponi settlements in the East were in the process of dispersing. Of course, for a hunting and gathering people, physical mobility was not out of the ordinary. But as also noted previously, many of the Virginia Siouans seem to have been adapting to a more sedentary lifeway. It seems more likely that the Tutelos and Saponis were beginning to experience the effects of a slow but steady European colonial thrust inland. Although these groups remained relatively isolated (indeed, their movements may have been an attempt to maintain such isolation), colonial activities in the period from 1650 to 1700 had profound effects on them, not only in terms of Indian-white relations but with regard to intertribal affairs as well.

Mooney (1894) suggests that the tie between the Tutelos and Saponis was so close that "[u]nder either name, their history begins in 1670" (p. 37). In making such a statement, Mooney reflected the Eurocentric view that the aboriginal peoples of this continent were devoid of their own unique histories until the coming of Western concepts of documentation. Nonetheless, it is worth examining the colonial experiences of the Tutelos and Saponis collectively after 1670, as these tribes and their activities are the best documented of the Monacan affiliates. The period from 1670 to 1740 marked a time of transition and uncertain mobility for most of the Tutelos and Saponis. In 1675, Virginia and Maryland colonists overthrew the powerful Susquehannocks, who had previously acted as a formidable buffer between the Five Nations and the Virginia tribes. This precipitated an increase in Iroquois raids from the north, and the Tutelos and Saponis in Campbell and Nelson Counties found themselves in a vulnerable position. Soon thereafter, some of them moved from their settlements along the Otter River and joined their Occaneechi allies at the confluence of the Dan and Staunton Rivers. However, this location proved to be equally vulnerable, as it lay directly in the Iroquois' route to their southernmost enemies, the Catawbas (Schaeffer, 1942: p. ix).

The fall of the Susquehannocks prompted a state of flux within the Virginia Indian country. Intertribal warfare trickled into colonial settlements that were beginning to penetrate the Piedmont, thus sparking white fears of a general Indian uprising. In 1676, a citizen army under the command of Charles City planter Nathaniel Bacon, without the approval of the colonial government, proclaimed open war on all Virginia Indians. In truth, Bacon's Rebellion was a frustrated reaction to the failure of colonial authorities to regulate tobacco trade tariffs. Although the Iroquois initiated most Indian raids on colonial settlements, Virginia tribes became the targets of retaliation. Bacon's men first sacked the Pamunkeys near Richmond, then turned southwestward and virtually annihilated the peaceful Occaneechis and their recent neighbors at the confluence of the Dan and Staunton Rivers.

Bacon's choice to attack the Occaneechis is difficult to grasp. Many accounts say that he decided to turn on the Occaneechis when they refused to turn over some "Manakins" (Monacans) to his command, even after they had aided him in overpowering a party of Susquehannocks (Washburn, 1957: pp. 43–46). His decision may also have been influenced by the fact that the village was an important center for fur trade. Whatever the case, the Occaneechis, and other Siouan peoples in their midst suffered greatly before Bacon's Rebellion was suppressed by colonial troops under Governor Berkeley (Mooney, 1894: p. 38; Schaeffer, 1942: p. viii; Houck, 1984: p. 71).

Bacon's Rebellion had the potential to spark a formidable Indian uprising, as the only Indians his forces had killed were those deemed "friendly" by the General Assembly (Washburn, 1957: p. 43). The rebellion also brought about a lull in the western fur trade, while internal strife in England (which ultimately led to the Glorious Revolution of 1688) created a shortage of regular British troops in America (Rice, 1970: p. 15). Perhaps in an effort to appease these tribes and to gain their alliance for the protection of European settlers, the colonial government negotiated a treaty with most of the known Virginia tribes in 1677.[6] This was the first colonial treaty to which any of the Siouan groups of Virginia were a party. Its terms were rather liberal toward the Indians, except that it required that the signatory "Indian Kings and Queens . . . acknowledge to have their immediate dependency on, and Own all subjection to the Great King of England" (Stanard, 1907a: p. 290). The treaty also acknowledged that the signatory tribes held their land in fee patent, and that they were to pay no rent for it other than twenty beaver skins and "three Indian arrows" from each tribe, to be delivered to the governor "in acknowledgment that they hold their Crownes, and Lands of the Great King of England" (Stanard, 1907a: pp. 291–93). It is interesting that the tribal insignia of the Monacans (the three arrows) were appropriated as a symbol of their subordinance to the British Crown. Although the treaty promised the Indians ample protections from encroachments on their land and injustices committed against them by non-Indians (Stanard, 1907a: 291–93), the overriding rhetoric of subjugation to the crown (e.g., the implication that their lands ultimately belonged to the King), foretold an impending state of dependency for the signatory tribes. One Monacan chief and two Saponi chiefs signed the treaty, though there is no reason to believe that they represented the entire complement of the Monacan confederacy, many of whom had migrated westward and southward into the Carolinas.

Neither Bacon's Rebellion nor the 1677 treaty inhibited Iroquois raids. Ironically, these raids seem to have perpetuated the dependence of many of the southern tribes on an otherwise common enemy—the colonists. By 1700, most of the Siouan tribes in Virginia and the Carolinas were leaving their initial settlements as a result of increased Iroquois raids (Byrd, 1929: v. 1, pp. 120, 188; v. 2, p. 220). In 1701, surveyor John Lawson reported that larger tribes in North Carolina were building palisaded villages for protection, while smaller tribes were consolidating and seeking protective alliances with other tribes or with colonists. Among the smaller tribes he encountered were the Occaneechis (near present-day Hillsboro) and the Tutelos and Saponis on the Yadkin River (present-day Salis-bury). Lawson reported that the combined population of the three tribes was about 750, and that as a result of their limited numbers, the latter two had sought protection from English settlers (Lawson, 1860: pp. 8, 334).

Due to steady Iroquois raids and uneasy relations with other Car-olina tribes, the Tutelos, Saponis, and Occaneechis continued to move around the Carolina Piedmont intermittently. Apparently, some of them entered agreements with the governor of Virginia to settle lands along the Meherrin River near the North Carolina bor-der in 1708 (Feest, 1974: p. 153). Then, around 1711, most of them returned to Virginia at the urging of Governor Spotswood, who of-fered them colonial protection at Fort Christanna in Brunswick County (also along the banks of the Meherrin). Although the Tute-los and their allies were enticed by the offer of protection, the mo-tives behind the Fort Christanna experiment were mixed. In con-junction with colonial authorities in North Carolina, Spotswood hoped that the settlement would draw these tribes away from alli-ances with "hostile" Indians (especially the Tuscaroras, who had just become engaged in a massive war with the colonists), and would provide a physical barrier between the hostile tribes and Virginia and Carolina settlers. With the Indians concentrated in one location, Spotswood attempted to implement a program of "civilization," sending missionaries and a schoolmaster to proselytize the Indians, and even sending a few to the College of William and Mary (Alex-ander, 1972: p. 157; Byrd, 1929: v. 1, pp. 75, 188; Mooney, 1894: pp. 42–44). This program was apparently short-lived, and the darker side of Indian-white relations became more prevalent.

The Tutelos and Saponis benefited very little from the Fort Christanna endeavor, as they constantly found themselves at odds with their Virginia Iroquoian neighbors, the Meherins and Nottow-ays, and faced continued raids from the Five Nations. Moreover, unscrupulous white traders from nearby settlements took advantage of the Indians' confined condition and used alcohol to entice them into unequal trade (Mooney, 1894: p. 43; Schaeffer, 1942: p. x). These problems were only exacerbated, no doubt, by the fact that the Virginia Indian Company (which had monopolized the Virginia fur trade for years) was permitted to operate a trading post at the fort (Alexander, 1972: p. 155). The Tutelo-Saponis continued to hunt and farm for subsistence, though existing records suggest an increasing dependence on agriculture (Bushnell, 1930: pp. 29–31). Although records are lacking to verify the extent to which they engaged in hunting, it is quite possible that the physical restrictions of Fort Christanna placed a strain on their physical environment. As White (1983) points out in his study of the Choctaws, Pawnees, and Navajos, alcohol, coupled with the negative demographic impact of Old World diseases loosened certain social taboos and increased reliance on nonaboriginal technologies for survival among these tribes. As a consequence, overhunting within a given territory for the sake of procuring European trade goods became common. Given the lack of physical mobility that the Fort Christanna Indians faced (reinforced by the threat of Iroquois attacks), it is possible that a similar process developed among the Tutelo-Saponis. In fact, the influx of alcohol did have adverse affects on their demographic and social order. Lawson (1866) reported that five-sixths of population among the Indians he visited along the Virginia-Carolina border in 1701 had died of alcohol related illnesses or European diseases such as smallpox (pp. 3–4, 119).

To the extent that paternalistic concerns of colonial authorities for the Fort Christanna Indians existed at all, they seemed only peripheral. Evidence of this lies in the words of the Huguenot traveler John Fontaine, who accompanied Governor Spotswood to the Fort in 1716. Fontaine described the "Saponey" town in subhuman terms: "They live as lazily and miserably as any people on earth," and "[t]hey look wild, and are mighty shy of an Englishman, and will not let you touch them" (Alexander, 1972: pp. 96–97). As ethnocentric as these words are, there is probably a strong element of truth in them insofar as the Tutelos had ample reason to be wary of their colonial overseers. Fontaine noted that the Indian leaders made various complaints to the governor about raids from other tribes and the depredations of white traders, but received only modest material compensation for their troubles (Alexander, 1972: p. 93).

The Tutelos and Saponis, it seems, were ultimately pawns in a scheme to stifle Iroquoian hostilities directed at white settlements. Indeed, the Iroquois did cease their southward thrust, but on their own terms. In September of 1722, representatives of the Iroquois League met in Albany with colonial governors and representatives from other tribes, north and south, including the Fort Christanna Indians. The product was a treaty in which the Iroquois agreed not to cross the Potomac River to make war (Mooney, 1894: p. 45). Evidently, the Iroquois regarded the treaty as an acknowledgment of their own political dominion, for at a 1744 council in Lancaster, Pennsylvania, a spokesman for the Five Nations denied any claims that the British had conquered any of the Virginia tribes other than those of the Powhatan alliance, and asserted that the tribes at the foot of the Blue Ridge were considered to be Iroquois subjects (Alexander, 1972: p. 22).

Apparently, the Tutelos and Saponis concurred with the Iroquois assertion of hegemony, for by 1740 they were trickling out of Fort Christanna to place themselves under the protective umbrella of the Five Nations. Their decision to join their old enemies serves as a likely testament to their unpleasant colonial experiences vis-à-vis the Virginia colonists. In addition to being subjected to the whims of unscrupulous white traders, the Fort Christanna Indians had to contend with the imposition of conflicting cultural values by colonial authorities, not only through missionaries and teachers, but through an alien justice system as well. William Byrd wrote of an incident that apparently provoked many of the Fort Christanna Indians to abandon faith in the capacity of Virginia authorities to protect their interests. In 1728, an unidentified chief at Fort Christanna murdered another Indian while intoxicated. The colonial authorities promptly dealt with the situation by hanging the assailant. The Indians were outraged by this method of dealing with criminals. According to Byrd, it violated a spiritual taboo in which it was believed that a person must die in such a manner that his or her soul would be allowed to leave the body through the mouth (Byrd, 1929: v. 1, p. 185). It is possible, however, that the Tutelos and Saponis would have sought an alternative means of *restitution*, as opposed to *retribution*, had they dealt with the situation in their own way. Traditionally, in many tribal societies (notably the western Siouan tribes) offenders such as murderers were often required to compensate for their crime by assuming responsibility for the welfare of their victim's family. In this manner, community harmony was given priority, and death was prescribed for only the most heinous offenses, such as rape or incest (Deloria and Lytle, 1983: pp. 83, 111).

The Tutelos and Saponis seem to have slowly trickled northward from Fort Christanna to their new home with the Five Nations, and as they did, their identity as separate peoples faded. By 1745, they were reported to be established in the village of Shamakin (near Salisbury, Pennsylvania). At that time their population was said to be around 150 (Hale, 1883: p. 6) although there is no evidence that this number represented the entire membership of these tribes. Once there, the Iroquois posted sentinels to monitor the influx of traders and liquor. While these precautions were only partially successful, the Tutelos began to realize a renewed sense of autonomy in their relations with the Iroquois. They were allowed to maintain separate settlements, and although they were officially adopted into the Cayuga Nation in 1753, they maintained a separate ceremonial complex for years thereafter. However, as a result of widespread intermarriage with the Cayugas, and of epidemic diseases, there are presently only faint vestiges of Tutelo culture among the Cayugas, including some linguistic survivals (Hale, 1883; Schaeffer, 1942: p. xiii).

The Tutelos and Saponis were but a portion of the Monacan alliance. What became of the other affiliated tribes, such as the Monacans proper? Unfortunately, the historical record is all but silent here. It is known is that in 1699, the governor of Virginia arbitrarily extended a land grant to a colony of French Huguenots at the site of the village of Mowhemicho, then known as Manakan Town. Fleeing religious persecution in France, these Protestants were granted asylum by King William III, who arranged for their trip to the British colonies. Upon reaching the apparently abandoned Manakin Town, the Huguenots repaired the existing Indian dwellings and cleared the Monacan old fields for their own use (Winfree, 1975: pp. 65–67). As late as 1702, a small group of displaced Indians was known to have lived nearby, and to have entered the Huguenot colony on occasion to trade furs, corn, and pottery. However, they are said to have vanished from the area by 1722 (Beverly, 1705: p. 245; Virginia Historical Society, 1883: pp. 42–43, 51; Bushnell, 1930: p. 9). Mooney suggested that they probably joined the Tutelos and Saponis and ultimately ventured north (1894: p. 30). It is quite possible, however, that instead they ventured farther upstream along the James and settled there permanently.

Colonialism and Dependency: A Preliminary Analysis

The paucity of historical and ethnographic data on the Virginia Siouan tribes in the early colonial period (1608–1740) makes it difficult to draw solid conclusions about their colonial experiences or the extent to which they became economically dependent on external forces. However, it can be assumed that these processes were intimately related.

In this period, it can be said that the Monacans were a colony in the classic sense. They were invaded by foreign entities, treated as subordinates—if not outsiders—to the mother country (Britain), and subjected to doctrines of racism that at their extreme took the form of cultural and physical genocide. Even so, it is possible to view the various parts of the Monacan Confederacy differentially based on the intensity of their colonial experience.

The easternmost portion of the Confederacy (i.e., the Monacans proper in the town of Mowhemicho) probably felt the greatest thrust of British colonial activity in the early years. It is into their territory that Newport first ventured in search of minerals, and Lederer's account seems to indicate that they were the first to procure European trade goods, especially firearms. Undoubtedly they were among the first Virginia Siouan tribes to fall prey to the General Assembly's policy in the 1620s of exterminating Indians. The afore-mentioned census of 1669, listing no more than 120 Monacans, serves as evidence. And yet the Monacans proper remained in the vicinity of Mowhemicho into the early 1700s, notwithstanding the arrival of the Huguenots. The Huguenots seem to have maintained relatively peaceful relations with their Monacan neighbors, and the records seem to indicate that the Indians had become quite dependent on European trade goods by this time.

As for other tribes of the Monacan Confederacy, it seems likely that those farther inland were the last to feel the effects of the British colonial thrust, while others, such as the Tutelos of Monahassanugh (Nelson County) and the Saponis of Monasukapanough (Albemarle County), began to abandon their villages for more westerly positions as colonial intrusions became imminent. In this manner, many were able for years to avoid succumbing to the colonial process. Ultimately, it seems that colonial relations with other tribes contributed to their demise. The defeat of the Susquehannocks in the 1670s triggered a chain reaction of Iroquois invasions that were met with colonial hostility. These weakened the Tutelos, Saponis, and Occaneechis, forced them into the Carolinas, and ultimately into a state of dependence on colonial largess at Fort Christanna. Restricted in movement, the Fort Christanna Indians faced conditions that allowed only a minimal reliance on game for subsistence, and left them vulnerable to disease and the invading foot of unscrupulous traders and Iroquois raiders. As their dependence on an indifferent colonial government increased, Governor Spotswood made a marginal effort to assimilate the Fort Christanna Indians through missionary and education programs. Likewise, the Indians found themselves subject to the colonial justice system, which ostensibly dealt with them in the same manner as non-Indian citizens. At that point, it might be argued that the Fort Christanna Indians were beginning to resemble an internal colony of Virginia, as their aboriginal culture was not held in high esteem, but the governor seemed to be making an effort to integrate them. However, their dependence on the colonial Virginia government was supplanted by relative dependence on the Iroquois League. Under the Great Peace of the Iroquois, the Tutelo-Saponis were able to salvage a great deal of their autonomy and to evade the forces of Euro-American colonialism for several years to come.

What is missing in this historical puzzle is an account of those members of the Monacan Confederacy who did not make the journey to the Five Nations. The assumption of many scholars is that all of the Virginia Siouan tribes either migrated north with the Tutelos or became extinct. Most of these accounts, however, were written without knowledge of the Indians of Amherst County (and surrounding areas for that matter), whose colonial experience had far from reached its zenith at the time of the exodus of the Fort Christanna Indians.

2 TOBACCO ROW

Development of a Colonial Enclave

History is laced with cruel ironies. In 1492, Cristobal Colón (known to the English-speaking world as Christopher Columbus) accidentally arrived off the coast of the Americas while searching for a westerly passage to India. In Spanish, the name Colón translates into "farmer." Hence, the word *colonialism* for the concomitant attempts to justify colonial processes as progress. Thus, the process whereby Europeans and their progeny have systematically dispossessed the indigenous peoples of the non-Western world is aptly named like the one who initiated it on the eve of the modern era. Nearly three hundred years later, an American continental general named Jeffrey Amherst contrived a scheme for exterminating Indian tribes on the frontier by sending them gifts of smallpox-infested blankets (Rice, 1970: p. 56). In 1774, the government of Virginia honored this military "hero" by naming a county on the upper James River after him. In the two centuries to follow, Amherst County would play host to one of the most peculiar and denigrating set of colonial circumstances ever to face indigenous people in North America.

Before the advent of railroads and highways, rivers provided the vital means of transportation and communication in the southeastern highlands, and for the Monacans and their confederates the

49

James River served as the primary artery. Several early explorers encountered Monacan groups living near the upper James in the vicinity of present-day Amherst County, and in neighboring counties, and the archaeological record confirms these settlements (Bushnell, 1930; Hantman, 1990). However, until recently it was assumed among scholars that when the last of the Indians from Fort Christanna trickled into the Iroquois Confederacy, Virginia was cleared permanently of Siouan peoples.

A deeper scrutiny of colonial records and local traditions, however, reveals strong evidence of Indian occupancy in Amherst County and adjacent areas long after the exodus to the Iroquois Confederacy. On the eve of the French and Indian War, the Virginia cartographer Lewis Evans drafted a map depicting the location of known Indian tribes along the frontier. In the vicinity of the Tobacco Row Mountains (present-day Amherst County), he wrote the names "Monacan" and "Tuscarora" (Evans, 1755). Likewise, in 1787 Thomas Jefferson—reflecting on an encounter with Indians visiting a burial mound on his property circa 1750—located the Monacans "on the upper part of the James River" (Jefferson, 1982: p. 97). Houck (1984: p. 35) points out that local traditions tell of two or three Indian villages in the vicinity of Lynchburg (which lies across the James River from Amherst) as late as 1781, though no specific tribal affiliation is given. However, in 1935 a local historian specifically referred to Indians known to be living near Madison Heights in the late eighteenth century as "peaceful Indians belonging to the Monagan tribe" (Yancey, 1935: p. 9).

The nineteenth and early twentieth centuries are seemingly devoid of any written reference to the Monacans or their confederates living in Virginia, although in 1914 Bushnell speculated that the Indians of Amherst County were of Monacan or Tutelo descent and suggested that further research be conducted (p. 112). Although this suggestion went unheeded until the 1980s, in 1934 a man named Samuel Johns (a common surname among the present-day Monacans) from neighboring Rockbridge County wrote to Frank Speck, who was then conducting research on the Tutelos in Canada, and informed him that he was of Tutelo descent (Johns, 1934).[1]

Beyond these scant bits, very little information exists from which to reconstruct a history of the Monacans in Amherst County between the time of European contact and the early twentieth century. Therefore, the ensuing historical analysis is based largely on an amalgam of census data, incomplete genealogies, and oral histories. Although many Monacans lived in areas adjacent to Amherst County, this analysis will be restricted to Amherst County because of the peculiar exploitative schemes that developed and diffused from there. These schemes reflect the profound relationship between the politics of race and the political economy of the region. The emphasis in this chapter is on Indian-white relations as they developed with the coming of Euro-Americans to the upper James River, how these relations affected the lives of the Amherst Indians over time, and the resultant feudal political economy that flourished in the county well into the twentieth century.

Euro-American Settlement of the Upper James

The 467 square mile area that became Amherst County is situated along the north bank of the James River and straddles a dividing line between the Piedmont and the Blue Ridge Mountains. The eastern segment of the county comprises rolling hills, which today do not appear as formidable obstacles to travel but in colonial times (especially before virgin forests were cleared) kept travelers close to the river. As one moves westward, a set of rugged peaks known as the Tobacco Row Mountains sprout from the horizon. Here is the eastern extreme of the Blue Ridge Escarpment in Amherst County, and the more rugged terrain of this area has resulted in its being the most isolated (in relative terms) and least populated section of the county. Yet the Tobacco Row Mountains, particularly Bear Mountain, have served as a focal point for Monacan life for centuries.

These mountains, however, did not inspire the covetous eyes of European speculators and yeoman farmers until the latter half of the eighteenth century. For one thing, even the Piedmont sections of present-day Amherst County contained only marginal soils, leeched by time. Moreover, although white settlers had moved farther west in some sections, the area of Amherst County was considered part of the frontier until at least 1760, as evidenced by the aforementioned map by Evans (1755). Thus, the area of Amherst County provided a physical and cultural barrier in which the remnant Virginia Monacans were able to enclave themselves until at least 1774, when Albemarle County was partitioned to form the county of Amherst (Houck, 1984: p. 31).

At the vanguard of Euro-American movement into the upper James region were fur traders. William Byrd was perhaps the first non-Indian to enter the area (in the early 1700s), followed by a trader named Hughs in the 1720s, who settled with his family along Otter Creek, where earlier explorers had reported Monacan settlements. While it is difficult to determine the effects these traders' activities had on the Indians of the area, they certainly had a profound impact on Monacan society through intermarriage. Hughs is reported to have married a local Indian woman, as did William Johns, the son of Richmond trader Robert Johns (as noted earlier, a common surname among present-day Monacans), who settled along the upper James in the 1750s (Houck, 1984: pp. 31, 51).

Houck (1984) points out that across the Tobacco Row Mountains in Rockbridge County, a large concentration of Monacans were settled along Irish Creek and remain there to date. But the origin of the name "Irish" deserves close scrutiny. Most likely, this creek was labeled as such as a result of a significant number of Scotch-Irish settlers who had entered the area from the Shenandoah Valley via the upper James in the 1740s (Leyburn, 1962: p. 209; Evans, 1965). While there is no indication of hostile relations between these settlers and the Monacans, their relations were probably marked by a significant degree of intermarriage, as intimated by contemporary works (Vest, 1992).

What appears to be most striking about the early years of Euro-American settlement of Amherst County is the fact that there is no indication that Indian-white relations were particularly turbulent. Certain later settlers such as Ned Branham, whose surname is also common among Monacans, were also known to have married Indian women. Evidence of a peaceful cultural interchange is seen in a local cemetery near Salt Creek, dating back to 1820, in which Indians and non-Indians are buried side by side (Houck, 1984: pp. 45–46). But to whatever extent Indian-white relations were harmonious in the late eighteenth century in Amherst County, they did not remain so. As the fingers of Western commerce prodded into the region, racial tensions began to escalate.

The Colonial Thrust: Commerce and Racial Disenfranchisement

However benign the sentiments of the early traders along the upper James River were toward Natives, they ultimately paved the way for systematic encroachment on Indian lands and rights by more aggressive settlers. The first trading posts established in the area emerged as commercial centers, which ultimately served as springboards to distant markets. Although the arable land in Amherst County was not the best, it was more than adequate to produce valuable cash crops such as corn, oats, and especially tobacco. The latter crop can be credited with speeding the early growth of the city of Lynchburg directly across the James River from Amherst County.

One of the first commercial centers to emerge in Amherst County was the small village of Bethel, along Salt Creek at the foot of the Tobacco Row Mountains. The site was originally a trading post in the 1750s, and in 1767 Nicholas Davis purchased the site and built a gristmill there. It then emerged as a small commercial center for Indians and white settlers. Subsequently, a tobacco warehouse was constructed and a ferry began transporting goods down the James River to markets. As more settlers moved into the area, similar commercial centers emerged along tributaries of the James (Houck, 1984: pp. 45–52). Thus the initial groundwork was laid for the influx of new settlers into the county and for the siphoning out of resources.

Increasingly after 1750, the droves of settlers who came to Amherst County were not interested in trade with the local Indian population, much less in equitable relations with them. As far as they and the colonial Virginia government were concerned, the lands they settled were previously unoccupied. These settlers brought with them an entrepreneurial desire to join the ranks of the plantation South, or at least to compete within the emerging agrarian economy. Thus the primary resource sought by these foreigners in the impending colonial process was the land itself.

By 1790, Amherst County's population had reached 13,703, of which 5,296 were slaves. The fact that nearly half the population consisted of slaves indicates the predominance of plantation agriculture in the county. Notably, this ratio did not change significantly until the institution of slavery was terminated after the Civil War (U.S. Bureau of the Census, 1908: p. 9, 1864: p. 155). Unfortunately, the early census enumerators were neither consistent nor thorough in recording data concerning agricultural production, but it is clear that the Amherst County economy did not depend on a single crop. While the 1820 Census does not elaborate on types of crops grown in the county, it does list 3,152 people (out of a total population of 10,932—a momentary decline) as being engaged in agriculture (U.S. Bureau of the Census, 1821: p. 206). These numbers, of course, do not account for the 5,567 slaves whose labor fueled agricultural production, but they do serve as a testament to the intense importance of agriculture in the local economy.

The 1840 Census is more detailed and reveals a rather diversified agricultural base. Crops such as corn, oats, and wheat were each produced in quantities exceeding hundreds of thousands of bushels. Cattle, sheep, and swine were also raised and sold to a significant degree and continued to play a major role in the local economy throughout the nineteenth century (U.S. Bureau of the Census, 1841: pp. 155–56, 1864: p. 155; 1895: p. 311). Although cotton was never "king" in Amherst County, as it was in lower parts of the South, tobacco was perhaps the number one cash crop well into the twentieth century. In 1840, 2,106,149 pounds of tobacco were produced in the county, marking it as one of the top producers in the state, and by the inception of the Civil War that number climbed to 2,847,209 pounds of tobacco (U.S. Bureau of the Census, 1841: p. 155; 1864: p. 155).

Given the considerable distance of Amherst County from major markets at the time, the question arises as to how commercial agriculture was able to flourish so rapidly. The answer lies in that pivotal conduit through which the Monacans had previously controlled the copper trade with their eastern neighbors along the James River. During George Washington's tenure as President, he expressed a desire to link east with west via a manufactured waterway reaching from the Atlantic Ocean to the Mississippi River. This grand scheme came to a limited fruition in the 1800s in the form of the Kanawha Canal. Although the canal fell far short of reaching the Mississippi, it became an important transportation route between Fincastle and Richmond, both in Virginia. Paralleling the James River (on which the canal depended for its supply of water) the route between Lynchburg and Richmond was completed in 1840, touching the commercial town of Bethel along the way and fanning the flames of a blossoming tobacco industry at the foot of the Tobacco Row Mountains (Houck, 1984: p. 42). In its prime, the Kanawha Canal carried the largest tonnage of agricultural produce and natural resources of any transportation company in the United States. As late as 1880, its freight tonnage to Richmond was greater than that of all the Virginia railroads combined (Striplin, 1981: p. 31).

The Kanawha Canal, then, provided the crucial link between Amherst County and distant markets, which in turn stimulated the development of an agrarian economy in which the bulk of local lands and resources were controlled by a few individuals. In 1850, for example, only 780 farms were reported in the census for Amherst County, amidst a population of 12,699 (U.S. Bureau of the Census, 1851: p. 322). By 1880, after the slave labor system on which the plantation system depended was outlawed, and an increasing number of blacks were able to secure property or tenancy of their own, the number of farms in the county more than doubled (U.S. Bureau of the Census, 1883: p. 94).

Conspicuously absent from the early United States census data on Amherst County are references to Indians. The same is true of local records, and with good reason. The legal designation of "Indian" was not possible where prior indigenous titles to the land had not been acknowledged (i.e., through treaties). Census figures for more easterly counties list Indians whose land titles had been acknowledged by colonial Virginia through various treaties and agreements. In 1800, for example, four small reservations were left in eastern Virginia, two of which were soon divided and sold (Rountree, 1977: p. 29).[2] Thus, the history of the nineteenth-century Monacans of Virginia must, for the most part, be considered in the larger context of a broader legal designation—the "free colored" population of Amherst County.

The Colonial Watershed: Virginia and Amherst County in the 1800s

The nineteenth century saw the beginnings of blatant efforts to eradicate the history of the Monacan people in Virginia. Equitable relations with early settlers made it possible for the Monacans to stay in Amherst County, but the question still remains as to why they were overlooked—at least as "Indians"—in historical records and census enumerations. Had Governor Spotswood been aware of their presence along the upper James during the early 1700s, one can only speculate that he may have attempted to negotiate land titles with them as he had with other Monacan confederates. Then again, it is possible that some of the Indians of Amherst County were descended from Saponi inhabitants of Fort Christanna.[3] Of course, it is just as likely that colonial officials would have assumed, however incorrectly, that the Indians of Amherst County were previously represented by the handful of Saponi and Monacan parties to agreements such as the Treaty of 1677. Whatever the case may have been, with the exodus of the Fort Christanna Indians to the Six Nations, colonial officials evidently assumed that the Monacans and their confederates were no longer in Virginia.

Perhaps the most potent force behind the obscuring of Monacan history was the increasing marriage between the law and the doctrines of racism in antebellum Virginia. As proposals for removing Indians to the West gained popularity and eventually became reality, the presence of Indians in the East was increasingly frowned upon.[4] As Rountree suggests, "There were still people living along the Blue Ridge who knew they were of Indian descent. . . . All of these Indians followed a kind of lifestyle that by 1800 had come to be more like that of their small farmer neighbors. And this got them into trouble with these neighbors; the Indians no longer seemed like 'real Indians' to many Virginians" (1977: p. 28).

Why didn't the Monacans seem like "real" Indians and why did it get them into trouble? As Rountree suggests, they had *seemingly* assimilated to a lifestyle more akin to Euro-American culture. But it seems more likely that the real issue centered around the intermarriage of Indians and whites, which, as previously noted, was not infrequent in the early days of Euro-American settlement in Amherst County.

Historically speaking, there has often been a peculiar (albeit sparsely studied) pattern involving interethnic sexual relations in Western colonial endeavors worldwide. John Rolfe married Pocahontas partly "for the good of the Plantation" (Kaplan, 1990: p. 126). In the nineteenth-century colonies of France and the Netherlands, the practice of European men taking native concubines was actually institutionalized as a symbolic and substantive form of conquest (Stoler, 1989). Such unions, however, produced children whose mixed heritage raised questions among colonial officials as to the extent of their rights of property and enfranchisement, and these material questions merged with growing racism, ultimately resulting in the prohibition of such unions. Several scholars have suggested that such miscegenation laws in the United States largely developed in an effort to keep property in the hands of a privileged few. Evidence of this lies in the fact that such laws were most frequently enforced when white *women*—the perceived progenitors and nur-

turers of the privileged class who could not easily conceal preg-
nancy—were involved in sexual relations with men of color (Saks,
1988; Pascoe, 1989).

This pattern was readily apparent in Virginia from colonial times
to well into the twentieth century. In 1784, Patrick Henry unsuc-
cessfully proposed legislation in the Virginia House of Delegates to
financially reward whites who married Indians in an effort to stifle
frontier hostilities (Kaplan, 1990: p. 128). Years later, Thomas Jefferson cheerfully suggested to a group of Indians that "You will mix
with us by marriage, your blood will run in our veins" (Kaplan, 1990:
p. 129). While some of these real and idealized unions were born of
sincere and benign sentiments, many must have been born of a colonial effort to legitimize or protect Europeans on this continent.[5]

Naturally, sexual unions between Indians, whites, and blacks produced children whose mixed heritage confounded lawmakers who
themselves belonged to the privileged class of property holders. In
1691, the Virginia Assembly responded to this development with the
passage of Virginia's first miscegenation law, which decreed that any
English man or woman who engaged in sexual union with a "ne-
groe, mulatto, or Indian," would be, "banished and removed from
this dominion forever" (Henning, 1823: v. 3, p. 87). As an added pre-
caution, the law required that all freed slaves be transported "out of
the country," a provision that technically remained in effect until the
American Revolution. To be sure, this provision was instrumental in
preventing the acquisition of property by people of African descent,
but it did not address the question of the rights of people of Indian
descent.

What eventually led to the ultimate dispossession and disenfran-
chisement of Virginia Indians was the subsequent elaboration of
classificatory provisions in miscegenation laws. Rice argues that the
statistical decline of the Virginia Indian population in colonial times
can be attributed largely to the use of the legal term "mulatto" in
census records (1991: pp. 15–16). A 1705 Virginia law proclaimed
that the offspring of any Indian "should be deemed, accounted, held

and taken to be mulatto" (Henning, 1823: p. 252). After American independence, the state of Virginia added detail to earlier miscegenation provisions through a 1787 law stating that "any person of whose grandfathers or grandmothers . . . is, or shall have been a negro, although all other progenitors . . . shall have been white persons, shall be deemed mulattos" (Henning, 1823: p. 184). An 1823 law added further elaboration: "Be it enacted and declared . . . that the child of an Indian and the child, or great grandchild of a Negro, shall be deemed, accounted, and taken to be a mulatto" (Virginia Assembly, 1823: p. 252).

Evidently, the popular misconception that Indians only lived on reservations had already taken root in Virginia during the formative years of the American republic. While census enumerators often identified individuals as "Indian" by marking a letter "I" by their names, this was never the case in Amherst County, where free people of color were identified with the letter "M" for "mulatto," or "B" for "black." Interestingly, after 1880, enumerators increasingly supplanted the letter "M" with the letter "B" in Amherst, until 1900, when the distinction of "mulatto" was no longer to be found in county records (Rice, 1991: p. 18). This suggests that the Virginia miscegenation laws gave enumerators license to classify the race of individuals on the basis of their own biases and perceptions of phenotypic features.

Although the "free colored" population of Virginia was eventually permitted to own property, a 1793 law required that all such persons be registered in the counties in which they resided (McLeRoy and McLeRoy, 1993: p. 7). Among those names registered in Amherst County between 1822 and 1864 were several Monacan surnames: Johns, Branham, Adcox, Redcross, Hicks, and so forth. Typical of entries in the register of "free colored" people was the following:

30 December 1831—*Patrick Henry Redcross* a free man of Color, aged about twenty one years, brown complexion 5 feet 4 3/4 inches high with a scar in the edge of his right eyebrow occasioned by a cut with an axe. (McLeRoy and McLeRoy, 1993: p. 58)

Such detailed information made these entries resemble contemporary FBI records kept on individuals suspected of illegal or subversive activities. Incidentally, in the same year as this entry, Nat Turner led his infamous slave rebellion in Southampton County, which compounded governmental efforts to account for free people of color, black and Indian alike (Houck, 1984: p. 56). Moreover, free people of color carried the contradictory burden of paying taxes while being prohibited from voting. In this manner, the Indians of Virginia were treated as freed slaves rather than members of the original sovereign nations of this continent. At that point, however, mere survival took precedent for the Monacans of Amherst County over the assertion of their sovereign rights.

Adapting to Institutionalized Racism: The Bear Mountain Settlement

How many Indians actually lived in Amherst County in the nineteenth century? This is a difficult question to answer, considering that they were not listed as "Indians" in census records and due to the paucity of other historical data dealing specifically with Indians in the county. Between 1810 and 1860, census records report the number of "free colored" individuals fluctuating between 198 and 393, or from 2 to 3 percent of the county's total population (McLeRoy and McLeRoy, 1993: p. 215). Until more rigorous genealogical research is conducted, one can only speculate that most of these were Indians. Evidence of this proposition lies in the disproportionate decrease in the number of slaves in the county between 1800 and 1810 as compared to the slight increase in the "free colored" population. In 1800, there were 7,462 slaves in the county, compared to 5,207 in 1810. The "free colored" population in 1800 was 138, but was 198 in 1810 (U.S. Bureau of the Census, 1811: p. 54). While the declining number of slaves might have been due to several factors (e.g., health problems, momentary lapse in agricultural production, movement of planters and their slaves into western territories), it might also be attributable to out-migration by freed slaves. Unless their former owners had deeded them land, it is plausible that freed slaves would have migrated to a region where farming was not the only niche open to blacks. The Monacans, on the other hand, had been legally classified "free colored" from the inception of such laws and many of them owned property.

What land Indians owned in nineteenth-century Amherst County, however, was not recognized as deriving from an aboriginal title. Rather, it came to the Monacans through their association with early white settlers. While it is difficult to say precisely how much land was held by individual Monacans, the history of the Johns family at Bear Mountain serves to illustrate this point.

As previously noted, trader Robert Johns came to the area from Richmond in the 1750s. His brother Thomas, who accompanied him, acquired 218 acres, 100 of which he deeded to Robert in 1778 (McLeRoy and McLeRoy, 1993: p. 38). Robert's son William, who somehow evaded the miscegenation laws and married a Monacan woman, eventually inherited his father's tract.

Previously, the colonial government had granted lands only to white settlers, and with the exception of a few tribes on the Tidewater, would not acknowledge Indian reservations. Most of Virginia's lands west of the Tidewater were deeded to white settlers and speculators prior to American independence, and even if a free person of color could afford to buy land, it was unlikely that a white owner would sell it to such a person. Realistically, then, almost the only way Indians could become landowners was through intermarriage with whites. In this manner a portion of the Monacan people became legally landed, and preserved for a time a portion of their homeland and their culture.

In 1833, William "Will" Johns purchased 400 acres located on the northeastern edge of the Tobacco Row Mountains at Bear Mountain. Previously, he had purchased 42 acres of adjacent land and this combined acreage soon developed into a home for several of William's Monacan relatives outside of his immediate family (Houck, 1984: p. 52; McLeRoy and McLeRoy, 1993: p. 38). In 1856, Will Johns divided "The Settlement" (as it is often called) among his sons and daughters. The land remained in the family for years, until individual members either sold out or were forced to relinquish their claim when unable to pay property taxes (Houck, 1984: p. 54). What is significant, however, is that for several years *Indians* owned The Settlement. Other similar settlements may have existed in the area, as Monacan surnames appear at irregular intervals in county land ownership records (McLeRoy and McLeRoy, 1993). As early as 1778, for example, a "free colored" family by the name of Beverley (another common Monacan surname) is mentioned in county tax records as owning 115 acres of land (McLeRoy and McLeRoy, 1993: p. 38).

With the establishment of the Johns Settlement, Bear Mountain became a focal point for Monacan homesteads. However, the vast majority of Monacans were not property owners. Instead, they either lived with landed relatives (such as at the Johns Settlement) or occupied as virtual squatters vacant lands owned by white settlers. Because the land surrounding Bear Mountain was too rugged for large-scale agriculture, squatting could be practiced without incurring the wrath of non-Indian owners. Arthur Gray made a reference to such practices in 1908: "Their [the Monacans] houses are merely little log cabins . . . and one such cabin will sometimes be the home of two or three families. . . . They live scattered about on the land of the white people" (1908: p. 1). Today, the remains of such "squatter" settlements lay strewn around the remote hollows of Bear Mountain and adjoining Sweet Briar Mountain. Decaying cabins are clustered near numerous aged cemeteries with occasional markers bearing names such as Johns, Branham, and Redcross, amid a plethora of unmarked graves. Some of the Monacan participants in this study told of growing up in such a situation and a handful of older Monacans still live rent free on the lands of non-Indians (Cook, 1996a; 1996b).

Although Bear Mountain may have been sacred to the Monacan-Saponis in precolonial times, the settlement patterns that developed in the nineteenth century ultimately made the mountain a symbol of Monacan identity. The issue of Monacan identity will be covered in greater depth in the next chapter, but it is important to note that the process by which a Monacan cultural enclave developed around Bear

Mountain in the nineteenth century might be viewed as a form of passive resistance to the dominant society of the colonizer. In other words, Monacans did what they had to do to survive. If they appeared outwardly to assimilate to the material culture of non-Indians, the appearances shielded the efforts of Indians at Bear Mountain to maintain bonds of community that had sustained them in earlier years. It was a process through which Monacans preserved and articulated a fluid sense of *peoplehood*.[6] Edward Spicer suggested that such processes of indigenous cultural endurance vis-à-vis the colonial development of nation-states are made possible by a condition of "cultural blindness" on the part of the colonizers (1994: p. 48). In short, colonial agents have often assumed that their subordinates were incapable of being like themselves, or were inherently inferior to themselves. Thus, they either ignored cultural persistence, or mistook cultural adaptation for assimilation (Spicer, 1994: p. 35).

Spicer's argument, however, points to the fact that "peoplehood" is not a given, but something that is constantly being negotiated, disputed, constructed, and reconstructed by members of a group and even by outsiders. Anthropologists have often used the term *ethnogenesis* to describe such historical processes of group self-distinction based on sociocultural and linguistic heritage (Sturtevant, 1971: p. 92). In recent years the concept of ethnogenesis has been broadened as "an analytical tool for developing critical historical approaches to culture as an ongoing process of conflict and struggle over a people's existence and their positioning within and against a general history of domination" (Hill, 1996: p. 1; Sider, 1994). For example, some of the most salient cases of the historical emergence of new peoples in the context of domination are those of the various Maroon societies in the Caribbean—societies formed from an amalgam of disparate colonized peoples, some of whom were transported from Africa (Bilby, 1996).

Ethnogenetic processes may take many forms, ranging from the redefinition of a single group's relationship to others, to the merging of several disparate groups to form a new ethnic configuration. As I will illustrate in subsequent pages, the emergence of the present-day Monacan Nation must be understood in terms of a process of ethnogenesis fueled in large part by a history of colonial domination. For instance, Hantman (1998) alludes to the possibility of various Monacan-affiliated groups merging in response to colonial pressures as early as 1650 when he states that by that time the Monacans were probably "renamed by colonial powers as the Saponi and the Tutelo, among other names" (1998, p. 14). A century later, many Saponis and Tutelos dealt with the inevitable Monacan diaspora by seeking asylum with—and ultimately integration into— the Six Nations, which itself constituted a separate process of ethnogenesis. For the Monacan-affiliated groups left in Virginia (namely, those in Amherst and surrounding counties), the process ultimately gained an extra layer of complexity with an increasing rate of intermarriage with non-Indians. This fluid construction and readjustment of group boundaries and identity over the years probably contributed significantly to the Amherst County Indians' failure to be recognized by colonial forces as a distinct tribal (and hence political) entity. Thus, the situation confronting these Indians circa 1750 and afterwards was similar to that described by Albers (1996) regarding various Algonquian conglomerate groups on the Northern Plains in the 1870s who were denied political recognition "because their hybridized ethnic backgrounds and identities did not match the picture of the policymakers, which was a notion of tribal blocs with exclusive memberships and territories" (p. 116).

With the possible exception of phenotypic differences, the Indians at Bear Mountain did not appear as "Indians" to their non-Indian neighbors in the nineteenth century. They lived in dwellings similar to those of their less affluent white neighbors, they raised the same crops and wore the same style of clothes. To the outsider, they were merely free people of color. But inside the community, a sense of peoplehood was flourishing—that is, a negotiated but shared sense of ancestry and history that was probably strengthened by a shared experience of marginalization. This situation is illustrative of Sider's argument that many native communities in the colonial Southeast were able to remain relatively autonomous because their autonomy "lay in a social 'invisibility' based on copying the outward appearances and economic activities of small Euro-American hamlets" (1994: p. 111). Although they did not fit the mold of popularly misconceived images of "real Indians," some of the more tangible elements of their culture persisted within the community. Some of the older Monacan participants in this study recall their grandparents speaking fluent "Indian," some as late as the 1950s. And to date, several tribal members retain an acute knowledge of the medicinal and other uses of wild plants passed on to them from prior generations (Cook, 1996a; 1996b).

It might be argued, then, that the period from about 1800 to 1860 marked a time of relative stability for Monacans around Bear Mountain. Life was not easy, to be sure, and they were by no means first-class citizens. Yet they were able to function as a community with little interference. Moreover, the thousands of black slaves living in the county afforded them a certain level of artificial prestige in the overall colonial hierarchy. All of this would change abruptly with the conclusion of the Civil War.

The Enduring Fiefdom of Amherst

It is all too easy to overlook the existence of slave labor in pre–Civil War Appalachia because the mountains for the most part inhibited any widespread occurrence of a plantation system. Amherst County, containing considerable amounts of workable land east of its mountainous sections, was the site of a rather prolific plantation economy in the antebellum South. As the slave population accounted for nearly half of the county's inhabitants prior to the Civil War, the "free colored" population of Amherst received a small degree of prestige in the dominant social hierarchy, since they were not at the bottom of the scale. Yet when the institution of slavery was terminated, free people of color in the South became merely "people of color," a legal category which now included former slaves.

In scrutinizing American miscegenation laws, Eva Saks (1988) has argued that after the Civil War, such laws in the South (which she maintains were designed to keep property in the hands of a privileged few white families by ensuring that their perceived "inferiors" could not gain such privileges through intermarriage) effectively internalized the prewar "feudal" economy. Although the termination of slavery had a crippling effect on the plantation economy, many large landowners were able to supplant the former system of unpaid labor with an almost equally oppressive system of sharecropping.

This was particularly true in Amherst County, where a quasi-feudal economy can be said to have existed into the 1960s. What is most striking about the situation in Amherst is that the termination of slavery drew greater attention to Monacans as a "mixed-race" people as perceived by local landowners and government officials. As so-called "mixed-race" people, they were seen as having violated miscegenation laws, and thus were relegated to the lowest category in the newly configured local power structure. In this manner, the Monacans became the most exploited people in the county and enjoyed even fewer legal rights and privileges than they had prior to the Civil War.

The use of the term "feudal" in reference to post–Civil War race relations in the South is really an exaggeration in most cases. The relations Saks applies this term to were between former slaves entering the capitalist system as wage laborers, and white power brokers who controlled local economic and political affairs. After the war, most former slaves (and many poor whites) found sharecrop farming to be their only prospect for survival short of migrating out of the South. Unlike serfs, who had certain rights and privileges, the only thing distinguishing many nonwhite tenant farmers from slaves was that they earned some income. Such a situation is best described as a state of peonage or at best, patronage. In fact, the peculiar racially-based tenant systems that developed in Virginia have been characterized as "capitalist patronage" systems (Shifflett, 1982). On the other hand, the relationship between lord and serf in classic feudalism was in some ways one of guardian to ward. Serfs had certain rights and a degree of usufruct access to land. Serfs paid tribute to the lord in return for military protection and certain welfare provisions. This was not the case in most tenant systems in America, as tenants were treated basically as labor.

A true feudal system is the quintessence of a tributary mode of production (Wolf, 1997: pp. 79–88). Under this type of social arrangement, states Eric Wolf, "the primary producer, whether cultivator or herdsman, is allowed access to the means of production, while tribute is exacted from him through political or military means" (1997: pp. 79–80). This definition automatically renders the use of the term "feudal" problematic in relation to the tenant system in the postbellum South, as one of the hallmarks of the capitalist mode of production is the alienation of producers (laborers) from any rights to the means of production. Moreover, it is difficult to argue that "political or military means" were used to exact tribute from most tenant farmers and sharecroppers, unless one considers the broader definition of politics as social power, and not merely the conventional understanding of state political or legal systems. However, Saks argues that miscegenation laws served as the primary political means by which an otherwise archaic mode of production remained intact. The case of the Monacans does illustrate this point.

The situation confronting many Monacans after the Civil War might be considered quasi-feudal. The relationship between Amherst County landowners and Indian sharecroppers resembled that between feudal lords and serfs in some respects. For example, in addition to working landowners' crops, many Indians were required to pay landowners a form of tribute that they drew from their own crops. Moreover, the tenant system (at least where Indians were concerned) was rigidly stratified, with no opportunities for upward mobility. The critical difference was that, unlike feudal lords, Amherst County landowners made no pretense of providing for the welfare of Indians. Their primary interest was in cheap labor. I suggest, then, that such a system is best described as "capitalist feudalism," or "colonial capitalism" (Alavi, 1980; Althusser and Balibar, 1971).

Saks (1988) suggests that miscegenation law can be viewed as an autonomous discourse—that is, as a way of giving meaning to the world; something that dictates what is right or wrong. So it was in Amherst County, where the Indians were increasingly viewed as having violated the norms upon which miscegenation laws were based. As noted, some of the Monacans had intermarried with early white settlers. Whether any of the Monacans had engaged in such relations with blacks is a point of contention, though just prior to the Civil War a settlement of freed slaves was established just two miles below Bear Mountain in Peters Hollow (Houck, 1984: 76). Whether the Indians had intermarried with non-Indians, however, did not necessarily influence the Monacans' own perception of themselves as much as it influenced the perceptions of local elites. Gray reported at the turn of the twentieth century that the Monacans fervently referred to themselves as "Indian men and Indian women" (1908: p. 1). Although vague, this observation nonetheless provides evidence of an ethnogenetic process in motion. The Monacans were *actively* differentiating themselves from former slaves— not to be treated as such. To their white neighbors, however, they were merely darker skinned people. While there was no overt enforcement of miscegenation laws in Amherst County in the later nineteenth century, census enumerators certainly held up their end of the law. As previously noted, the free people of color in the county were never recorded as "Indians" in census and tax records, but as either "black," or more frequently "mulatto." The term "mulatto" was undoubtedly applied most frequently to Indians, thus labeling them as violators of the sexual norms of the dominant society. Apparently, as the Monacans became more assertive of their Indian identity in the late 1800s, census enumerators decided to erase them from the record once and for all. By 1900, the term "mulatto" had been entirely replaced in census records by the designation "black" (Rice, 1991: p. 18). One speculates that these documentary changes reflected the fears of white elites and state officials concerning their own perceived loss of power if people of color were treated as equals.

It was probably during this period that the term "Issue" became more extensively used by non-Indians in reference to the Monacans.

The term "Issue," or "Free Issue" was generically used in reference to any free people of color prior to the Civil War, deriving from the fact that they had been "issued" their papers for freedom (Houck, 1984: p. 77). It remained in the vocabulary of many southern counties after the war, but in Amherst it gradually seems to have been applied only to Indians.[7] "They [the Monacans] dislike the name very much," noted Arthur Gray at the turn of the twentieth century, and it is no wonder (Gray, 1908: p. 1). The term "Issue" was derogatorily applied by local non-Indians to designate a virtual caste of individuals whom they perceived to be hopelessly inferior as a result of racial admixture. While miscegenation laws may have discouraged former slaves from engaging in sexual unions with whites (and thereby confounding questions of heirship), they provided a means of justifying the inequitable treatment of those who were perceived as having violated them in the past—those whom local non-Indians called Issues.

The emergent "caste system" placed the Monacans in the very bottom echelon of a semifeudal political economy. While many Indians around Bear Mountain had lived relatively autonomously on the land of non-Indians prior to the war, this became increasingly difficult for a couple of reasons. First, some of these lands were being partitioned and/or falling into the hands of new owners. As previously noted, the number of farms in Amherst County doubled after the Civil War, in part due to the breakup of plantations with the collapse of slavery, and also due to an increasing free population. However, the amount of land actively farmed also increased. While in 1860 there were 111,969 acres of improved farmland, that acreage rose to 205,691 by 1925 (U.S. Bureau of the Census, 1864: p. 126; 1925: p. 126). A good portion of this newly "improved" farmland was in the area of Bear Mountain.

But perhaps the most significant factor leading to the increase in farming along the Tobacco Row Mountains was the booming orchard industry in Amherst County. It is not surprising that orchards would gain prominence in the area. Earlier crops were extremely depletive of the nutrients in soil, and by 1900 the time-leeched soil of Amherst County was suffering from nearly a century and a half of cultivation. Formerly prominent modes of agricultural production fell into a sharp decline after the Civil War. While 16,294 farm acres of Amherst County land were devoted to cultivating corn in 1890, that number had dropped to a mere 152 acres in 1925 (U.S. Bureau of the Census, 1895: p. 388; 1925: p. 105). A similar pattern was seen in livestock production, which could be as damaging to the soil as nutrient draining crops. In 1860, for example, 17,179 swine were reported in the county, but only 4,642 were reported in 1925 (U.S. Bureau of the Census, 1864: p. 155; 1925: p. 152). The dawn of the twentieth century, however, brought forth an explosion in orchard production in Amherst County, particularly of apples. In 1890, there were 64,261 apple trees in the county producing 134,132 bushels of apples. By 1925, that number had more than doubled, with 136,703 trees producing 293,644 bushels (U.S. Bureau of the Census, 1895: p. 533; 1925: p. 165).

Apple and other fruit trees are extremely adaptable to diverse environments, and require little more than water and pruning to prosper. It is not surprising, then, that orchards diffused into the Tobacco Row Mountains almost overnight. The proliferation of the orchard industry in Amherst County is almost legendary in local history. People who lived in Amherst in the 1950s recall a time when most of the county's landscape—particularly in the western portion—consisted of nothing but orchards. Older Monacans recall a time when High Peak Mountain (which is now covered with secondary growth forest), was covered with nothing but fruit trees and small tracts of pasture (Cook, 1996a). Alienated from their homes and having nowhere else to go, many of the Monacans were forced to seek a meager living through tenancy on the orchards.

Monacans probably made up a minority of the total population of tenant laborers in Amherst County. In 1925, there were reported 447 white tenants in the county and 300 "colored" (U.S. Bureau of the Census, 1925: p. 126). It is difficult to say how many of the "colored" tenants were Monacans, but if Gray's (1908: p. 1) earlier estimate that there were 325 "of these mixed blood people" is at all accurate, then it is possible that Monacans made up the bulk of the "col-ored" labor force in the orchards. Although there were also blacks working in the orchards, they were kept separate from Indians in the orchards as a result of racial hostilities (Houck, 1984: p. 77).

Life as a tenant farmer can rarely be considered easy under any circumstances. But for the Monacans, it was particularly harsh, pos-sibly more so than for black tenants in Amherst County. There is ev-idence that Indian workers often received less pay than blacks, and in some cases received no pay at all. At best, pay was often irregular for Indians, and arbitrarily doled out by orchard owners, especially in the days before the minimum wage was established. When pay did come, the amount varied, but it was always low—too low, in fact, to sustain families. One man considered himself fortunate to make one dollar for a ten-hour workday in the 1930s, and $1.25 a day in the 1940s. Another Monacan man, aged eighty-eight, recalled making up to ten dollars a month in the 1940s (Cook, 1996a; 1996b: p. 72). And one Monacan woman, age fifty, who spent her childhood in the orchards recalled of her parents: "I remember, Mom used to say, there were times when they made twenty-five cents a day when they first started in the apple orchard. They was just a married couple, and wouldn't get no more than twenty-five cents a day for what they done."

The greatest premium Indians received for their work in the or-chards was not the meager wage they earned, but the provision of a house to live in and space to grow a garden and graze personal live-stock for subsistence. And even this came at a price. The following words of an elderly Monacan man who lived and worked on the High Peak Orchard most of his life are very revealing of the semi-feudal situation in which many Monacans found themselves in the early part of the twentieth century:

> I was sixteen years old when I started working in the apple orchard. I had about twenty-five hands helping me to pack apples, and pick ap-ples, pick peaches, pack them. And didn't none of us have nothing! They even owned our clothes on our backs. They even owned our

house. Just as I told you, we owned our chickens, hogs, milk cows, horses. But still we had to pay the rent for our horse so he wouldn't go over on the next man's place. It was fifteen cents a day for horse to graze. . . .

And the big man, he was the one that owned all this land. Took the money, and we got the land to work. We had to rent that land from the man that owned it. And the crop would come. And he took half, and we took half. Anytime you're workin' for somebody else, and ain't able to work for your own self—that's a horrible living. He was get-tin' it all sittin' down, watching out the window. And if your plot was-n't taken care of, he'd tell you about it. Or else he'd make you leave the land. We kept goin', though.

High Peak Orchard employed primarily Indians. Probably more of the Monacans worked there than anywhere else. As the above words reveal, the Indians at High Peak were essentially paying to work on the orchards. Certainly the wages they made were not enough to live on after paying for house rental and grazing fees. Additionally, they were required to give half of their crops—or the money they made from selling these crops at farmer's markets in Lynchburg—to the owner. Such a situation evokes images of the feudal estates of me-dieval Europe, except that the Monacans were tenants-at-will rather than hereditary tenants.

As the above quote also indicates, Indians living and working on the orchards grew their own crops and raised their own livestock for subsistence purposes. Without exception, all of the Monacan partic-ipants in this study who grew up in Amherst County prior to the 1960s said they relied heavily on gardens, livestock, and hunting for survival. It was, quite simply, a necessity, and yet it was a way of life to which the Monacans were accustomed. This points to an interest-ing economic trend that was occurring not only in the orchards of Amherst County, but elsewhere in Appalachia.

In the early part of the twentieth century, the coal mining indus-try was able to expand and prosper in large part due to the precar-iously low wages that were paid to miners. In considering how the industry was able to get away with paying low wages, Salstrom

(1994: pp. 67–68) notes that most miners and their families relied significantly on subsistence farming for their livelihood, as they had previously. They entered the coal-mining work force primarily because they needed extra cash to maintain the lifestyle to which they were accustomed, and particularly to pay taxes on their farms. Thus, Salstrom argues, the miners' family subsistence practices actually *subsidized* the coal industry in the early years. The situation in Amherst County was similar. The subsistence practices of the Monacans allowed the orchards to prosper while paying a pittance for labor costs. Indeed, it is probably safe to assume that as long as the Monacans were sustaining themselves through subsistence, the cost of maintaining labor was even less of a burden on the orchard owners than the costs of maintaining slaves had been for the antebellum planters in the county.

Another parallel to the central Appalachian coalfields found in Amherst County in the early part of the twentieth century was a peculiar form of debt peonage, documented here for perhaps the first time. The parallel of which I speak is to the company store system of the coalfields, in which workers were issued scrip in lieu of cash when they were in debt. Scrip was redeemable only at the company store, where prices were often considerably higher than at other outlets, thereby keeping miners in a perpetual cycle of debt. Although the Amherst County orchards did not maintain their own commissaries, there developed among orchard owners and various general store owners a sort of tacit agreement concerning the distribution of merchandise to Indians. Quite simply, if an Indian family needed certain staples—such as sugar, salt, or coffee—but had no money to purchase it, they would ask the orchard owner for a "contract," as some have called it. This was simply a note from the orchard owner to a storekeeper asking that he be billed for specific merchandise requested by Indians, but usually forbidding the purchase of additional items. Although the provisions of such contracts varied, the recipient of the goods signed the agreement. Typical of such contracts was the following, which was found among others in a store ledger:

March 29, 1912
Mr. Smoat
Dear Sir,

I This day agree to Stand for Allix Johns to get as much as
$2.00 per week until he get the amount of 25.00 dollars Then
you let Me Know and I will draw money on said Allix Johns
tobacco and pay you for Same.
Respectful,
W. J. Faulkner

This Contract don't include no dry good at all as follows
meal. flour. meat. coffee. sugar
I This day agree to do what contact reads
Allix Johns (his mark).[8]

Unlike company scrip, these contracts restricted the types of merchandise Indians could obtain on credit. There is even some indication that orchard owners sometimes arbitrarily made these contracts with Indians in lieu of wages (Cook, 1996a). The same elderly
man quoted above recalled vividly the procedure and humiliation involved in obtaining such contracts:

> We could get as much as ten dollars a month. Then, if we got any
> more than that, the man that lived here and owned that place, he'd
> write a note to the stores, tell the merchant to let you have coffee,
> sugar, flour, or something like that. And really, we couldn't get no
> thin' on credit. And so—that was in the forties—and the man that we
> was livin', workin' for . . . we'd run out of sugar, coffee, or something
> like that. We'd go to him, and he'd give us a note. Said let us have
> sugar, coffee, flour, or what we need— 'til the thirty days was up.
> Then we paid him. We didn't have no say so, like now. We didn't have
> hardly any say so on our living. Somebody had to sing for us. And
> that's the way we lived, people lived, around Bear Mountain.

The last three sentences concisely sum the situation confronting the
Monacans with the growth of the orchard industry. Somebody had
to "sing" for them because they were integrated into a wage labor

structure designed to sustain a quasi-feudal set of economic relationships. Moreover, at that time (early to mid–twentieth century) it
was nearly impossible for *anyone* who was poor to obtain credit virtually anywhere in the United States. While those living on the orchards ultimately relied on subsistence practices rather than wages
for survival, even these practices would not have been possible without a place to live and the small amount of cash needed to buy the
staples they could not produce. In short, the growth of the orchard
industry (and to a lesser degree, other tenant-supported cash-crop-
ping) thrust the Monacan people into a state of utter economic dependency.

At the micro level, however, the degree of dependency in which
individual Monacan families found themselves sometimes varied.
Relatively speaking, some were economically better off than others,
though none could claim to have had an equal opportunity to better
their economic condition in the larger capitalist economy. On the
orchards, for example, Monacan men who served as foremen might
receive slightly higher wages than other workers, though they were
ultimately subject to the same restrictions imposed by owners.
Other Monacans were able to find work outside the orchards,
though most commonly in other agricultural settings. One man,
who considered himself fortunate to have grown up and worked on
the dairy farm belonging to Sweet Briar College, recalled that his
family was treated fairly, or at least on equal terms with non-Indians
working there:

> I think that the wages was comparable to any of the rest of the farms
> in the area, dairy farms in the area. But then you gotta remember,
> we're talking about back in the 1950s. I didn't work by the hour, I got
> paid by the week. Which, as you know and I found out, if you're in a
> salary position, there's no restriction on the hours. They can work
> you as long as they want to. And I used to work from sun up until
> sundown for twenty-five dollars a week. But so did everybody else
> there. And on other farms in the area they did the same thing. So as
> far as me being Monacan, and that being an influence on my wages or
> hours, I don't think that had anything to do with it.

But I will say this: I think that due to the fact that we were on that farm—a dairy farm—we were probably financially better off than some of the other Monacans in this county that worked in the apple orchards. And sharecropping, stuff like that.

There were still other Monacans who neither lived nor worked on the orchards full-time, but were considered—at least by local non-Indians—to be the poorest people in the county. These were the last of the "squatters" (for lack of a better term), people who lived rent-free on the remaining undeveloped lands belonging to non-Indians in the Tobacco Row Mountains. Though few in number, these Indians—perhaps more than anyone else in the county—relied most heavily on subsistence for survival, and they engaged in wage labor activities only infrequently. This mode of living existed into the 1970s (Houck, 1984: pp. 114–15; Cook, 1996a). One woman recalled growing up at a cabin in a remote hollow of Sweet Briar Mountain (northwest of Bear Mountain) in the 1950s. The owner of the land— Sweet Briar College—had agreed to let her family live on the land as long as they desired. Although her family raised some hogs and milk cows, they relied primarily on wild game for meat, and on their garden for vegetable subsistence. To acquire the cash necessary for sugar, salt, and other store-bought staples, her mother worked odd jobs such as cleaning houses, and occasional janitorial work at Sweet Briar College (Cook, 1996a). Neomarxist theorists have applied the term "articulating modes of production" to discuss such arrangements. Althusser and Balibar (1971) argue that colonial domination, accompanied by forced capitalist integration, does not necessarily bring about the eradication of precapitalist modes of production. They suggest that colonial contexts have, in fact, merged capitalist and noncapitalist modes of production into varied modes of coexistence, which do not resemble in any clear way the classical modes of production. In this case, an indigenous mode was preserved by a handful of squatters who engaged in wage labor primarily at their convenience, relying most frequently on their own autonomous activities for survival.

While outsiders regarded the Monacans engaged in this latter mode of living as the most "backward," they were, in a sense, the freest Indians in the county if one gauges freedom by the degree to which people are able to evade capitalist integration. Unlike the Monacans on the orchards, they did not have to pay rent on houses and grazing land, nor did they face the threat of eviction if their crops failed. Even today, a handful of elderly Monacans continue to live in this manner by choice, engaging in wage labor as they please and pursuing with a passive recalcitrance a subsistence-based mode of living. Nonetheless, such a lifeway was and remains the most precarious practiced by Monacans in Amherst County. Given the fact that it is primarily elderly Monacans who are the most reliant on an indigenous mode of production, it seems likely that it will soon succumb to a purely capitalist mode.

Regardless of how Indians lived or where they worked in Amherst County, in the long run they were all the same in the eyes of the law. This law, in turn, reflected the will of the vast majority of non-Indians (particularly Euro-Americans) living in the county, if not the state. The law effectively deprived Monacans of opportunities—especially education—which would allow them to escape the grasp of the semifeudal economy in which they were so disadvantageously integrated, as will be discussed in detail in the next chapter. However, with the disintegration of such laws (among other notable factors) the quasi-feudal economy in Amherst County fell into decline.

The Decline of Feudalism

The lifeblood of the oppressive tenant system that evolved out of the postbellum economy in Amherst County was a self-sustaining, self-reproducing labor force, in which local farmers and orchard owners needed to invest a minimal amount of capital. By the 1960s, several factors converged to render this arrangement increasingly unfeasible.

First, as will be discussed in the following chapter, a renewed fervor on the part of state and local officials for elaborating and enforcing miscegenation laws had a particularly adverse effect on the Monacans. Beginning in the 1920s, several Monacan families migrated out of the county into nearby Lynchburg and other parts of Virginia, and even out of the state in search of greater opportunities in areas where they could either conceal or assert without repercussions their Indian identity (Houck and Maxham, 1993: p. 128). Although it is not yet possible to determine the extent to which Monacans left the county over the years, out-migration was extensive. Approximately half of the individuals currently registered on tribal rolls (approx. 350–400) are out-of-state residents (Cook, 1996a). This exodus must have had an impact on the availability of cheap labor, particularly on the orchards, which were primarily worked by Indians. Orchard owners may have found it necessary to make increases in wages.

Wage increases did come with the incorporation of minimum wage laws in the 1960s. Although Congress passed the Fair Labor Standards Act—the first minimum wage law—in 1938, it initially (and not surprisingly) applied only to those industries with the longest tradition of labor unions (e.g., mining). Following a series of amendments beginning in 1961, the act was finally expanded to apply to agricultural workers on large farms (Editorial Staff of Labor Relations Reporter, 1967: pp. 8–9). A Monacan man who lived and worked on the orchards as a child in the late 1950s and early 1960s recalled:

> I was raised in an apple orchard, and I've been working ever since I was ten years old, you know, during school and after school, and in the summer time. I always bought my own school clothes since I was age ten, and paid for my books. That was the way I helped out my mom and dad. I can remember when the minimum wage went up to a dollar thirty. And the man that my dad worked for, you know, you would think they asked him to cut off his legs or something. He was paying them seventy-five cent an hour, and it went up to a dollar thirty. Like I say, you'd think he got shot or something.

It is no wonder the orchard owner reacted negatively. The minimum wage law signaled the end of an epoch in which the laborers' own subsistence practices could be expected to subsidize the industries in which they worked. Yet orchard owners still continued to cut the corners of labor costs from every possible angle. As the above quote suggests, orchard owners were not averse to using child labor. Moreover, the same man recalled:

> We lived in a house, we had electricity, but we didn't have running water, or any plumbing whatsoever. And that didn't change 'til after I was married for a year [in the late 1960s]. But that was the case with a lot of our people that lived in Amherst County. Some of the older ones can tell you that they didn't have electricity, and my mom could tell you the same thing. But we were very fortunate to have electricity.

By the 1960s, even those industries historically reputed to be the most exploitative of workers—mining, for example—at the very least had bathhouses for workers on company property. In the coalfields, such amenities were required by law. In Amherst County, the law apparently overlooked or provided loopholes for such details. As late as 1970, 13.5 percent of the children in the county between ages fourteen and fifteen were engaged in the labor force; specifically, 14.1 percent of "Negro" children (which may well have included Indians) were engaged as such (U .S. Bureau of the Census, 1973: [I–48] p. 424). Granted, even contemporary child labor laws in Virginia contain exemptions for "work outside of school hours on farms, in orchards, or in gardens performed with the consent of the child's parent or guardian" (Virginia Department of Labor and Industry, 1988: p. 1). Interestingly, the 1966 amendments to the Fair Labor Standards Act made minimum wage requirements applicable to children at work on large farms (Editorial Staff of Labor Relations Reporter, 1967: p. 10), which may explain their diminishing number in the recorded county labor force after 1970.

However, long before the implementation of the minimum wage law, local ordinances prohibited the free grazing of livestock. After the Civil War, "Southern agriculture became land-intensive and labor-extensive, rather than labor-intensive and land-extensive [as was formerly the case]" (Atack and Passell, 1994: p. 378). In addition to coercive tenant systems, livestock fencing laws became the most effective means of ensuring the optimum productivity of restricted lands by reducing the damage caused by cattle to lands not reserved for grazing. This meant that lands that were formerly regarded as "commons" (i.e., for grazing) were often made available for cash crop production (Kantor, 1998).

For years, Monacans and some of their non-Indian neighbors had set their cattle loose in the mountains to graze on natural fodder. Although those living on the orchards often had to rent pasture space for their horses, they still set other livestock loose in the mountains to feast on the highly nutritious mast of nut-bearing trees. In fact, although stock laws were in place in Virginia by 1875 (Kantor, 1998: p. 116), each county had the option to enforce such laws as it saw fit. In western Amherst County, livestock ranging restrictions were evidently contingent on the growth of orchards in the mountains. As the county's population began to increase, and agricultural and suburban developments began to encroach upon the forests, the law prohibited the free ranging of cattle lest they destroy private property. Although some Indians in the remoter sections of the Tobacco Row Mountains continued to free range livestock into the 1970s, most were forced to cease this practice and either purchase feed (which they could not afford), or rely on store-bought meat (Cook, 1996a). This sudden loss in a vital means of subsistence for workers translated into higher labor costs.

Meanwhile, the later twentieth century saw a slow but steady trend toward urbanization in Amherst County as towns such as Madison Heights were transformed into suburbs of metropolitan Lynchburg. Between 1960 and 1970, the population of Amherst County rose from 22,953 to 28,072. Out of a total work force of 9,401, only 477 people were engaged primarily in any kind of agricultural work (U.S. Bureau of the Census, 1973: [I–48] pp. 15, 448). Faced with increasing labor costs and a rapidly growing population, many farmers and orchard owners in the 1960s and 1970s found that their best financial alternative was to sell out to real estate de-

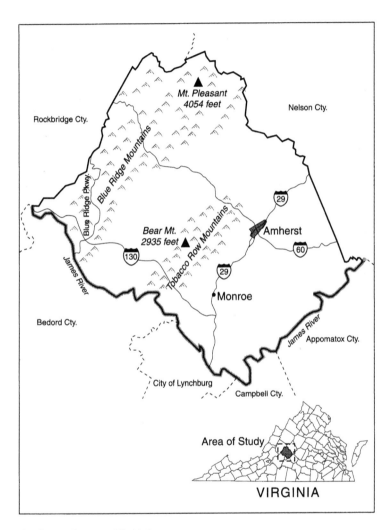

Amherst County, Virginia

velopers. Today only one small orchard remains in the county (Cook, 1996a).

But perhaps the most significant factor leading to the demise of the exploitative agricultural economy in Amherst, at least in terms of changing power relations, was the opening of greater economic opportunities for Indians. Because of their precarious legal status as "mixed blood" people, the Monacans were not allowed to attend high school in Amherst County until the 1960s. Even after desegregation, their successful matriculation in the public school system was delayed by blatant racial discrimination. The circumstances and implications of the Monacans' experience with public education will be discussed in detail in the next chapter, but it is important here to point out that once Indians began graduating from high school in Amherst County, a range of new opportunities opened for them. Something as fundamental as a high school education—which many people take for granted—allowed Indians in Amherst County to find new and more equitable employment alternatives closer to home. And with the birth of these opportunities came the death of capitalist-feudalism in Amherst County.

Colonialism and Dependency

This chapter began by describing the conditions under which the foundations of a firmly entrenched colonial structure emerged and embraced the Indians of Amherst County. Its emphasis then moved to a primarily economic analysis of a semifeudal system on which the Monacans became utterly dependent. The initial resources sought by the colonizers were land and labor, which were transformed into agricultural products to be unilaterally siphoned into distant markets. I have argued, and will further illustrate in the next chapter, that a higher degree of integration into the wage labor force due to greater educational opportunities provided a crucial means by which the Monacans were able to break the bonds of dependency. In other words, contrary to many applications of dependency analysis, fuller capitalist integration was ultimately a positive thing for the colonized people in this case. What I have not discussed in detail were

the discursive underpinnings of the colonial situation confronting
the Monacans, the cultural biases and implications of oppressive legal and economic structures in Amherst County, and how the
Monacans contended with and ultimately confronted these structures. The next chapter, then, will focus on the twentieth century,
the most turbulent period in Monacan history—but ultimately a liberating one.

3 LEGAL RACISM, RESISTANCE, AND RESURGENCE

The Monacans in the Twentieth Century

The post–Civil War capitalist-feudal economy did not develop overnight in Amherst County. Rather, it was inseparably integrated into a larger colonial process in which Indians bore the brunt of exploitation. As noted in the previous chapter, the legal foundation for such a system was built on miscegenation laws that cast Indians as marginalized "others" by questioning their very existence in the state of Virginia. Most non-Indian Virginians, especially in Amherst County, could not accept the possibility that Native Americans still resided in the state, particularly "racially pure" Natives. Yet the question of how to deal, legally and ethically, with so-called "mixed-race" peoples in the state was still not fully resolved by the turn of the twentieth century. As late as World War I, for example, Amherst Indians were drafted into the armed services as "whites," as was the practice at that time for all ethnic groups other than blacks (Murray, 1987: p. 223). By the time of the Second World War, however, Virginia miscegenation laws would be elaborated with a fervor previously unmatched, and the Monacans would face the most brutal colonial assault in their experience. But as the century approached its end, conditions would improve markedly for Indian people in Amherst County, and the Monacans would begin to reclaim their heritage and legal identity as Indian people. Nonetheless, things worsened before they got better.

The Confounding Question of Race

It is ironic that the Monacan draftees in World War I would be legally recruited as "whites," for they were otherwise treated as equal, if not inferior, to blacks in a state where Jim Crow laws were rigorously enforced. As noted previously, after 1900 the Amherst Indians were not even afforded the dubious "mulatto" distinction in census records, but were classified as "black." Theoretically, this entitled them to the same "privileges" as blacks but such was not necessarily the case in Amherst County. For example, by the turn of the twentieth century separate schools had long been established for local blacks, and the Monacans were given the choice to attend these schools or do without. Almost without exception, the Indians opted to refrain from indulging in an education system that would deny them equal opportunities with other individuals regardless of race, and more critically would deny their existence as Indians. Even after the Episcopal Church built a mission school at Bear Mountain in 1908, it was years before the county agreed to provide any funding or resources for this facility, and subsequent support was limited and reluctant (Houck, 1984: pp. 95–104).

Although they were technically citizens of the United States and the state of Virginia, Monacans were seldom treated as such. Of course, the same situation was true for the black citizens of the county. The picture in Amherst County in the first half of the century was in some ways typical of situations confronting people of color throughout the South. An elderly Monacan man recalled: "One time they even wouldn't let Indian people go in a white restaurant and eat. And we just went on by and we didn't say anything." At the turn of the twentieth century, Edgar Whitehead (1896) noted that an 1830 racial segregation law was still enforced in Amherst churches, where Indians and blacks were required to sit in a separate section if allowed to attend at all. Few Indians are alive who experienced this first hand, as the establishment of St. Paul's Mission in 1908 provided them with a place to worship. Nonetheless, these public restrictions remain alive in oral tradition, as evidenced by the following words of a Monacan woman who grew up on the threshold of desegregation: "I can remember Mom tellin' that they'd go into [the town of] Amherst to the churches, or over to the little country church that's near our subdivision. And they'd all have to sit in the back. You never was allowed to go to the front of the church. If you wanted to be in the church service you had to sit in the back pew. And the restaurants and things was the same way. They had black and white. And if your skin was dark as I was, you sat in the black section, you weren't allowed in the white. And there was things that happened back then. Like I say, they didn't accept no race as being Indian."

As if these social restrictions were not enough to reduce the people of color in Amherst to second-class citizenry, local officials sometimes crossed the boundaries of legal prohibitions and sought to disenfranchise Indians outright. Older Monacans recall a time when Indians were not welcome at the election polls. One man recalled, "Yes sir, yes sir. That was back in the forties. They would try to have every kind of word, or name, or something, to make against us." Sensing their own lack of efficacy in the local political system, many Indians prior to the 1960s did not bother to attempt to vote. This tendency would reverberate into the future. As one tribal official noted, "Very few of our older people vote."

But if Indians and blacks in Amherst County shared a common experience of limited access to the public domain, they did not share a sense of solidarity. Most often, they tried to dissociate themselves from one another. While Indians did not appreciate being identified as "blacks" in the dominant social and legal hierarchy, blacks were not hesitant to ridicule Indians for their perceived status as "mixed-race" people. Whitehead (1896) noted that most Indians refused to attend churches where they were forced to sit with blacks. Although contemporary Monacans who wish to leave the mistakes of the past behind do not speak freely of past tension with blacks, several acknowledge that it existed. One elderly man recalled black children waiting every Sunday near the gates of High Peak Orchard to pick a fight with an "Issue." He related that he fought constantly with black children while growing up, though he took no pride in it (Cook, 1996a). Tensions between blacks and Indians grew so immense that local farmers had to establish separate sections for the two groups of workers in the fields and orchards (Houck, 1984: p. 77).

Why were such tensions so rampant, and why did the Monacans seem to bear the greatest burden in the overall scheme of racial oppression in Amherst County? The answer revolves around their being perceived by local non-Indians as "mixed-race" people. The corpus of miscegenation laws that had accrued since colonial times in Virginia had made it possible for Indians, particularly in Amherst County, to be classified as "mulattos." But as noted above, "mulatto" was a transitory status in the legal hierarchy of Amherst, and by 1900 all Indians (or in legal terms, "mulattos") were *legally* classified as blacks. If it is possible to say that those who identified themselves as blacks in Amherst were not as harshly chastised as Indians, then it is because in the minds of local whites, these people had "accepted their place in society." The Monacans, however, neither perceived themselves as "blacks" nor did they want to. They were Indians, and as the law, as well as the attitudes of local non-Indians, moved one step farther away from recognizing them as such, they asserted their Indian identity with a renewed fervor. In 1908, Arthur Gray wrote that the Amherst Indians were "proud of their Indian blood, though generally not attempting to put themselves on equality with whites" (p. 1). Nearly forty years later, local attorney William Allen remarked that the people of Bear Mountain "have never obtruded themselves upon the white race. They have lived apart for over a quarter of a century among themselves, associating with neither the white nor the negro race so far as they could control the situation" (Murray, 1987: p. 225). Embedded in these vague remarks is evidence of a process of ethnogenesis in motion in which the Indians of Amherst County were forging a history (and hence identity) unique from all other groups in the county—a history influenced and aggravated by domination. Unfortunately, this attempt at separating themselves as Indians got the Monacans in deeper trouble with their non-Indian neighbors.

Thus, the first half of the twentieth century in Amherst County would see the development of a tumultuous and cyclical chain reaction, in which miscegenation laws would become more elaborate as Indians asserted their identity as Natives with greater vigor. Such laws propelled the Monacans ever deeper into dependence on the semifeudal economy, and led to the sanctioning of a virtual witch-hunt to eradicate Indians from the state of Virginia once and for all. There were a handful of non-Indians, however, who were not threatened but instead were fascinated by the Monacans' Indian identity.

The Missionary Zeal

The turn of the twentieth century marked a unique time in North American Indian-white relations. Popular sentiment in the late nineteenth century espoused the view that with the closing of the frontier, Native Americans would either assimilate into the mainstream of American society or cease to exist altogether. Accordingly, federal policies toward those Indians whose existence was recognized by the national government sought to partition Indian lands and entice Natives toward assimilation through private property ownership and formal education. The "Vanishing American" image propelled a barrage of social scientists and philanthropists who believed that what was left of America Indian culture must be recorded for the benefit of science and society before it disappeared completely. However, out of this movement to preserve the images and facts of aboriginal culture there emerged, by the turn of the twentieth century, growing pockets of appreciation for Native culture as something ideal and exotic. And a few individuals began to laud indigenous societies as something to be protected from annihilation.[1]

At the turn of the twentieth century, the Monacan Indians had long vanished in the eyes of their non-Indian neighbors. However, the growing national fascination with Indians as the exotic "other" did manage to diffuse into the county when, in 1896, Captain Edgar

Whitehead wrote an article for a Richmond newspaper describing the Amherst Indians as descendants of Cherokees (Whitehead, 1896). Although the historical accuracy of this lengthy article is questionable (indeed, Whitehead's link to the Cherokees seems embellished, if not fabricated), it marked the first time that anyone had acknowledged—at least in print—that the Monacans were Indians.

Whitehead's fascination with the Monacans opened a new and bittersweet chapter in Indian-white relations in Amherst County through the medium of Episcopal missionaries. From the inception of European contact, Christian missionaries have frequently acted as cultural intermediaries between Indians and non-Indians, often serving as agents for colonial policies toward Natives (see e.g., Spicer, 1962: pp. 288–98; McLoughlin, 1984). As late as the 1870s, missionaries were officially sanctioned to "Christianize and civilize" Natives on western reservations, contrary to the constitutional mandate for separation of church and state (Hoxie, 1987; Prucha, 1976, 1990: p. 135). But the situation at Bear Mountain was somewhat different, though paradoxical. The missionaries who came to Bear Mountain were among the few non-Indians in Virginia who recognized the Monacans as Indians, not as "mixed-race" people. They came with a sincere concern for an oppressed people, and yet they addressed their problems and dealt with the Indians through methods entrenched in mainstream Western cultural biases.

At Whitehead's urging a young seminarian named Arthur Gray began mission work at Bear Mountain in 1908. Previously, itinerant Methodist and Baptist missionaries had ventured into the area to proselytize to the Indians but none had stayed (Gray, 1908). With the backing of Amherst County resident J. J. Ambler, Gray purchased a small tract of land along Falling Rock Creek at the foot of Bear Mountain and began construction of a mission. Evidently, he was immediately well received by a number of Indians, for Monacans themselves collected $150 for building supplies (Gray, 1908: p. 1; Houck, 1984: pp. 95–102).

The immediate task at hand for Gray was the establishment of a permanent school. In 1889, Amherst County had begun sending a part-time teacher to Bear Mountain, but prior to that African American schools provided the only channel for Indians to obtain an education in the county. Most Indians refused this kind of schooling. "There are 150 children under 16 years of age," lamented Gray, "who are capable of taking a good education, some of them being especially bright" (Gray, 1908: p. 1). Thus, he began holding classes in an old log cabin that had been deeded to some Monacans after the Civil War and the cabin continued to serve as a classroom until public schools were integrated. By the time he left Bear Mountain in 1910, Gray had managed to obtain a few teachers with the help of the Episcopal diocese, and the mission church and school served an estimated 350 Indians (Houck, 1984: p. 95).

After Gray's departure, a series of deaconesses and Captains of the Episcopal Army (surrogate ministers) staffed St. Paul's Mission. The school obtained financial and infrastructural support from three primary sources: The Episcopal Church (in particular, the Diocese of Southwest Virginia); neighboring Sweet Briar College, which was associated with the Episcopal Church; and the county school board, which reluctantly offered limited fiscal support for the school after continuous prodding by mission staff (Houck, 1984: pp. 100–101). However, in the fifty years that it was in operation, the school provided education only up to the seventh grade for Monacans, and they remained alienated from public high schools until the 1960s.

The influence of St. Paul's Mission on the Monacan community over the years is a controversial subject. While many Indians and non-Indians believe that the Monacan community could not have survived without the mission, others argue that it was yet another colonizing agent. For years the mission provided a source for spiritual consolation, education, clothing, food, and health care that had previously been unavailable to Indians in the county. On the other hand, it is sometimes argued that these fundamental amenities made the Monacan people too dependent on the church (Houck, 1984: p. 96). Both sides provide arguments that deserve elaboration.

Undoubtedly, the mission provided educational opportunities for Indians that they would not otherwise have had prior to the desegregation of public schools in the 1960s. In fact, various deaconesses and Episcopal officials confronted county officials aggressively to secure the entry of Indians into public high schools, as will be discussed in a later section. Perhaps most significantly, the staff at St. Paul's was willing to accept the Monacans as *Indians*, or at least as people of salient Indian ancestry, reinforcing to some degree a sense of indigenous pride in the community. Concomitantly, the mission itself provided a physical space where Indians could gather as a community, casting aside any fear of racial persecution. Some Monacans who attended the church and school still express a deep sense of indebtedness to St. Paul's. One woman who attended the school in its final years reflected on the role of the church:

> I don't know if any of our people ever stopped and thought about it—where would we be if it hadn't been for the Episcopal diocese? Where would we be? They came here in 1908 and they took that church over, and they been here ever since. And where would we have been if they hadn't? Would we be a people like we are, so drawn together, and a loving people, and a fellowship people, and be able to give and do and be where we are today?
>
> And that's another thing that's a big part of our life is land being here for us to be able to stay here. Because most of them might have left just like all the rest of them did. If we didn't have this focal point that we could come to and have our schools, and have our church, and a place to play and different things like that, to associate with each other.

Implicit in this statement is the idea that the Mission provided, for those who attended it, a mechanism for preserving (as opposed to creating) a communal sense of peoplehood. One Monacan man offered a similar view: "if that church hadn't been there, and with the real close community ties, and if that hadn't been sustained, I don't think we would have the Monacan tribe in the position it's in today. And especially the people that were born and raised here, they are probably more aware of that." In other words, those Monacans who attended St. Paul's on a regular basis found there a source of repose and solidarity in which existing community ties were maintained. The physical space on which the mission was built, though technically owned by the Episcopal diocese, instilled in the congregation a sense of proprietorship stemming from their preexisting relationship with the land. The mission was not another means of segregating Indians from the public domain, but it was something that was exclusively theirs.

Even after the Amherst County school system became integrated, the mission continued to serve as a focal point for Indians, as integration did not mark the end of racial discrimination in the county. One man who was among the first children to enter the newly desegregated schools, recalled, "We'd come down here and have a good time, played like kids, didn't have to worry about what was going on outside. This was our little safe place."

But the idea of the mission being a safe haven from racial persecution has drawn criticism from certain parties inside and outside the Monacan community. The argument is that the Indians who attended St. Paul's became overly dependent on the protective shadow of the church, and that church officials were too controlling of the lives of Indians. One elderly man recalled going to school at the mission for one week before his father pulled him and his siblings out to help support the family in the orchards. Although he continued to go to the church, he did not find the experience entirely liberating: "Only Indians went down there to St. Paul's. In the schools, the teachers was white. May be an Indian teacher in the Sunday school. We just didn't have no say so whatever." Still, he did not deny the positive influences of the church.

The above quote, however, prompts certain questions regarding the cultural underpinnings of missionary activity at Bear Mountain. Several scholars (Plaut, 1979; Whisnant, 1994; Batteau, 1983) have applied cultural systems analysis to demonstrate that externally generated social and economic development activities in Appalachia have often entailed an imposition of mainstream middle-class values (such as individual achievement, impersonal relations) against local grass-roots values (community orientation, interpersonal relations, for example). Whisnant in particular describes Christian missionary zeal as attempting to better "backwards" people in the mountains at the turn of the twentieth century. Such was the case at Bear Mountain, where missionary work was guided by an air of paternalism from its outset. Despite his sincere concern for the welfare of the Monacans, Arthur Gray espoused an attitude of superiority in his description of the Indians: "The moral conditions under which they have multiplied have been of a very low standard. . . . They seldom mix with the other races, as they have done, and almost every home now has a marriage 'stiffizy' as one of them called the certificate" (1908: p. 1).

But at least Gray acknowledged the Monacans as Indians, though he referred to them as a "Cherokee remnant." Some local supporters of the mission, however, did not share this view. J. J. Ambler and his family, who had initially purchased the land for the mission and who prided themselves on their sense of noblesse oblige toward "Issues," never acknowledged their Indian ancestry (Houck, 1984: p. 99). J. J. Ambler IV made this painfully evident in a 1956 letter to Deaconess Florence Cowan, rebuking her for her stand against miscegenation laws and segregation: "Your statements of their being 'Indian-white' is the FIRST time I have heard that. It is just another step in publicity of making the freed negro . . . into Indians, and now 'Indian-white.' This they are NOT. As to their 'high cheek-bones' you mention, to me that is just wishful thinking. Knowing them and their characteristics in the past, they never acted like Indians. They have always been more or less cowards, never war-like at all" (1956). If this man had any benign sentiments at all toward the Monacans, these words still reflected prevailing perceptions that non-Indians had concerning Indians in Amherst. Since the missionaries did not share in these sentiments, one wonders why the Ambler family took such an interest in their endeavor. It is possible that they saw in the mission yet another channel for preserving the social caste system that existed in the county.

Over the years, St. Paul's developed a close relationship with Sweet Briar College, which was associated with the Episcopal

Church. As noted, Sweet Briar was known to employ Indians at an equitable wage, thereby distinguishing it from other employers in the county as more "progressive" in its treatment of Indians. However, some of the most destructive and denigrating rhetorical assaults on the Monacans in the twentieth century were launched from Sweet Briar, sometimes in conjunction with St. Paul's. In the early 1920s, Sweet Briar professor Ivan McDougle, joined by eugenicist Arthur A. Estabrook of the Carnegie Institute set out to study the Amherst Indians as an example of the genetic evils of interracial unions. Believing that the Monacans were "tri-racial" people, they produced a book called *Mongrel Virginians* (1926), which cast the Monacans as backwards, retarded people possessing an inferior gene pool due to interracial marriage. Although they used pseudonyms for people and places, they betrayed the trust of a people whose confidence they had initially won and produced a widely circulated book in the process (Houck, 1984: p. 78). Most significantly, they were working for the national Eugenics Records Office, which meant that their work was used to justify the proliferation of miscegenation laws (Smith, 1993: p. 83–84).

Two years later, University of Virginia graduate student—and former Sweet Briar undergraduate—Bertha Wailes produced a thesis that seemingly repudiated the conclusions in *Mongrel Virginians*, but still espoused an ethnocentric view of the Monacans. Wailes continued to use the same pseudonym that Estabrook and McDougle had coined for the Indians: the "WIN Tribe"—an acronym for "White, Indian, Black"—thereby perpetuating the notion that they were "tri-racial." "That these people are backward no one disputes," wrote Wailes. Although she refuted the argument of genetic retardation while lamenting their isolation from the trappings of modern society, "Their manner of living, their habits and customs have changed but little since those early days. They live in log cabins of one or two rooms, sometimes with a lean-to termed 'cook-room.' These cabins are frequently quite difficult to access" (Wailes, 1928: p. 61). Wailes concluded that a change in their social and economic environment would save the people of Bear Mountain, suggesting that if the Indians owned land they would be more industrious. This thesis marked perhaps the first scholarly application of Eurocentric modernization theory to the Monacans. Nonetheless, Wailes must be commended on her brave critique of Eastabrook and McDougle in light of the politics of her time.

While the aforementioned studies were not conducted through St. Paul's Mission, another "philanthropical" endeavor based at Sweet Briar was directly connected to it. From the 1920s to the 1960s, a Sweet Briar sorority visited the mission every week, engaging in volunteer activities ranging from playing games with children to fund-raising for the congregation. Although their motives may have been benign, it is disturbing to note that the members of this group called themselves the "Bum Chums," which carried denigrating implications concerning their perceptions of the Monacans (Cowan, 1956: p. 6; Houck, 1984: p. 103). Many contemporary Monacans who recall the presence of the Bum Chums during their childhood have only fond memories of them, though some say that, in retrospect, they realize how demeaning the name of this organization was (Cook, 1996a).

What about the missionaries themselves? Was their influence on the Monacan community positive or negative? On the one hand, the various Episcopal representatives who staffed the mission over the years served as staunch advocates for those Indians who attended St. Paul's. As will be illustrated, they often launched aggressive assaults against miscegenation laws that threatened to incriminate many Monacans, they lobbied relentlessly for the integration of public schools on behalf of Indians, and they provided certain services and opened doors to social and economic opportunities that otherwise would not have been available to Amherst County Indians until much later.

On the other hand, some criticism has been leveled at the missionaries and at Sweet Briar College for not making more opportunities available to the Monacans—in essence, for trying to make them comfortable with their lot in life. It is also argued that the missionaries attempted to impose middle-class values on the Monacans, while ignoring the value of indigenous culture. Some have even suggested that various missionaries showed favoritism toward "lighter skinned" Indians, or at least toward those who seemed more willing to assimilate toward mainstream values and alienated "darker" Indians (Cook, 1996a). To the extent that this later assertion may be true, however, it must be noted that rifts based on skin color probably existed within the Monacan community before the coming of the missionaries. Gray, in fact, remarked that "those who have most negro blood and least Indian are not in the same social standing as others" (1908: p. 1). It may have been that those with "most negro blood" were actually phenotypically more "Indian" but were snubbed because non-Indians perceived them as "mixed Negroes." Whatever the case may be, it is possible that certain missionaries, particularly through the imposition of middle-class values, perpetuated such rifts in the community.

In all fairness, it should be pointed out that the missionaries at St. Paul's came to Bear Mountain with good intentions, cultural biases not withstanding, and in so doing placed themselves in a very precarious position vis-à-vis local non-Indians. Regardless of skin color, anyone bearing a Monacan surname was an "Issue" to local non-Indians, and anyone who respected the Monacans' claim to be Indian was not apt to receive a warm welcome because it threatened the local status quo. Although there are no recorded reports of threats against the missionaries, a nonresident farmer who purchased land near Bear Mountain in the 1950s is said to have received threats to his life when he offered Indians a fair wage to help him clear the land (Cook, 1996a). One can only imagine that the missionaries received their share of tongue-lashings, as evidenced by the above letter from Ambler to Deaconess Cowan. And in the long run, the mission did provide a space from which the Monacans developed several tribal programs and a successful campaign for state recognition as a tribe.

Whatever praises or criticisms may be leveled at St. Paul's, it cannot be denied that the mission profoundly influenced the destiny of the Monacan people. This will be further explored in the following pages. However, while the positive influences of the church on the

Monacan community must be acknowledged, previous writers (e.g., Houck, 1984; Smith, 1993) have tended to overemphasize its role in preserving the community and bolstering the prosperity of the Monacan people, without giving due credit to the people themselves. Thus, it is necessary to consider how the Monacan people reacted to and dealt with the conditions of colonialism and dependency during the first three-quarters of the twentieth century.

Subsistence and Resistance

Although the missionaries at St. Paul's may have provided a modest education to some Monacans and served as their political advocates about critical issues, they did not feed the families around Bear Mountain. The mission did provide a food and clothing bank to help Indians supplement what they had, but the Monacans had survived as virtual exiles in their own land for years without charity. And they continued to survive, with or without the missionaries. Whatever factionalism may have existed within the Monacan community, there remained mutually enhancing cooperative networks and family subsistence patterns that were at the heart of the Indians' survival. As will be illustrated below, the missionaries often sought to improve elements of the Indians' lives where many Monacans themselves saw no need for improvement.

It might be argued that the mere survival of a people is a form of resistance. From an economic standpoint, survival for the Monacans in the context of a semifeudal structure meant adapting old subsistence practices to new conditions. Although subsistence agriculture and other practices were a necessity in the absence of adequate wages, they were also something that Monacans were accustomed to, and that were woven into community social activities.

Whether living on the orchards or in the hollows of the Tobacco Row Mountains, nearly every Monacan family prior to the 1960s had a large kitchen garden. This garden supplied the bulk of a family's vegetable diet, and any surplus was stored for the winter. Some families additionally raised cash crops such as tobacco, wheat, and oats to the extent that they were able to balance such endeavors with work in the fields and orchards. An old High Peak resident recalled, "Everybody . . . put the tobacco in. We'd take the tobacco, put it on a wagon, with two horses. Drive to Lynchburg to the warehouse, and that's where we'd sell tobacco. And we would take tobacco, wheat, corn, oats—we would bring a bit of everything. We would try to hook up and do it the best way." These supplementary activities, however, were only possible when there was no work to be done on the commercial orchards and fields. Subsistence agriculture in itself can require long hours of labor and it certainly became an exhausting necessity as Monacan families were more deeply integrated into the commercial agricultural economy. However, gardens were not merely an essential component for survival but also served as a symbol of individual family autonomy, an indication that a family was holding its own. Evidence of this lies in the continued growing of large gardens by older Monacans today, who despite their improved financial condition, scoff at the option of store-bought vegetables (Cook, 1996a).

Personal livestock was also an essential component of Monacan subsistence prior to the 1960s and continues for some today. Prior to the prohibition of free ranging, many Monacans let their livestock feed on the rich, natural fodder in the mountains. As the previously quoted gentleman recalled, "Oh, yes sir. That's the only pasture we had. And we done that a good fifteen years. Then we kept our chickens, had hogs, kept our horses. That's what everybody had." The restriction of grazing lands had the heaviest impact on cattle; it meant that even milk cows would be hard to maintain. Fortunately, many Monacans were able to get milk from the dairy at Sweet Briar College in exchange for labor (Cook, 1996a). Other livestock were easier to maintain in a small area and could be fed with table scraps. Individual households relied very heavily on these modes for survival.

Most households pooled the incomes of all family members to make ends meet. Many of the older participants in this study said that they rarely attended school, if at all, as they had to help support their family. Even to this day some children work after school to contribute their earnings to the household. If this sounds oppressive, it should be noted that none of the participants in this study voiced any regrets but were instead grateful for the experience of being able to appreciate what they had accomplished through hard work (Cook, 1996a; 1996b).

Household initiatives, however, were not always enough to compensate for deficient wages. Thus, reciprocal exchanges between families, friends, and relatives within the community served as both a means of survival and solidarity. Many Indians engaged in inter-household exchange strategies of what LaLone calls "cooperative labor and gift giving" (1996: pp. 58–60). For example, families might exchange commodities such as sugar or livestock to the mutual benefit of each party. Or, if someone had a surplus of food, they might simply pass it on as a gift to another family whose fortune had not been so good. One woman noted that such practices are still common within the community: "People will—if my garden's got more than I can put up, then they give it to somebody else. . . . That's called making do. The people here make do."

Cooperative labor exchanges served the dual purpose of allowing people to get essential work done quickly and bringing them together in a communal social event. The types of exchanges that took place exemplify what anthropologists call balanced reciprocity (Polanyi, 1944; Sahlins, 1965; Schneider, 1989: p. 99). For example, if a family had a large crop of corn to harvest, they would invite other community members and relatives to join them in a "corn husking." Neighbors would bring food and would provide the necessary labor to husk and prepare corn for storage. Similar gatherings might occur for the planting of crops or slaughtering of livestock. Interestingly, these practices were brought to my attention by older Monacans while attending community social events during the course of my fieldwork. Many spoke of how cooperative labor gatherings often involved a feast and dancing afterward. People would bring fiddles, banjos, and other instruments, and contests would be held to see who could husk the most corn, and so forth (Cook, 1996a). A family might host such an event one week and in return would supply its own labor to neighbors the next week.

On a more fundamental level, the Monacans engaged in strategies of generalized reciprocity to survive the hard times brought on by the semifeudal economy (Polanyi, 1944; Sahlins, 1965; Schneider, 1989: p. 99). Quite simply, they helped each other out with no expectation of a return favor. For example, if someone needed money for a medical bill, or if a community member was out of work, other families might take up a collection or provide space in their own homes for those down on their luck. Reflecting on his experiences in the 1940s and 1950s, one man recalled, "There were Monacans in this comity that didn't have a heck of a lot. But I don't think that anybody ever went hungry or without clothes. Because it was always someone helpin' someone out. And I believe that that's the reason we've been such a close-knit community. I think it was because we had such close ties. And I don't know of anyone that was ever homeless. Because someone would always take you in, take care of you." It is no mistake that this man momentarily shifted his recollections to the present tense. During the course of my fieldwork, a tribal member was laid off from his job and his family was in danger of losing its home. Other tribal members promptly came together like a well-oiled machine, pooled cash and food, and helped this family through the next few months without making the situation so visible as to damage the family's dignity (Cook, 1996a).

These survival strategies have been well documented throughout the Appalachian region at various times (Eller, 1982; LaLone, 1996). However, it should be noted that although some of these practices were appropriated *in form* from non-Indians, they were incorporated into and possibly emerged from a continuum of aboriginal community life. It is known, for example, that among the Tutelos, harvest time marked the occasion of a pivotal ceremony (Kurath, 1953). If this ceremony was lost in form to the Indians of the Tobacco Row Mountains, it continued in spirit through corn huskings and similar gatherings. Moreover, as noted in the previous chapter, the establishment of the Johns Settlement at Bear Mountain was in itself a cooperative endeavor to preserve the existence of at least a segment of the Monacans.

Although the household and communal practices of the Monacans prior to the 1960s were a necessary means of coping with an oppressive economic structure, they represented a familiar way of life to the Monacans long before the semifeudal economy developed in Amherst County. However, the missionaries at St. Paul's were misled by their own cultural biases, for they assumed that the conditions of isolation and simplicity under which the Monacans lived were a sign of their deprivation and not a functional way of life. Precourt (1983) has suggested that capitalist society *needs* a poverty population to define its own standards, and he succinctly illustrates that definitions of poverty imposed upon certain populations do not always derive from their standard of living, but from the values of metropolitan society. Thus, preindustrial forms of subsistence that exist for the most part outside of the national economy (e.g., family based subsistence, independent commodity production) become defining elements of poverty in the minds of the dominant society.

The Monacans were the victims of such a characterization from both missionaries and less sympathetic non-Indians, though the latter saw this perceived poverty as the Indians' destiny. But the Monacans themselves, though they were cognizant of their subordinate position in the local power structure, did not view their economic condition as one of deprivation. When the participants in this study were asked if they thought of themselves as being "poor" when they were growing up, the uniform response was no. There were, however, variable interpretations. As one woman who grew up on High Peak Orchard recalled:

You can look at me and tell that I did not go hungry. And I might have went to school with rubber bands around my socks. My grandmother made me a mini dress out of flour sacks. She'd take them and steam 'em and wash 'em real good, and take the material and make me a mini dress. And I don't know if you remember that song Dolly Parton put out at one time, it's called "Coat of Many Colors." Well, that song means a lot to me, because my grandmother made my first coat, and it had many colors. . . .

But one thing you learn, that material things are only here for you to use. You can't take 'em with you. But thank the Lord for the love that your parents had for each other, and the love that they carried for the children, and they done the most important things. And that was to love you, to have a roof over your head, and for you to have something to eat. And when you think about it, they're the most important things in life. . . . I mean, there were times when I'd say, "Hey mom, why can't I have this, and have that?" But like I said, as I sit back and look on it today, I was far richer than a lot of people out there.

A man who worked on the Sweet Briar farm as a youth recalled, "I felt like at that particular time, in the fifties, and me being young and working hard, you know, I never felt like I was poor. I felt like basically I had everything I needed. Years later I realized that I didn't have everything I needed, because I didn't get the education that I needed."

Education, or at least increased exposure to different ways of living and higher economic standards, brought about slightly different perspectives about poverty, as seen in the words of one of the first Monacans to graduate from public high school: "We were poor, you know. I realize that now, but back then I didn't. You know, I always had plenty of food, I always had clean clothes. I didn't have a bunch of clothes, but they were always clean. . . . But you know, we were happy. I think now that you can have too much. You know, you start to think about what you want instead of what you got. Like I said, I don't remember going hungry or having to wear dirty clothes. But at the same time there were Monacans that were a lot poorer than we were."

All of the above perspectives on poverty are bound by the common theme of contentment with a lifeway based on simplicity and hard work. As one elderly man put it: "I don't mind wallerin' in the dirt. I come from dirt, dust. And that's where I'm comin' back to." And in spite of increased opportunities and a higher standard of living (in metropolitan terms) among contemporary Monacans, there are still older people who, by choice, pursue a simple, subsistence-based lifeway. Although they draw their water from springs and cook and heat their homes with wood, they are by no means poor, as evidenced by the fact that one such individual recently paid to have a road on tribal property resurfaced with money out of his own pocket (Cook, 1996a).

What all of this suggests is that, while the semifeudal economy that developed in Amherst County placed onerous demands on Monacans in their effort to subsist, it did not inhibit the subsistence practices and cooperative lifeway to which the Indians were accustomed. Indeed, the local economy relied on these practices to sustain a low-cost labor force. Although the semifeudal economy imposed formidable restrictions on the autonomy of Monacans in terms of where they lived, how they spent their income, whom they associated with, and so forth, in the long run it probably served to reinforce family-based subsistence patterns and communal ties among the Indians. The tenant system escalated the urgency for people to pool their resources to survive, and Indians had no one to turn to besides each other. To the extent that St. Paul's was a source of relief, it was primarily a space appropriated by some Indians to continue unencumbered the cooperative activities in which they had been engaged for years.

Nonetheless, if the semifeudal economy served in some way to reinforce communal ties among Monacans, other elements of the overall colonial scheme in Amherst County had the opposite effect. Miscegenation laws had been used for years to obscure, if not exterminate Indian identity in Virginia, and in the 1920s the most devastating of these emerged. It was then that the Monacans faced the most brutal assault on their community and on their legal existence.

The "Final Solution" in Amherst County

If the proliferation of miscegenation laws to keep power and property in the hands of the privileged few was justified by Eurocentric moral arguments in the nineteenth century, proponents of such laws found a new source of justification in science in the twentieth century. When Herbert Spencer posited his evolutionary scheme of "survival of the fittest" in the 1860s, he specifically applied this concept to human beings, arguing that humans of "superior Stock" should reproduce only with each other. In 1883, Francis Galton seized Spencer's ideas to coin the term "eugenics," which he described as a "science of race improvement." Eugenics rapidly gained popularity among conservative privileged classes in Europe and the United States as a means of justifying poverty. So called "degeneracy studies" were used to "scientifically" prove that the deprived social conditions of poor families were the result of intermarriage with people of inferior stock, most often with nonwhites (Smith, 1993: p. 1–4). By the early twentieth century, eugenics became an influential force behind racial segregation laws in the United States.

Among the most influential Virginia public figures aligned with the eugenics movement was Dr. Walter A. Plecker, who became the state's first Director of Vital Statistics in 1916 (Houck, 1984: p.72). Although space allows only a cursory glance at the highlights of Plecker's career, his shameful treatment of people of color (particularly Indians) and his obsessive manipulation of the law in the name of "racial purity" could easily be the subject of a lengthy volume.[2] In thirty years, Plecker managed single-handedly to do more to erase Virginia Indians from the legal record than over two centuries of miscegenation law had accomplished. In his mind, interracial unions led to the dilution of superior human stock; perpetuating racial segregation literally became his mission. The existence of Indians complicated this scheme, as it was much easier to separate black from white. Thus Plecker espoused the view that all Virginia Indians had intermarried with blacks and therefore should be considered "Negroes": "It goes to say that any person claiming to be Indian by heritage is to be classified as Negro or colored" (1925: p. 19). His attitudes concerning race and particularly as regards to Native Americans is succinctly stated in the titles of several of his publications, such as *The New Family and Race Improvement* (1925), and *Virginia's Vanished Race* (1947).

Plecker's influence as a eugenicist was national if not international in scope. Throughout the 1920s, organizations such as the American Public Health Association and the National Museum of Natural History called on him to speak on racial purity, and it is said that the "scientific" system he devised to determine the racial origin of individuals was adopted by Nazi Germany in advance of the "Final Solution" (Smith, 1993: p. 61). Plecker's influence in the state of Virginia was profound. Enlisting the aid of his friend John Powell—a key founder of a white supremacist organization known as the Anglo-Saxon's Club—who had powerful friends in the state legislature, Plecker successfully secured legal sanction for a grand scheme to keep the races separate and to legally delete Indians from Virginia through a process which J. David Smith aptly refers to as "legal racism and documentary genocide" (Smith, 1992).

Plecker was the author of the 1924 Virginia Racial Integrity Law, which was the most elaborate of the state's miscegenation laws to that date. The act read in part: "It shall be unlawful for any white person in this State to marry save a white person, or a person with no other admixture of blood than white or American Indian. For the purposes of this act, the term 'white person' shall apply to the persons who have no trace whatsoever of any blood other than Caucasian; but persons who have one-sixteenth or less of blood of an American Indian" (Virginia Assembly, 1924: p. 535). By "American Indian" Plecker did not mean any of the aboriginal people of Virginia, as he indicated throughout his career. Employing divide and rule tactics, he enlisted the support of the American Indian Association (AIA), a western organization of Native Americans themselves opposed to racial admixture (Smith, 1993: pp. 78–79). In a letter to AIA representative Dr. Red Fox St. James, he insisted that there "are no pure Indians unmixed with negros in the State," excepting a few who had moved from out of state, and he proceeded to warn Red Fox not to make alliances with Virginia Indians: "Should you admit any of these, the thinking white people will immediately put you in the same class as them" (Plecker, 1926a). Although the AIA endorsed the Virginia Racial Integrity Law, Plecker revealed his true sentiments toward all Indians in a letter of the same date to Charles Davenport, director of the Office of Eugenics: "I think . . . they are very eager to lose themselves in the white race" (Plecker, 1926b). The law, in essence, gave Plecker license to classify all Virginia Indians as "black," thereby making the task of segregation easier. As Smith points out, the law really only addressed the issue of "white integrity," as it did not prohibit interracial marriages between nonwhite groups (1993: p. 59).

The first legal test of the 1924 Racial Integrity Law came in the same year and involved a Rockbridge County woman named Dorothy Johns, who was of Monacan descent. The county clerk had refused to issue Johns a marriage license on the grounds that she was of mixed racial heritage. While witnesses testified that the only nonwhite progenitors in her lineage were Indian, Plecker himself emerged with documents showing some of her ancestors to be "colored." Judge Henry Holt of the Eighteenth Circuit Court of Virginia reluctantly upheld the clerk's refusal, criticizing the Racial Integrity Law for being too vague (Smith, 1993: p. 71). In November of 1924, Holt seemingly backpedaled in the case of *Atha Sorrels v. A. T. Shields, Clerk*, again involving a woman of Monacan descent being denied a marriage license. This time Holt ruled in favor of the plaintiff, criticizing the Integrity Law for its poorly defined concept of race, but recommending an appeal to clarify the law (Smith, 1993: pp. 71–72).

The *Sorrels* decision infuriated Plecker and his ally John Powell, though they declined to appeal to a higher court for fear that the Racial Integrity Law might be declared altogether unconstitutional (Smith, 1993: p. 75). Nonetheless, Plecker continued to manipulate records with relentless fervor in an effort to protect the integrity of the "white race." Eva Saks (1988) has argued that the term "blood" in miscegenation law was most often a metaphor, and that legal definitions of race could contradict the social meanings of these terms. Plecker's campaign against the Indians of Virginia provides excellent evidence for this argument. Plecker and his clerks devised what he termed a "scientific" system for determining race by tracing surnames through birth records dating from 1833 to 1896. If the classi-

fication of "Negro," "mixed," "colored," or similar classifications
were listed, county clerks and registrars were ordered to classify
persons bearing those surnames as "Negro" unless they could prove
otherwise. Of course, the designation "colored" or "free colored" as
noted in the last chapter, could have been applied to any number of
minorities, including Indians or their offspring with whites, which
reveals the immediate flaw in Plecker's "scientific" method (Houck,
1984: p. 73; Smith, 1993: pp. 89–93).

Very early in his career, Plecker developed a particular vendetta
against the Indians in Amherst County. He was especially infuriated
by the fact that 304 people in the county had been listed as "Indian"
in the 1920 census enumeration and he fired dozens of letters at the
United States Census office in an attempt to have this corrected
(Houck, 1984: p. 73; Cook, 1996a). In fact, he kept such a watchful
eye on the Amherst Indians that his obsession bordered on paranoia.
Although there is no confirming evidence of such an occurrence,
Plecker reported an uprising of Amherst Indians that threatened to
turn into a full-scale race riot in the aftermath of the 1924 case involving Dorothy Johns. Most likely, he was trying to inhibit the
threat of future litigation in the wake of the *Sorrels* case, as evidenced
by the fact that he requested information on the litigants in that case
from the Amherst County clerk (Smith, 1993: pp. 91–92). Very little,
it seems, escaped Plecker's attention. In 1940, for example, he wrote
a threatening letter to a Rockbridge County official for listing a
newborn Monacan baby as white: "I am amazed that you would register one of these Amherst negroes as white.... Somebody has made
himself liable to the penitentiary" (Plecker, 1940).

As Plecker was launching his program of documentary genocide,
Estabrook and McDougal were conducting fieldwork in Amherst
County for *Mongrel Virginians*. In the preliminary report for the
study, Estabrook wrote that "the low mental level [of the people of
Bear Mountain] is no doubt due to the preponderance of Indian and
negro blood" (Estabrook, 1924). Ignoring the limitations of the local
power structure, he offered as "proof" of the Indians' low mental capacity the fact that a school had existed for them for years but had

yet produced no teachers or preachers (ignoring the fact that the mission school offered only seven grades under the best of circumstances). This set the tone for the study, which was published in 1926, and it became widely circulated among eugenic policymakers such as Plecker. Plecker's interest in the study was compounded by the fact that despite measures of confidentiality, he knew that it took place in Amherst County, and he pressured the authors first for a manuscript, then for a key to break the pseudonyms. The authors, however, believed Plecker to be a dangerous man and never consented to his requests (Smith, 1993: pp. 84–87). But even before the study was released, Plecker falsely claimed to have knowledge of its findings and informants, as exemplified by a threatening letter he sent to a Rockbridge County Indian in 1924: "I don't know you personally . . . but I do know that an investigation made some time ago by the Carnegie Foundation of the people of mixed descent in Amherst County found [your] family one of those known to be mixed" (Plecker, 1924).

In 1942, Richmond attorney John Randolph Tucker threatened Plecker with litigation if he did not send birth certificates for several Amherst Indians free of racial notation (Smith, 1993: pp. 95–96). Plecker responded by approaching his powerful friends in the General Assembly and securing the passage of amendments to the Racial Integrity Law, which gave him unlimited discretionary power in determining race on records of persons "for whom the records are such as to leave the Registrar to doubt the correctness of the racial designation or designations contained in the certificate" (Virginia Assembly, 1944: p. 53). The grand colonial thrust led by the state of Virginia against the Monacans had reached its peak.

Plecker's Legacy in Amherst County

The 1924 Racial Integrity Law was unlike prior miscegenation laws in Virginia, for in addition to being more explicit it was also more rigorously enforced than previous laws. Its effects on the Monacans were immediate, though incremental. The first complication Indians in Amherst County faced under the new law was the fact that prior birth and death records had classed some of them as "Indian," some as "black," and some as "white." This meant that under the provisions of the new law, certain people within the Monacan community could not be legally married to each other, regardless of how they identified themselves (Houck, 1984: p. 73). Moreover, the persistence of many Monacans in identifying themselves as Indians got them into deeper trouble with Plecker and probably led to the disproportionate amount of attention he focused on Amherst County.

The first step was to correct what Plecker perceived as erroneous census enumerations listing a "formidable" Indian population in Amherst County. He wrote numerous letters to national and district census officials, insisting that "They [the Monacans] are under no circumstances entitled to be called Indians" (Plecker, 1925) and conducted an "investigation" of his own to offer proof of this assertion. Perhaps as a result of this pressure, the census enumerator for the 1930 census simply left the race category blank on the records for many Amherst Indians. Several Monacans wrote to the district census office to report this, notably asserting their Indian identity, at which point Ernest R. Duff, director of the district census office launched his own investigation. Reporting to his superior in Washington, W. M. Stewart, Duff stated "that should this colony of mixed Indians be listed as Negroes, a grave injustice would be perpetrated upon a defenceless people" (Duff, 1931). Stewart, in turn, was satisfied that the Indians were Indians, and dismissed the barrage of letters from Plecker and his allies in Amherst County.[3]

Stewart's decision, however, was but a hollow victory for the Monacans, as it did not stand in the way of Plecker's tampering with vital records. At the county level, Plecker found enthusiastic allies among prominent Amherst officials and citizens. William Sandidge, who served as county clerk for most of Plecker's tenure, was instrumental in seeing to it that the vital statistics of Amherst Indians listed them as nothing other than "Negro" (Smith, 1993: p. 95–96). Prominent businessmen and farmers, such as J. J. Ambler IV, whose family had been patrons of St. Paul's Mission, made public their views that the "Issues" were more "Negro" than anything and acted as lobbyists in support of Plecker's allegations against the Census Bureau.[4] In 1943, Plecker sent a letter to all county clerks and registrars in Virginia stating that his "scientific" scrutiny of vital statistics records was complete and he presented his "hit list" of surnames that were thereafter to be classed as "Negro." In Amherst County, all of the prominent Monacan surnames were listed: Johns, Branham, Adcox, Hicks, Hamilton, Redcross, and so forth (Houck, 1984: p. 73; Smith, 1993: p. 89).

Although the Monacans offered no overt resistance to Plecker, he became more aggressive in his efforts to alter records, and the effects of his policy were more devastating to the Monacan community than any prior colonial thrust. Not only did it legally deprive them of their identity, but it provided an indirect legal sanction for the blossoming semifeudal economy and the racist assumptions on which it was built. There was simply no escaping the legal designation of "Negro," and in the wake of the eugenics movement the term "Issue" became synonymous with "tri-racial," or inferior stock. This led not only to increased marginalization of the Monacans within the dominant social hierarchy, but gave rise to rifts within the community as well.

In his landmark *The Wretched of the Earth* (1963), Frantz Fanon wrote extensively of the tendency of colonized people, faced with a condition of hopelessness and powerlessness, to internalize their subaltern condition. This internalization manifests itself through attempts by colonized people to emulate the colonizers, or through acts of violence upon each other. What happened to the Monacan community during Plecker's reign seems to exemplify such trends very well. Many Monacans quite simply became ashamed of their Indian heritage and took every practicable measure to conceal it. As one woman noted of her childhood in the 1950s and 1960s: "I can definitely sit here and say there were times when I was going through school, and things was happening to me and people was treating me like they was, there were times I didn't want to hear the word Indian. And I truthfully admit to it today. . . . There was a time in my life, that I can't say I was proud of who I was. I wasn't because of the discrimination that was going on, and the people the way they were, you know, the things they would say to hurt their feelings. And I can't say I was proud then."

It was probably during this period that the last known vestiges of the Monacan language in Amherst County died, simply because people were afraid to teach it to their children. A handful of middle-aged Monacans have vague childhood memories (during the late 1950s to mid 1960s) of grandparents who could speak a few "Indian words." One elderly man said of his grandfather in the 1920s that "he could speak 'em [Indian words] just like those Indians from down in North Carolina [presumably Cherokees]," implying that his grandfather was fluent in the indigenous language. However, the same man recalled of the Plecker years: "If you will join me—people didn't want to be learned to speak Indian. They didn't want . . . wanted to do it a different way. I think a person, being stuck in this county—and they had no reading and writing at the time—and they was pushed down to dirt and dust. Just like the dirt we come from."

In many instances, whether they continued to self-identify as Indians or not, most Monacan parents attempted to shelter their children from the ominous realities of racial oppression in the county. One man recalled of his childhood: "I'll tell you something—it's sad. But I basically left the state of Virginia when I was eighteen and a half years old, and probably about as naive as some guy that had lived back in the mountains for thirty years and never been out. Because we had three school systems in this county, and I didn't even recognize it. I didn't even recognize it. Because, you know . . . the elders kind of protected the younger people coming up. You know, even though there was all this racial prejudice directed toward the Monacans, your families kind of kept it from you." In other words, Monacan children indirectly internalized the colonial hierarchy in the county because their parents shielded them from the realities of its oppressiveness. This is not to say that they developed a false consciousness of the situation because once they grew older—and this was particularly true of those who later entered the public education system—many became eminently aware of their condition.

Other Monacans left the county, if not the state altogether. Some attempted to maintain their Indian identity, though most moved to places like Glen Burnie, Maryland; Johnson City, Tennessee; New Jersey; and West Virginia where they could register and marry as "white" (Houck, 1984: p. 103; Cook, 1996a). It is difficult to determine how many Indians left the county during the Plecker years, but it is possible that at least half of the Indian population migrated during those years.

In 1946, St. Paul's Deaconess Isobel Wagner wrote to the diocese voicing her concern that "Until . . . the Virginia Racial Integrity Law was passed, the social status of these people [the Monacans] did not seem to cause them any great concern" (Houck, 1984: p. 103). She noted that the law had caused a decrease in the number of marriages and an increase in out-migration. In truth, the mission probably enhanced the visibility of the Monacans in the county, thereby making it easier for Plecker and his political allies to implement his hit list. Meanwhile, it seems that the preexisting rifts within the community escalated, and "darker" Indians were chastised by "lighter" Indians and accused of being mixed with blacks. Some of those attending the mission who asserted their Indian identity are said to have denied that those with darker skin were Indian, but were in fact "Negroes." Still others denied their Indian identity altogether and made every effort not to associate with those who claimed to be Indians. These increased rifts, however, may have also been based on the willingness and ability of some Indian families to attend the mission and attain some semblance of a Western education, while others less fortunate had to devote their lives to labor (Cook, 1996a).

Yet the 1940s ushered in the beginning of Monacan opposition (however indirect) to Plecker's campaign for racial purity. Although the Monacans had been permitted to serve in white units during World War I, during World War II the Selective Service decided to allow local draft boards to determine whether local draftees would be placed in "white" or "colored" units. Predictably, the Amherst County draft board registered Monacans as "Negro." Several Virginia Indians voiced opposition to such a placement, but the Selective Service decided to leave the decision in the hands of local draft boards when Plecker intervened (Murray, 1987: p. 222). Several Monacans flatly refused to enter the service, and in 1940, when seven Indians were drafted as "Negroes," Bertha Wailes (who was then a professor at Sweet Briar) wrote the Selective Service on their behalf arguing that they were Indians. When this failed, the Indians enlisted the aid of local attorney William Allen, who eventually initiated a suit in the United States Western District Court of Virginia. In the 1943 case of *Branham v. Burton*, the federal court held that the Selective Service had no right to assign these men a racial designation against their will, thereby declaring the criterion for racial determination as self-identification (Murray, 1987: pp. 222–27). While this decision applied only to the Western District of Virginia, it did reflect a growing federal willingness to challenge racial integrity laws.

The Racial Integrity Law met its final demise in 1967 after a lengthy series of court battles involving an interracial couple who had married out of state and moved to Virginia. The case was initiated in 1958 in a lower Virginia court, and upon the couple's guilty plea, the presiding judge revealed the sentiments then prevalent in the state: "Almighty God created the races. . . . The fact that he separated the races shows that he did not intend for the races to mix" (388 U.S. 2 [1967]). Nearly ten years later, that case of *Loving v. Virginia* (388 U.S. 1 [1967]) reached the Supreme Court, where it was unanimously held that the Virginia Racial Integrity Law (and all miscegenation laws, for that matter) was unconstitutional, as it violated the equal protection and due process clauses of the Fourteenth Amendment.

Although Plecker retired long before this decision was rendered, his policies of racial purity and documentary genocide were nonetheless carried forth by his successors, even after the 1967 decision. Several Monacans recall that well into the 1970s they had to struggle with local clerks and hospital officials to make sure that birth certificates and other records listed themselves and their children as "Indian" (Cook, 1996a; 1996b). But the 1970s would see the beginning of a new and positive direction for the Monacan community. In the interim, they had one more pivotal legal battle with which to contend.

Public School Integration

Fourteen years before the *Loving* decision, the U.S. Supreme Court rendered the opinion in *Brown v. Board of Education* (347 U.S. 483 [1953]), which mandated the end of racial segregation in public schools. Like many southern states, Virginia was slow to defer. The old Democratic leadership in the legislature pursued a policy of "massive resistance," and Governor Lindsay Almond attempted to sidestep integration by introducing "freedom of choice" legislation in 1959 (Houck, 1984: p. 104). By the late 1950s, all counties in Virginia had integrated Indians into their public school systems—except for Amherst.

Prior to integration, Amherst County had offered limited support to the Bear Mountain school, paying the salaries of three part-time teachers and providing school bus service. When Florence Cowan became head deaconess at the mission in 1952, she began to demand more resources and equity, and when the county failed to follow up on the *Brown* decision, she launched an aggressive campaign for the integration of Monacans into the public school system. The county school board first responded by offering correspondence courses for Indian students and even offered to partially finance private school education for Indians if other benefactors could be found (Houck, 1984: pp. 104–6). When Cowan renewed her attack on the school board in 1963, the board attempted to avert the issue once again by proposing a thirty thousand dollar bond issue to build a separate high school at Bear Mountain. Cowan bluntly called this measure a "pacifier" and used every ounce of her influence to make the situation as visible as possible (Cowan, 1963). As Cowan pointed out, busing the Indians to a public school would have cost the county a fraction of the cost of building a new school. Considering the fact that black children were already being integrated into public schools, it is evident that at this point the Monacans were the most marginalized and disenfranchised people in the county. Nonetheless, as Cowan's campaign became more salient, and as the federal government became increasingly dominated by liberals, the county conceded. The first Monacan children were integrated into public schools in the fall of 1963 (Houck, 1984: p. 107).

Integration into the public schools, however, by no means signaled an end to racial persecution of Monacans. Instead, it brought about an increased and painful awareness of discrimination among children who had previously been sheltered from such treatment by their parents and the church. For many children, it marked the first time they heard themselves directly referred to as "Issue," and it was not a pleasant experience. One man who entered the school system in the third grade recalled:

> The first couple of weeks were about pretty good. But after a couple of weeks you sort of noticed that the people you were playing with were sort of shying away from you. And when you asked them why, it was something like, "well, my mom told me not to be playin' with you," or, "my parents said we shouldn't be playin' with you." And you know, that kind of hurt. Then shortly after that, the names. You know, they started callin' names and stuff. . . .
>
> Now when I went to Elon School, which was the elementary school, I was in at least two or three fights a week. But my dad told me never to start a fight. And I can't say that I ever started them, and I was in a lot of 'em.

This particular man managed to finish high school, becoming one of the first Monacans to graduate from public school in 1972. The very first, in fact, did not graduate until 1971. But more dropped out in the early years of integrated schools than graduated. The county school board itself did little to discourage discrimination against Indians, as evidenced by the fact that many participants in this study reported that the school bus drivers often refused to pick them up when they first started school. One woman recalled how her particular experiences with the county school system prompted her to drop out:

When we were segregated into the white schools, I started in the ninth grade. But I did not finish high school because of the discrimination and everything that went on in the schools. I just couldn't stand that. I went to the tenth grade, and was going on to the eleventh, and that's when I quit. . . . I think it was five high school kids, and the rest of them was elementary children. And out of the five, didn't have one of us graduate. . . .

I remember going to school the first two days—I think it was two days—that I stood up on the school bus to school and from school. No one would let me sit down. . . . You did have a few friends, you had a couple of them that had something to do with you, or talk to you. And then you had some of them just pure-down HATEFUL, you know, in treatin' you the way they did.

Nonetheless, as harsh as the initial entry of Monacan children into the Amherst County school system may have been, racial tensions in the school system dissolved rapidly over the next twenty years. One of the first Monacans to graduate from high school in the early 1970s recalled several of his non-Indian classmates apologizing to him in high school for the way they had treated him earlier (Cook, 1996a).

It seems, then, that school integration served as one of the key factors in diminishing racial tensions in the county, partially due to the fact that Indian and non-Indian children began to be exposed to each other during the formative years of their childhood and began to foster a greater tolerance for each other. Moreover, the entry of Monacan students into the public school system in Amherst County helped to usher in the beginning of a new epoch of resurgence and revitalization for the Monacan Nation.

Challenging Colonialism, Severing Dependency

Although racism was by no means peculiar to Amherst County in the 1960s, the particular way in which it had become institutionalized was.[5] Indeed, Amherst seems to have been the last deteriorating outpost of Plecker's eugenic agenda. One Monacan recalled that when he was dating a non-Indian woman from nearby Lynchburg in the late 1960s, she had no idea of the implications of the word "Issue," or that people were identified as such and chastised on the basis of surnames: "I told her about the situation in Amherst and I don't think she really believed me at first. I told her about the way they [county clerks, etc.] went by the last names in Amherst County." This situation was losing momentum and the way was being paved for a Monacan resurgence for several reasons.

First, the desegregation of public schools opened doors to new opportunities for Indians in areas that other people had taken for granted. The mere attainment of a high school diploma allowed several Indians to expand their career opportunities and find jobs that paid fair wages. While few attended college until recently, they were able to better their standard of living within the area as they became more engulfed by the capitalist system.

Second, the nationwide desegregation of public schools came in the wake of a growing Civil Rights Movement. The relative success of this movement reflected a growing distaste among Americans for racial discrimination, which became manifested in federal policies. The *Brown* decision had legally stigmatized institutionalized racism, and later national policies such as the 1961 Area Redevelopment Act (75 St. 47) and the Office of Economic Opportunity (OEO) of the War on Poverty tended to favor minorities (Cornell, 1988).

Related to the Civil Rights Movement was the waxing political activity of Native Americans nationwide. For perhaps the first time in history, Native Americans across the continent came in closer contact with each other and were able to effect a greater degree of solidarity than ever before—a solidarity that transcended tribal distinctions. Attaining higher degrees of education through the OEO and other programs, and having learned from federal efforts to reorganize the tribal governments of federally recognized tribes in the 1930s, tribal leaders were able to put greater legal pressures on Washington. Meanwhile, pan-Indian organizations such as the American Indian Movement (AIM) made more overt demonstrations, such as the cross country Trail of Broken Treaties Caravan in 1972, and the occupation of Wounded Knee on the Pine Ridge Reservation in South Dakota in 1973.[6] Federal policymakers responded to these pressures, if not out of benevolent concern then as a measure of co-optation, with favorable policies such as the Indian Self-Determination and Education Assistance Act of 1975 (88 St. 2203), which purported to recognize a greater degree of sovereignty in federally recognized tribes (Cornell, 1988; Gross, 1989). Since the Monacan Nation was not federally recognized, it was not eligible to benefit from most of these policies. However, it did derive certain positive benefits from the increased salience of Indians in the national media. Although the media did not always cast Natives in a favorable light, Native American culture was viewed in a more positive manner by mainstream society, though often for what non-Indians perceived as its exotic character rather than its humanity.

Finally, the integration of schools and the nullification of miscegenation laws by the Supreme Court coincided with the decline in large-scale agriculture in Amherst County for reasons noted in the last chapter. While this decline potentially meant the loss of employment for Indians, it ultimately signified their liberation from the semifeudal economy that had prevailed for over a century. Moreover, the declining agricultural base was accompanied by the extension of suburbs from nearby Lynchburg, and with it, the diffusion of more mainstream "popular" values and attitudes among non-Indians, which were more tolerant of minority populations. Indeed, even William Sandidge, who had faithfully executed Plecker's orders for years while serving as Amherst County clerk, went on record in the *Washington Post* as saying "the Indians have a good record. I'd say local authorities have had less trouble with them . . . than with the other two races" (O'Neill, 1969). What is significant about this remark is the fact that one who had for years denied the existence of Indians in the county publicly acknowledged their existence. Thus, it became increasingly possible for Monacans to find equitable employment close to home.

The aforementioned external factors contributed significantly to the arrangement of circumstances that would facilitate the revitali-

zation of the Monacan community after nearly two centuries of colonial barriers. As the economic structure shifted in Amherst
County, and as national social and political trends favored Indians,
many Amherst Indians began to express a greater pride in their heritage. However, the revitalization of the Monacan community would
not come overnight. The shackles of colonialism had to rust away
slowly, and there were still many open wounds in the community inflicted by years of oppression, especially those resulting from
Plecker's campaign to erase the Monacan heritage. The healing
process would have to come from *within* the community.

At this point, a word on the changing role of St. Paul's Mission in
the Monacan community is necessary. Some tribal and nontribal
members have often expressed the sentiment that the tribe and the
church (meaning St. Paul's) are inseparable. Although the church
had a very profound and intimate involvement in the Monacan community from the time the mission was established, this assertion has
become less true in recent years. However, in the years immediately
following integration and continuing into the 1980s, it would have
been easy for an outside observer to come to that conclusion.

In 1965, Captain John Haraughty became the director of St.
Paul's and remained there until the late 1980s. Haraughty is both a
celebrated and controversial figure among the Monacan community,
but for some of the Monacans at least, his influence was decisively
positive. As a skilled lawyer, minister, and businessman, he was instrumental in lobbying for the abolishment of Plecker's racial classification system. In 1970, as the orchard industry was falling and
many Monacans were faced with unemployment, loss of homes, and
invading real estate developments, Haraughty used his influence to
purchase a two hundred acre tract of the old High Peak Orchard for
a Monacan housing development. This development was largely financed by money pooled by members of St. Paul's. He then secured
a low interest $114,000 loan from the Farmers Home Administra-
tion for the construction of modest but comfortable homes in what
became known as Orchard Hills Estates. Thus, a portion of the Mo-

nacan community was able to secure land of its own in their ancestral homeland (Hock, 1984: pp. 113–15; Green, 1987: p. 27; Cook,
1996a).

In the mid-1970s, Haraughty was instrumental in securing federal funding for a job training program (JTPA) under the provisions
of the Comprehensive Education and Training Act (CETA, 87 St.
839). This program was administered by tribal members and it
served Indians not only in Amherst but in surrounding counties
such as Rockbridge, Nelson, and Campbell. While the records are
incomplete on how many Indians were served by this program, and
on its results, several individuals stated that it was an essential step-
ping stone for them toward vocational careers (e.g., as electricians).
Moreover, it might be argued that this program, which was housed
and administered out of the St. Paul's parish hall, laid a tentative
foundation for the modern tribal government.

Both the establishment of Orchard Hills and the JTPA program
were conducted out of the church. For this reason, Haraughty's initiatives have been criticized by some for excluding those Monacans
who were not associated with the church, thereby exacerbating rifts
within the community. There was a time when certain community
members referred derogatorily to Orchard Hills as "Hooterville," or
"the Hill," and it is understandable that Indians who did not attend
St. Paul's might have felt alienated. Prior to the mid-1980s, whatever
semblance of a tribal government was closely associated with the
church vestry. However, it must be remembered that such rifts existed in the community long before Haraughty's arrival, if not before
the arrival of the church. Thus, to imply that such rivalries were
solely caused by the church would be to portray the Monacans as
mere reflections of exogenous forces and not as agents of their own
destiny. If the exercise of such agency was restricted in years past, it
was never extinguished, and in recent years the community has, of
its own volition, gone far to overcome age-old rifts. Now when
people refer to "the Hill," it is rarely with a malevolent tone. In fact,
for a period of about four years (1995–98) tribal bylaws prohibited
church vestry members from serving on tribal council in order to

ensure that church matters did not dominate tribal business, and to accommodate the interests of those who did not attend St. Paul's. While this sanction may seem discriminatory, most tribal members agreed that it was a wise compromise at the time, and vestry members voiced little resentment.

But how did the Monacans manage to initiate the healing process within their community? This is a complicated question to answer, and it will be dealt with in detail shortly, but a couple of rallying factors can be identified at this point. The first was the 1984 publication of Peter Houck's book, *Indian Island in Amherst County*. Houck, a local pediatrician who served several Monacan families, was not convinced that they were Cherokees, as previous writers had contended. In fact, most Monacans simply referred to themselves as "Indian." Following Bushnell's (1914) speculation, Houck conducted historical and genealogical research that yielded evidence that the Amherst Indians were descendants of the Monacan confederacy. It should be noted that the use of the name *Monacan* in reference to the contemporary Amherst County Indians (or any contemporary Indians for that matter), after three centuries of not being in common usage, was a direct result of Houck's book. Although Houck is an amateur historian whose work may not meet the highest standards of trained ethnohistorians, it was nonetheless a commendable effort. What is more, at a time when the scholarly abuses of Estabrook and McDougal remained etched in the minds of many Monacans, Houck distinguished himself as the first scholar to treat them with dignity and integrity, without condescension.

Although Houck dealt primarily with Indians at St. Paul's, his book evoked a sense of pride in some Indians in Amherst and beyond who had remained hesitant to assert their Indian identity even after the positive turn of events in the 1970s. At St. Paul's an ad hoc tribal council was formed under the name of the Monacan Indian Tribal Association (which initially served as the official corporate name for the tribe as well), and the Monacans petitioned for official recognition from the state of Virginia as an Indian tribe. They received this in 1989, following the recommendation of the intertribal Virginia

Council of Indians (VA-House Joint Resolution 390). But even the prospect of state recognition did not spark a great deal of community solidarity. Those involved in the process recall that many Monacans, even within the church, were wary of the implications of the process and adopted a "wait and see" stance.

As the state recognition process was well underway, however, a phenomenal thing happened to the Monacan community. Many tribal members who had moved away during hard times, or were born in distant counties and states, began to move to Amherst County permanently. Some were drawn by the new research done on the tribe's heritage; others had just been waiting for favorable circumstances to develop in the county that would allow them to return home without fear of economic or racial oppression. Many returning home were equipped with tools obtained through higher education, thus bringing new and useful skills into the community. Moreover, many of those returning home had never been integrated into the matrix of the rifts existing in the community and were able to deal with different individuals with a degree of impartiality. They also brought with them a politically charged understanding of the implications of state—and eventually federal—recognition. One man had been active for years in the American Indian Movement as a staunch advocate of indigenous rights and became a charismatic force in the community. Although these individuals were initially received with mixed feelings by many tribal members who had lived in the county all their lives, their presence and outspoken pride in their Monacan identity ultimately had a congealing effect on the community. This is not to say that factionalism vanished, but many Indians who had either concealed their identity or had avoided the mission began to take greater pride in who they were.

The ability of tribal members to move back to Amherst County evokes an important point. As previously mentioned, the simultaneous growth of the Lynchburg metropolitan area and the decline of large-scale agriculture in Amherst County in the 1960s and 1970s actually provided unexpected opportunities for tribal members to find diversified and fair employment close to home. This trend has continued, and those who have returned to Amherst County from as far away as Florida have been able to find suitable employment. For some this has meant a substantial cut in salaries and relative standard of living, but in their minds and hearts it is a worthy sacrifice. In fact, although no comprehensive survey has been conducted on tribal employment rates, during the course of my fieldwork no one interviewed reported knowing of anyone in the tribe who was unemployed. The only exception was a tribal member who was laid off during that period. And most tribal members enjoy a comfortable, though modest, standard of living. Those who own land, own on average between one and five acres, though a few who have engaged in successful business enterprises own up to fifty acres.

It would seem, then, that capitalist integration has had a positive effect on the community insofar as entry into the local labor force has allowed tribal members to stay close to home. However, some adverse side effects exist. Work schedules often conflict with tribal gatherings and meetings, thus interfering with tribal members' full involvement in tribal affairs. If the tribe is able to establish a tribal enterprise of some sort in the future, this problem may be at least partially remedied. As it stands, tribal members have done a remarkable job of sustaining a community and government while having to make a living outside.

The issue of capitalist integration evokes another essential point concerning the cohesion of the Monacan community—namely, the effects of colonialism and changing economic conditions on gender roles. Several feminist scholars have argued that capitalist integration in many colonized societies created greater gender rifts when men were absorbed into the wage labor system to the exclusion of women (Bozzoli, 1983; Hansen, 1984). Specifically, some argue that the capitalist system, as a *cultural* system, reflects Western dualistic thought that draws a sharp dichotomy between men and women, relegating the latter to a subordinate position in society (Wallerstein, 1983: pp. 39–51; Scott, 1995). This, however, was not the case with the Monacans. Whatever else may be said of local orchard owners and farmers, they did not discriminate on the basis of sex when it came to hiring labor. They were only interested in production, and men and women worked side by side out of necessity. When the semifeudal system subsided, and greater education opportunities arose, both men and women within the tribe found more diversified employment opportunities.

However, it seems that an increasing number of Monacan women have left the workforce in recent years while their spouses support the family financially. Although this would seem to indicate the subordination of women through a gendered division of labor, a better answer lies in the work of Diane Rothberg (1980). Examining the integration of Iroquois men into the fur trade and then the wage labor force, Rothberg illustrates how the increased absence of Iroquois men in villages led to an expansion of women's authority in tribal affairs and that women became the primary conservators of community and tradition. A similar situation appears to have developed in the Monacan Nation. It was largely through the efforts of Monacan women that the tribe attained state recognition, and women have remained prominent in the tribal government since then. In 1996, a Women's Circle was formed with the intention of drawing the community closer together via the association of women, who could spend more time together than could men. "I think in society women are at the center," said one woman, "because they raise the kids . . . and they know what's going on. They're the ones that know, and once they really get involved in stuff, the men always follow" (Cook, 1996b: p. 55). The Women's Circle, in essence, serves as a "community watchdog." It is independent from the church and the tribal council, and yet it includes members from both entities, and informs them of what is going on in the community.

The tribal government itself is structured in such a manner as to facilitate maximum tribal participation in all matters of government. While the Monacan Nation is formally incorporated as a nonprofit organization, the tribe currently has what is known as a general council form of government (Deloria and Lytle, 1983: p. 109). In this system, a set number of tribal officials are elected by the tribe as a whole, but the officials have no substantive authority. The council (elected officials) meets twice a month on issues, then they bring them before the tota as a whole for discussion and approval or rejection. Tribal meetings are held on weekends to facilitate maximum participation, and there is even a seat on the council to represent the youth in the community. It is quite an informal institution, which is intended to give every member of the community a sense of empowerment. Although the tribe has no legal jurisdiction over criminal or civil matters, the council does administer notable welfare programs for tribal members in need.

The point of the foregoing discussion on community cohesiveness is to stress the fact that the Monacans *themselves* have taken the initiative to seize control of their destinies, notwithstanding any help they may have received from the church or other outside parties. In its relatively short existence, the tribal council has represented its constituents well, basically because the constituents ultimately are the government. Every year the tribe hosts a major pow wow and various fund raising activities. As a result, the tribe has established a scholarship fund with the hope that in the near future any Monacan who wishes to attend college will be able to do so. Although the fund is young, it enjoys modest but steady increases each month. The tribal council, now in conjunction with the Women's Circle, also makes emergency funds available to any families in need, and tribal meetings are often used to coordinate informal community efforts to help out tribal members down on their luck. Likewise, the Women's Circle maintains a lucrative food and clothing bank for both tribal *and* nontribal members. In essence, the tribal council has served as a medium through which preexisting community cooperative networks have become consolidated and somewhat institutionalized.[7] The tribe is also involved in an intertribal career development and training cooperative, Monacan-Pamunkey-Mataponi, Inc. (MPM), which serves as a conduit for federal grants for job training and financing among the three tribes. With funds from MPM, the Monacans have been able to establish part time jobs for tribal researchers, establish a summer youth employment program, and send several tribal members to community college. And although tribal programs are few and the infrastructure limited, they are both growing. In 1995 the tribe purchased 120 acres of the original Johns Settlement on Bear Mountain with the goal of buying back the whole mountain eventually. It is hoped that this land base will be the site of a new tribal complex and environmentally safe tribal agribusiness in the future.

The year 1995, in fact, saw some of the most positive events in Monacan history. Not only did the tribe reclaim a portion of Bear Mountain but on Columbus Day, the Episcopal diocese deeded to the tribe the 7.5 acres of land on which the mission was built (Hibbert, 1995: p. 1). The transfer reflected a changing relationship between the church and the Monacans, largely facilitated by changing attitudes among Episcopal representatives who believe that the people of the community should control their own destiny. With the transfer of the land, the parish hall officially became the tribal center. But perhaps most significantly, the event served as a symbol of the Monacan Nation's resurgence as an autonomous people.

Despite the positive developments within and around the Monacan community, there are still rifts within the community. At this point, however, the greatest challenge the tribe will face will be sustaining the community dynamic in the absence of legal power to protect tribal autonomy. This is a problem the tribe is beginning to confront as it prepares to file for federal recognition, which translates into a problem of history.

Although the Monacans' history is unique, the phenomenon of tribal resurgence is not. In fact, it should be noted that the Monacan story is in some ways the story of many Indian people in the East. In the mountains and beyond there exist numerous groups of indigenous descent who have maintained unique identities in the face of pejorative classifications or references by non-Indians, such as "almost white," "tri-racial isolates," or "racial hybrids" (Berry, 1963). This stigmatization and the concomitant indigenous responses point to a problem of history, or rather, to conflicting interpretations of history with no clear resolution. Many of these groups, such as the Lumbees in North Carolina (Sider, 1993) and the Mashpee Wampanoags of Massachusetts (Clifford, 1988: pp. 271–346), have consistently asserted their indigenous ancestry, and their contemporary identities are largely the product of racially charged histories of domination. However, because such groups have not in *recorded* history constituted neat "tribal blocs," their fluid group boundaries and dynamics do not match Euro-American concepts of "Indianness." Likewise, this fluidity of group definition has often been accompanied by a paucity of documentation to confirm these groups' ties to an aboriginal past. It is precisely this problem of history that has made the pursuit of federal recognition such a potentially legitimizing, yet perpetually confounding process for many tribes in the East.

The federal recognition process was another policy initiative generated from the activities of Indian rights activists within and without the government in the 1970s, and made it possible for tribal entities that had been overlooked in the process of treaty-making or negotiations between tribes and the federal government in the past to receive federal endorsement of their sovereign status (U. S. Office of the Federal Register, 1978: p. 39362). This process in itself is a double-edged sword. On the one hand, federal recognition means that the United States government—the de facto supreme colonial power on this continent—will acknowledge (if it so desires) that the Monacan Nation is a sovereign nation that predates any European presence on this continent. Conversely, if the federal government refuses to recognize the Monacan people as a sovereign nation, the tribe will lack any legal means of exercising certain sovereign powers, such as civil or criminal jurisdiction, should it so desire. On yet another hand, federal recognition could subject the Monacans to a new cycle of dependency on federal largess and increased bureaucratic control. Either way, the danger of a new phase of colonial intrusion is apparent.

The Monacan people, however, are well aware of the implications of federal recognition and the process of pursuing it, and they have expressed a remarkably pragmatic attitude concerning such an endeavor. One Monacan woman commented, "Whether we get it [federal recognition] or not is not really the point. What I see is that

striving for federal recognition will pull our community closer together. Because of all the research and stuff that's going to have to
be done. . . . That's like life. It's not the end, it's the in-between, it's
getting there from beginning to end."

Another man, who is very active in coordinating the federal recognition petition, made the following statement:

> We are who we are, because that's who we are. And nobody has to tell
> us that's who we are. The only people that can really give us sov-
> ereignty is ourselves. The federal recognition thing? I guess we seek
> it because that's the way the laws are laid out right now. And in order
> for us to have certain rights under federal laws we have to be rec-
> ognized as a group of Indian people, which is kind of ironic, because if
> anyone ought to be doing the recognizing, we ought to have to rec-
> ognize them as a government. . . . And to me, the only thing the fed-
> eral government does is divide people. They divide cultures, they di-
> vide individuals out, they separate people.

Even younger members of the tribe express such sentiments. According to one young man who is a senior in high school, "The government's only been here for two hundred years. Before that we were
still the Monacans, and after it we're still the Monacans." Others in
the tribe like the prospects of having access to certain federal services and funds but worry about federal bureaucracies interfering in
community affairs. Overall, however, there is little disparity within
the tribe about federal recognition.

The above opinions of the Monacan people concerning federal
recognition and their views of federal largess indicate that there is a
strong sense of peoplehood within the Monacan community—that
is, a shared sense of identity and experience distinguishing the Monacans from other people in the world. Taking into account the Monacans' unique and turbulent history vis-à-vis colonial forces, one
can interpret this emergent and impressive sense of peoplehood as a
contemporary stage in the process of ethnogenesis to which I have
alluded throughout. Intrigued by the degree to which colonized
peoples around the world had maintained a strong semblance of eth-

nic identity in the wake of severe cultural erosion, Fredrik Barth (1969) urged anthropologists to study these phenomena in detail. Barth suggested that in modern times, the total cultural configuration of a society is not as important in defining ethnic peoplehood as the particular cultural symbols the members of a given society exalt as unique to themselves. Anthropologists such as Edward Spicer (1971, 1980) and Robert K. Thomas (1990) responded to this call in their studies of North American indigenous groups. Thomas suggested that ethnic groups that managed to preserve their distinct identity in the face of colonization often exhibited four defining elements of peoplehood: a common language (or particularized use of a more dominant language); a common religious system; a sacred tie to a particular land—a homeland; and a sacred history that spells out the group's relationship to God, to the land, and to other people (1990: pp. 36–37).

While Thomas has been criticized for essentializing the boundaries defining tribes and other ethnic groups, he himself admitted that these criteria were flexible and that one may take priority over others. Indeed, Thomas's flexible typology provides a useful starting point for considering the manifestations of the ethnogenetic process behind contemporary articulations of Monacan identity (something that beckons future research, to be sure). While it is not within the purview of this study to apply Thomas's model to the Monacans in detail, it can be said that they do enjoy a sacred relationship to the land and a common sacred history.

That the land is sacred to the people is evident in the fact that the tribe pooled its resources to purchase the original Johns Settlement on Bear Mountain, and has as one of its top goals reclaiming the entire mountain. A woman who moved back to the area after many years expressed a common sentiment: "It just seemed like I had to be to the mountains, so that they surrounded me and that was my protection. This is where I'm supposed to be." A Monacan man who served two tours in Vietnam expressed the intimate ties between community and land when he recalled that during the hardest times of the war, he was able to keep going when his thoughts drifted back to Bear Mountain and the security he felt among people there: "The last time I was in Vietnam I was in a heck of a rough situation, and I really thought about this place. Thought about the church there."

As Thomas suggested, the relationship to the land and a common sacred history can be intimately related elements of peoplehood. Another Monacan man who had been absent from the Bear Mountain area for years expressed this connection while recalling his return: "I [went] out to the old mission and school, and went out to the old cemetery. And after walking around and going through the old cemetery I knew that—it's just a feeling we had to be here. Seeing the mountain and actually walking on the land. But once you've seen it and once you feel it you have to come back. It just reaches out and grabs you." It should be noted that this individual left a very high-paying job for the modest salary he now earns in order to be near Bear Mountain and the community. It was not just the land, but the fact that he shared a common history with the people and the land. As Spicer (1980) suggested, "Every people has a historical experience which no other people have undergone. Every people has accumulated experiences which they pass on from generation to generation. These experiences are associated with specific places . . . with friendly alliances, with persecutions and betrayals" (p. 346). For Spicer, a common history is one of the most important hallmarks of peoplehood, for it pervades the ever-changing boundaries defined by landscape, genetics, language, and customs, "so long as the common meanings of what has been experienced in relations with other people are known and felt, a people will persist" (1980: p. 347).

The Monacans do, indeed, share a common history, which they— as a community—have become increasingly cognizant of in the wake of positive changes over the last thirty years. If old rifts in the community die hard, they are certainly showing signs of mending as people in the community realize that they were once subjected to the same persecutions at the same point in time and place. Thus, differences like skin color or church affiliation have become increasingly superficial. The events, places, and people of sacred history need not always date back to ancient times. The common history, which is peculiar to the Monacans, might be compared to an epic, in which Walter A. Plecker is a salient antagonist, and countless unsung members of the Monacan community are protagonists. This is already seen today in the numerous stories told in the community of Plecker visiting a tribal member's home and being chased out by someone's father or grandfather.

Although it is unwise to attribute any form of good to oppression, it might nonetheless be argued that the Monacans' shared experience of persecution was ultimately a key factor in allowing them to preserve a strong sense of community and peoplehood. In his famous study of rites of passage, Victor Turner (1969) focused on the transition period of such rituals to derive a model that may be applied to society in general. Turner referred to the transition period in rites of passage (whether Jewish bar mitzvahs, college graduations, or initiations into priesthoods) as the liminal (meaning "threshold") stage. For the ritual passenger, this stage is likened to death, darkness, anxiety, or uncertainty—it is a feeling akin to that which children experience on their first day of school, though in varying degrees of intensity. People experiencing this state of liminality together, stated Turner, tend to develop an intense camaraderie, in which all social distinctions dissolve. Turner called this type of camaraderie "communitas," essentially, an unstructured community of equal individuals. Turner further suggested that communitas could exist beyond rites of passage, in the everyday lives of certain groups. Marginalized people in a given society (e.g., slaves, prostitutes) can be said to be experiencing a prolonged state of liminality, and hence share the experience of communitas. And so it is for colonized peoples, particularly those whose experiences have been as peculiar and denigrating as those of the Monacans. However, Turner concluded that although communitas outside of the ritual context is usually a brief state (as societies need *structure* to hold together), all societies need to experience some level of communitas in order to bolster solidarity. This was certainly the case with the Monacans during the first half of the century. Indeed, as one Monacan woman commented on Plecker's eugenic policy: "The only good thing that can be said about Walter Plecker is that he pulled our people closer together . . . because they had nowhere else to turn" (Bryant, 1997).

The colonial critic Edward Said has stated, "No one today is purely *one* thing. Labels like Indian, or woman, . . . or American are no more than starting-points, which if followed into actual experience for only a moment are quickly left behind" (1993: p. 336). It is true that none of us remains untouched by the globalization of the economy and the effects of communication. But the Monacan people have illustrated a remarkable capacity to resist, if not positively adapt to, those forces which could have potentially disintegrated the dynamics of their community, and their future prosperity as a collective entity will depend on the continuation of this resurgent sense of community.

In the strictest and oldest sense of the term, a nation is a people. Just as the Jewish nation maintained a semblance of peoplehood through thousands of years of persecution and migration, the Monacans have never ceased to be a collective entity whose existence predates the American republic, and unlike the American republic they can admit to a strong element of homogeneity. Although tribes in the eastern United States such as the Monacans are often ridiculed for having (seemingly) lost all tangible vestiges of aboriginal culture, the Monacans at least still retain that most important aspect of a tribal community—a knowledge of who they are and a sense of shared history. The name Monacan, of course, is merely a foreign appellative that they have appropriated as a symbol by which outsiders may identify them. Within the community, however, they more frequently refer to themselves as "our people," or "the people," which is precisely what some of their ancestors were saying when they called themselves *ye-sah.*

However, the concept of *nation* is not to be confused with the relatively recent and sometimes Eurocentric construction, *nation-state.* Nation-states come and go, some almost overnight (as seen frequently in postcolonial Africa). In order for a nation—or more appropriately, a people—to endure its boundaries and its criteria (im-

plicit and explicit) for membership must be incredibly fluid. Peoplehood (or the sense thereof) is a question of *group* identity, and the
rules are constantly changing. In sum, if one subscribes to Sider's
(1994) notion of "identity as history," then peoplehood must be seen
as an ongoing historical process. Early in the twentieth century
some of the Indians of Amherst County might have been content to
be "white," most distinguished themselves emphatically as "Indians."
Now they distinguish themselves from others overwhelmingly as
Monacans.

As an epilogue of sorts, it is worth emphasizing the fact that the
Monacan people are fully cognizant of the synonymous relationship
between nationhood and peoplehood. In June of 1996, the tribal
council convened a general tribal meeting to discuss, among other
things, what the official designation of the tribe would be. The
people of the tribe voted unanimously to change the name from
"Monacan Indian Tribe" to "Monacan Indian Nation." The people
thereby asserted a sphere of inherent sovereignty that no government or law can take away from them.

* * *

The future prosperity of the Monacan Nation depends on the maintenance of its sense of community, and this is something that is
threatened by the forces of capitalist integration. But economic and
political conditions are remarkably better for the Monacans than
they were at midcentury. The term "Issue" is very rarely heard in
the county; local political representatives are responsive to their
Monacan constituents. The local state representative, Vance Wilkins, for example, was instrumental in securing state recognition for
the tribe, and as noted, candidates for state and local offices cater to
the tribe during their campaigns for office. Virtually everyone in the
tribe is employed.

However, the legacy of colonialism and racial oppression is not
gone. In 1995, while a Monacan tribal member was addressing a
meeting of the local Daughters of the American Revolution, an
elderly woman stood up and publicly referred to him as "no more

than an Issue" (McKelway, 1995: p. G3; Cook, 1996a). Every few years a similar incident is reported. One can only hope that the woman's age is a testament to the line of thought associated with the use of the term. Recently, the tribe faced yet another battle to extinguish the legacy of Plecker, as it confronted the current state registrar, Deborah Little, over the issue of tribal birth certificates that still bear racial designations other than "Indian." Little agreed to change certificates only if those individuals requesting such a change paid a fee of eight dollars, and she claimed to have no record that the Office of Vital Statistics tampered with these in the past, despite incontrovertible evidence presented by J. David Smith and other researchers on behalf of the tribe (*News From Monacan Country*, 1996: pp. 5–6). However, fervent lobbying on the part of the Monacans and the Virginia Council of Indians prompted the state legislature to pass a law in March of 1997 allowing all Virginia Indians whose birth certificates had been altered by Plecker to have them corrected free of charge. These incidents serve as a reminder that as long as there are indigenous peoples on this continent surrounded by nonindigenous groups, no matter how peaceful relations are between the groups, and no matter how integrated the groups become, there will always remain a colonial residue. The real challenge lies in rendering such a residue inorganic.

1. Monacan Indian children in schoolhouse at St. Paul's Mission. This revealing photo was taken around 1914, two years before Walter Plecker became Virginia's state registrar. The mission school, which offered eight grades, was in operation from 1908 to 1963, and it was the only place that Monacans could seek a formal education in Amherst County until public schools were integrated (photo courtesy of the Jackson Davis Collection [MSS 3072], Special Collections Department, University of Virginia Library).

2. St. Paul's Mission today. Newer buildings now serve as the Monacan Ancestral Museum. The old log schoolhouse is now registered as a national landmark and will soon be restored and used as a visitor's center.

3. Monacan Tribal Center at Bear Mountain. Originally constructed as a parish hall for St. Paul's Church, the tribal center is a focal point for tribal meetings and other gatherings, such as the annual homecoming in October.

4. Monacan Nation annual pow wow, Elon, Virginia. The pow wow is not only a major fundraising event for the Monacan people, but for many it is a symbol of their resilience as Indian people in a county where Indian people have historically born the brunt of racial persecution.

5. Company town of Itman, West Virginia, ca. 1920. Named after veteran coal operator Isaac T. Mann, this subsidiary of Pocahontas Coal and Coke was famous for its palatial company store (stone building in the foreground), although the surrounding community had no bathhouse, and the employee

houses lacked running water. Today the company store serves as a homeless shelter and home for Wyoming County veterans of war (photo courtesy of Eastern Regional Coal Archives, Craft Memorial Library, Bluefield, West Virginia).

6. Miners at the entrance of Itman Mine, ca. 1920 (photo courtesy of Eastern Regional Coal Archives, Craft Memorial Library, Bluefield, West Virginia).

7. Pineville, West Virginia. The main street of the Wyoming County seat still hosts a continuous flow of coal trucks, despite a steady decline in the number of jobs in the mines in the county.

8. Former Red Jacket Coal and Coke company store. Once serving the community of Wyoming in the southern part of the county, the store closed in the late 1970s. It now hosts occasional weekend flea markets. Notice the abandoned train tracks. Only a few houses remain in the community.

4 A FRONTIER ISLAND

The Growth of Wyoming County, West Virginia

Some two hundred or so miles southwest of Amherst County lies one of the most peculiar counties in the Allegheny Plateau. Wyoming County, West Virginia, is situated squarely in the heart of the plateau, in the dead center of southern West Virginia, and is second to none in the amount of mineral wealth both contained in and extracted from its bowels. However, this region was also one of the latest and slowest to develop. Physiographic isolation coupled with cultural and political recalcitrance at the local level complicated the exploitative process of extracting coal from the county, whereas in many other central Appalachian counties, mineral speculators were able to manipulate local power relations to their favor with relative ease by the turn of the twentieth century. When development did occur, few of the native residents benefited substantially, and dependency on external economic forces was an ultimate conclusion. Today, Wyoming County is classified as one of the most economically distressed areas in the Appalachian region.

In order to understand how Wyoming County became so deeply entrenched in a condition of dependency, it is necessary to consider its historical foundation in the larger context of its relationship to the states of Virginia (of which it was originally a part) and West Virginia. This chapter will examine the history of Wyoming County in its formative years, taking into account who the first Euro-American settlers were, their ways of life, and their relationship with state and national political entities, and outside economic interests up to 1900. But first, it is necessary to develop a familiarity with the natural environment that so profoundly affected the way people lived in the county, as well as their relations with those outside the region.

Environment and Settlement
of the Upper Guyandotte Basin

The area that became Wyoming County was one of the last sections of the Allegheny Plateau to be settled by Euro-Americans, but in previous years it had been the home and territory of various indigenous groups. The county is known to have hosted settlements of Cherokees, Delawares, and Shawnees at various times prior to Euro-American settlement. In fact, although there were no longer tribes living in the area by the time the first white settlers entered the region, they reported a recently abandoned Indian village along what became known as Indian Creek (Bowman, 1965: pp. 1–4).

Whether Indian or non-Indian, those who ventured to settle in or even travel through this area faced formidable physiographic barriers. The 507.3 square miles that now compose Wyoming County may well be the most rugged of Appalachian counties in terms of terrain, climate, and fecundity. Elevations range from 927 feet at the mouth of Little Huff Creek to 3,536 feet on Bluff Mountain. The county is dissected by the once deep but treacherous Guyandotte River, into which all of the local streams feed. Even when the water was high, the Guyandotte was only marginally navigable by small vessels such as canoes or flatboats (Bowman, 1965: p. 11). In spite of the high elevations, the use of the term "mountain" in reference to bluffs in Wyoming County is somewhat deceptive. In geographical terms, there really are no mountains in the area, but rather, deep V-shaped gorges cut into the plateau by streams such as the Guyandotte. Thus, the bottomland so coveted for agriculture in the mountains is a scarcity in Wyoming County, though there are some rather uncharacteristically wide valleys along the Clear Fork and Little Huff Creek, tributaries of the Guyandotte.

With an average annual rainfall of forty-five to sixty-three inches, one would expect agricultural endeavors to flourish in the area (Clarkson, 1964: p. 3; Rice, 1970: p. 8). However, the steep slopes of these narrow valleys invite erosion, and the delicate soils (inceptisols), although rich in nutrients, require careful conservation to remain productive. Because of the high rainfall, steep slopes, and erosive quality of the soil, flooding has always been a problem in Wyoming County valleys.

Somewhat offsetting the restrictions and hazards imposed by the county's rugged terrain—at least in the days before mass industrialization—was an abundance and wide variety of vegetation and wildlife. The bottomlands abounded with various oaks, walnut, yellow poplar, sycamores, paw-paw, gum, ash, and other trees providing fruit and versatile woods. At higher elevations grew sugar maples, beech, yellow birch, red spruce, white pine, and especially chestnut (Clarkson, 1964: p. 1; Rice, 1970: p. 7). While all of the hardwoods provided durable wood that could be put to many uses, chestnut provided the most dependable wood for housing, fencing, and fires. After Euro-Americans settled the area, its nuts provided the most favorable natural fodder for free-ranging livestock. When the first Euro-Americans came to the area, they found (as had their indigenous predecessors) massive virgin forests of these trees, which housed a thriving population of squirrels, raccoons, rabbits, deer, foxes, turkeys and various other fowl, timber wolves, elk, and buffalo (Clarkson, 1970: pp. 11–12; Rice, 1970: p. 7).

In all, these elements combined to form an area of unsurpassed natural beauty, which offered the potential for a good living for those who were willing to endure and do without the amenities of urban life. However, present-day Wyoming County remained free of white settlers until the close of the eighteenth century. But the environment alone did not impede Euro-American settlement of the upper Guyandotte. Iroquois military activities inhibited settlers in the region into the 1760s, and various colonial laws restricted westward settlement until the Revolutionary War. Yet with the opening of the Shenandoah Valley for settlement in the 1730s, the gears were set in motion for the ultimate infiltration of the plateau. By 1750, the settlement of the Shenandoah Valley (primarily by Scotch-Irish and German immigrants) was complete, and new settlers began to follow the Appalachian Valley and its tributaries into Tennessee and Kentucky. Still, of the 125,000 trans-Allegheny settlers in 1796, only 20,000 were in what is now West Virginia (Rice, 1970: pp. 5–21).

Unfortunately, the settlement of the plateau was a fiasco that would have serious repercussions for residents in the future. The problem lay in the state of Virginia's haphazard manner of keeping land records between the competing interests of squatters, speculators, and soldiers who received land grants for military service. Quite often the state land office granted titles to land that overlapped preexisting titles. In 1779, the Virginia General Assembly attempted to ameliorate this problem through a land law, which gave squatters preemptive rights to four hundred acres each in the trans-Allegheny region, and gave pre-1778 settlers preemptive rights to an additional one thousand acres. However, the law also made military warrants transferable, which whet the appetites of numerous absentee speculators. Moreover, the law did not safeguard land titles from subsequent litigation, which meant that many settlers faced the possibility of having to pay handsome legal fees that they could not afford. In sum, the 1779 law opened the way for absentee speculators who established a historical trend in West Virginia that would culminate in the wholesale exploitation of the region by outside interests at the turn of the twentieth century (Rice, 1970: pp. 118–49).[1]

How did these developments and patterns in the settlement of the plateau affect the area that became Wyoming County? It is difficult to determine the extent to which squatters inhabited the area, though that occurred less than in other parts of the plateau because of the area's isolation. In fact, the first recorded settlement of the area did not occur until 1799, when John Cook moved his family from the Shenandoah Valley onto lands he had received for service in the Revolutionary War. However, at least one squatter was reported in the area during that period and there were likely more (Bowman, 1965: p. 6). Since the opening of this area to Euro-American settlement did not officially occur until after 1779, the preemptive rights of prior settlers would not have been an issue.

The earliest speculators, it seems, were settlers themselves, most of whom received their land through military warrants. Among the earliest recorded land grants in the Wyoming County area were those of war veterans such as John Cooke (1785), Thomas Huff (1781), and Edward McDonald (1784), the latter two receiving in excess of eight hundred acres each. These lands were among the best in terms of agricultural utility, being situated along the bottomlands of the Guyandotte and its tributaries (Bowman, 1965: pp. 6, 14). However, absentee speculators had also planted stakes in the area by that time, although not as extensively as in other parts of the plateau. Most notably, Philadelphia financier Robert Morris acquired 1,360,000 acres along the Big Sandy and Guyandotte Rivers in the 1780s, much of which was situated in what became the counties of Wyoming and Raleigh (Rice, 1970: p. 139). The transfer of this land to new absentee owners would play a pivotal role in opening the area to industrialization by the early twentieth century. Most land claims were much more modest than this, however, and were primarily in the hands of settlers. Between 1800 and 1850, when Logan County was partitioned to form Wyoming County, county records listed seventy individual land grants, very few of them over a hundred acres. By 1850, the population of Wyoming County was 1,645, and virtually every head of a household was listed as a farmer (Bowman, 1965: pp. 14–52). A cursory glance at land records suggests serious disparities between the number of individuals eligible to own land and the number of individuals actually owning land. But a more detailed glance reveals that several adult family members were included in the households of those under whose name lands were listed. This suggests a settlement and tenure pattern that must be considered in the context of who the first Euro-American settlers of Wyoming County were.

Settlement Patterns and Community Dynamics

The population that settled the area of Wyoming County was not entirely homogeneous. Although the bulk were Scotch-Irish, there were several English settlers and a few Germans. From the outset, disparities were evident in the ways different families lived, their political and religious tendencies, and their economic standards of living. And yet the isolation of the area from distant economic and political centers gave rise to a semblance of shared meanings among the residents in the area.

If the original Euro-American settlers had one thing in common, it was that none of them were from aristocratic or even bourgeois backgrounds. Whether German, Scotch-Irish, or English, all had either emigrated from Europe or were descended from those who had in order to escape conditions of poverty and/or ethnic oppression. Even John Cooke, the most salient (and ultimately very influential) English settler of the county had been impounded in England and brought over as an indentured servant (Bowman, 1965: p. 329). Likewise, all those who came to the area faced the common experience of trying to survive in an isolated, rugged environment. Perhaps this is why the Scotch-Irish settlers, directly or indirectly, played such a profound role in determining the character of the region.

From Euro-American settlement to the present, the Wyoming County rosters abound with names of Celtic origin: McDonald, Bailey, Morgan, Stewart, and the list goes on. Yet it is not enough to attribute their sheer numbers to the common threads of the social dynamics and economic practices of the area. It is important to recall that the Scotch-Irish were accustomed to surviving under the most adverse circumstances. Most were descended from vassals under British rule in the Scottish lowlands, who beginning in 1610 were persuaded, if not coerced, to move into Ulster, Northern Ireland. Thus, they essentially became pawns in a colonial process. But rather than gaining privilege as colonial agents, they were marginalized and often dispossessed. Land titles in Ulster, as had been the case in Scotland, were insecure at best, and the Scottish migrants often found themselves living a transient way of life. The "rugged individualism" that is so often attributed to the Scotch-Irish was something that developed while adapting to hard times. And yet, these individuals still realized the security and importance of family and community; they did, after all, face common experiences unique to themselves (Leyburn, 1962: 63–88).

The pattern of settlement and land tenure that developed in Wyoming County is quite possibly attributable to practices stemming from feudal Scotland. Prior to 1600, a peculiar relationship often existed between feudal lord and tenant. In many cases, lord and tenant were kin, and relations between the two parties were very personal. Vassals often lived in the same house with the lord, and their relation to the lord was less one of subservience than family responsibility (Leyburn, 1962: p. 69). Vestiges of this relationship may have endured in modified form in the peculiar practice among many families of titling land to a single name in an extended family in Wyoming County, while other adult family members lived on the land and were listed thereunder as "farmers." The following sample from the 1850 census is typical of such entries:

JAMES SHANNON, 63, FARMER, $5,616 [property valuation]
Mary Shannon, 47
Powell Shannon, 24, farmer
Augustus Shannon, farmer
Coshi Shannon, 20
Newman Shannon, 17
Fieldon Shannon, 15
James E. Shannon, 12[2]

What this entry indicates is that more than one nuclear family connected to the extended family was living on and making use of the land. The two other "farmers," sons of James Shannon, are listed as family members because their father was the recorded owner of the property. Bowman provides evidence that prior to the Civil War, land titles in the county were usually deeded to more than one family member—immediate or otherwise—if that person was male and of voting age (1965: p. 80). As Virginia law then required voters to be property-holding men, deeding land to a family member could help to sway local politics in the primary landowner's favor. This pattern was quite common in Wyoming County in the nineteenth century and existed even into the 1960s (Cook, 1996c). Significantly, when industrial forces later began entering the area, this manner of land ownership ultimately made it easier for absentee speculators to dispossess multiple families in a single transaction.

The Scotch-Irish also had a significant influence on subsistence practices in what became Wyoming County. The Ulster Scots had historically been accustomed to cultivating marginal lands, ranging from the bogs and vertical slopes of Scotland to the highly erosive terrain of West Virginia (Leyburn, 1962: p. 20). Once settled in the plateau, they and their neighbors often adopted indigenous slash and burn techniques to cultivate the land. Such practices were, however, extremely destructive to the soil when not carefully managed, and as bottomlands became exhausted, fields were often moved onto the slopes, thereby augmenting the vulnerability to erosion (Salstrom, 1994: p. 10). Such practices were common in Wyoming County (Bowman, 1965: p. 161), though not excessive. Most families only maintained what has been called the "Celtic dispersed farm" (Raltz and Ulack, 1984: p. 115). Cultivation was limited to a small kitchen garden for subsistence purposes, and—as had been the practice in Scotland—cattle were allowed to range freely in the hills. The practice of free-ranging cattle is reported to have continued into the 1940s in Wyoming County. Moreover, family kitchen gardens still exist today almost universally in the county (Cook, 1996c).

Another less tangible but equally potent contribution of the Scotch-Irish to the social configuration of Wyoming County was a staunch opposition to absolutism in government. This had been a principle of the Presbyterian Church to which many lowland Scots had belonged, and it is no wonder that many of the settlers of Wyoming County had earlier fought against the British Crown in the

Revolutionary War (Leyburn, 1962: p. 145). However, this wariness of government may have had adverse manifestations in the long run. In Scotland, the lowlanders had known no regular tax in the 1600s, and their descendants on this continent fought against excessive taxation in the Revolutionary War and in other contexts (Leyburn, 1962: p. 40). Although local taxes were irregular in the area prior to the Civil War, Wyoming County settlers still had to contend with taxes imposed by the state government. Wyoming County developed as a kin-based society at least at the level of various communities within the county, so that local tax assessors were often related to many people within the county. Hicks (1962) noted a tendency in the North Carolina mountains for local tax assessors to under-assess the property of friends and relatives, and it seems that this was not uncommon in most parts of Appalachia. This trend would have repercussions at the turn of the twentieth century when new state taxes became more strenuously exacted, and industrial speculators found an easy way of obtaining land through encouraging the collection of back taxes (Lewis, 1983: p. 183). Many farmers could not afford to pay back taxes and were forced to sell. Several participants in this study reported their families having lost their land in this manner in the early part of the twentieth century (Cook, 1996c).

Celtic or not, the fact remains that all of the early settlers of Wyoming County found themselves in an isolated, rugged environment where survival depended on individual determination and community cooperation. Kinship through extended families became the sinew of cooperative networks. Specific localities and communities quickly became associated with particular families soon after settlement: Indian Creek with the Morgans and Lesters, Oceana and Clear Fork with the Cookes, the McDonalds and Shannons on Huff Creek and the "roughs" of the Guyandotte. But in pre-industrial Wyoming County, the household was the basis of most activity.

Eller has suggested that preindustrial Appalachian society was unquestionably patriarchal in nature, particularly where the division of labor was concerned (1982: pp. 31–32). This is a questionable generalization, especially with reference to Wyoming County. It is true that certain activities were almost exclusively practiced by women or by men. Women almost always cooked, made quilts, sewed, nurtured children, and oversaw household affairs, while men were most frequently engaged in hunting and trapping, building houses, clearing fields, and so forth (Bowman, 1965: p. 163). However, survival in a challenging environment requires versatility; all hands must be prepared to engage in any task that needs to be done. Several of participants in this study who grew up in the twilight of preindustrial Wyoming County recall their mothers hunting and trapping, while male participants reported engaging in activities said to be traditionally relegated to women, such as tending crops and livestock, mending fences, curing meat, making soap, and so forth (Cook, 1996c; 1996d). In a society where civic and commercial life was severely limited and where the household was the locus of most human activity, it would seem that women's authority was much broader than in metropolitan society. The possible exception to this notable degree of authority and responsibility among women was on the three major plantations in the county. During the Civil War, most farms in the county were able to continue functioning and producing enough food and other necessities for their inhabitants to survive, as women and children were prepared to assume extra responsibilities. On the plantations, however, it seems that women and children were less adjusted to the labors and responsibilities of farming. This was especially evident when the men were gone to war and the slave population dispersed (Bowman, 1965: p. 163).

In early Wyoming County, most farms were at least a mile apart, and with families busy tending to the manifold tasks of survival, visiting between neighbors did not always occur on a daily basis. But even in the best of times, surviving as subsistence farmers required cooperative efforts among neighbors when there were crops to be harvested, fields to be cleared, or buildings to be raised. Thus, intimate systems of balanced reciprocity (Sahlins, 1965; Schneider, 1989: p. 99) existed from the inception of settlement in Wyoming County and continued into the twentieth century. Many of the same activities discussed in previous chapters—corn huskings, barn or house raisings, hog slaughterings, logrolling (clearing of timber), and fall sorghum molasses making—constituted important social events and served along with kinship ties as the sinews of community (Rice, 1970: pp. 171–75). Of course, there were also less formal cooperative networks of generalized reciprocity (Sahlins, 1965; Schneider, 1989: p. 99) in which favors were conveyed with no return favors expected. In times of birth, death, illness, or economic need, people simply came together and helped each other with gifts of labor, food, clothing, or moral support (Bowman, 1965: p. 103).

The settlement of Wyoming County coincided historically with the second Great Awakening—a movement of religious revivalism that swept through the eastern United States in the early nineteenth century. Although most Scotch-Irish settlers had been born into the Presbyterian faith, they and their neighbors were easily enlisted into new charismatic Christian denominations that offered messages of hope and liberty. Utilizing itinerant ministers, Methodist and Baptist sects spread the word of free will and a personal relationship with God to the remotest corners of West Virginia. Both groups espoused egalitarian sentiments that clergy need not be educated, only inspired to spread the word of God, thus gaining instant popularity. The Greenbrier Baptist Association (based in Greenbrier County) initially gained a significant following in the Guyandotte Valley— partially because the Baptists' initial call for religious freedom in the 1770s had evolved by 1800 into a zeal for political freedom (Rice, 1970: pp. 281–91). Moreover, Baptist clergy in the Guyandotte region made a better impression on local residents than did Methodist clergy. In 1814, for example, residents of the area scorned a young Methodist circuit rider as "proud, ambitious, and too aspiring" because of his fancy dress and presentation (Rice, 1970: p. 294).

Whatever the denomination, churches served as vital points for social gatherings. Whether through itinerant camp meetings or in permanently established meeting places, churches became perhaps the most important focal points of social activity and control in the early days of Wyoming County. Throughout central Appalachia, where civic infrastructures were lacking or county seats distant, churches often served in a limited, albeit effective capacity as arbiters of justice. It was not uncommon for domestic disputes, acts of violence, or excessive indulgence in spirits to be punished through the medium of the church, legitimized by community pressure (Lewis, Kobak, and Johnson, 1978: p. 116). In Wyoming County in particular, specific churches were associated with specific communities and families, so imposing sanctions on members was ensured a high degree of efficacy. Therefore, it is not surprising that church affiliation became tantamount to political preference as the nineteenth century unfolded (Cook, 1996a).

In sum, the society that developed in preindustrial Wyoming County was based on ideals of freedom and community, insofar as community may be described as a sense of shared experience and cooperation. The dynamics of kinship and community industry and cooperation made possible for most of the residents of the county a remarkably self-sufficient way of life based on subsistence. Situated in perhaps the most isolated reaches of central Appalachia, far from markets and centers of government, the early settlers and their progeny found subsistence a rank necessity.

Subsistence versus Commerce: The Local Economy

The area that became Wyoming County originally fell within the boundaries of Montgomery, Tazewell, and Giles Counties. Due to the extreme distances in this and neighboring sections of present-day southern West Virginia, the County of Logan was formed in the 1830s, and in 1850 Wyoming was partitioned as a separate county. Prior to that time, the area of Wyoming County was the most inaccessible part of the counties in which it was originally included. County seats such as Christiansburg, Pearisburg, and Tazwell were over a hundred miles away, which meant several days' travel just to pay taxes or to trade (Bowman, 1965: p. 163). Thus, self-sufficiency was a universal requirement for survival.

Due to a paucity of good roads and navigable rivers, commercial activities within and related to the county were extremely limited in preindustrial times. The first merchant did not appear in the area until 1845, and the average farm family usually visited the county seat once a year, at best, to pay taxes and trade. Even after Wyoming became an independent county and more merchants and artisans established trades there, transactions were most often made without cash. Farmers and their families instead took produce, meat, milk, butter, and various other items produced on the farm to trade for cloth, coffee, sugar, tea, spices, and other commodities that they could not produce themselves. Some of the earliest trade centers in the county, in fact, were public gristmills where farmers usually paid the miller with produce or other farm products (Bowman, 1965: pp. 165, 180; Rice, 1970: p. 165).

However, it is important to realize that the people who settled Wyoming County (as well as other parts of Appalachia) *came* from capitalist societies. If they were not fully integrated into the national economy, they certainly brought with them some of the trappings of capitalist society—among these, European technologies such as metallurgy and its concomitants, including water-powered mills. Local blacksmiths and millers were able to produce at home what people in metropolitan society or in societies lacking such technology had to obtain through increased trade ties with core regions. More often than not, the raw materials needed to produce metal implements and crafted wood tools were readily available, since various locales within the region held sufficient iron ore deposits for local consumption, and timber reserves were more than adequate to sustain a sparse population. As recent scholars have illustrated, the possession and knowledge of these fundamental technologies actually allowed Euro-American settlers of the region to evade extensive integration into the national market economy much longer than the region's Native American population could. The latter grew dependent on European implements such as guns and other metal items, but lacked the technology to produce these themselves. Thus, Indians became heavily involved in trade relations with Euro-Americans from the core sooner than did white settlers (Dunaway, 1996: pp. 38–39; Salstrom, 1994: pp. 129–30).

This is not to suggest that agriculture for commercial purposes did not occur. Indeed, the McDonalds, Shannons, and Cookes respectively owned three sizable plantations. However, the combined slave population at its peak in 1860 was only around sixty, which suggests that the physical terrain and isolation from the market were antithetical to commercial agriculture. These plantations, in fact, were self-sufficient entities within themselves, each containing a gristmill and blacksmith shop.

Of the 234 families listed in the 1850 census for Wyoming County, virtually every one farmed for a living (Bowman, 1965: pp. 54–58). Corn, potatoes, sweet potatoes, rye, turnips, and lesser quantities of wheat and oats were grown primarily for personal consumption, as was flax for yarn. Although tobacco was of some importance commercially, corn was the single most important staple for both commercial and personal use. Corn could be grown virtually anywhere, and before excise taxes were established and enforced, it could easily be transported when converted into distilled spirits (Rice, 1970: p. 155). Significantly, gristmills in the county were never idle, as flour was not commonly available until the turn of the twentieth century (Bowman, 1965: p. 171). Moreover, agricultural statistics reveal that corn production rose prolifically along with the county's population. In 1850, for example, with a population of 1,645, the county's farms produced 47,506 bushels of corn, and the output climbed steadily to a peak of 195,698 bushels in 1910, when the population reached 10,392 (U. S. Bureau of the Census, 1851; 1913). Actually, these figures indicate a very slow narrowing of the margin between population density and corn production, which, as will be discussed, was later narrowed much faster with the onslaught of industrial forces. The point is that corn production remained high enough to sustain the local population well into the twentieth century—as it had to do, given the distance from markets.

As noted previously, personal livestock also played a crucial role in the local economy of preindustrial Wyoming County. Hogs provided by far the most important source of meat, the ratio of farm swine to people in the county in 1890 being nearly two and a half to one. By 1910, however, when the county's population was 10,392, the number of farm hogs was only 7,792 (U. S. Bureau of the Census, 1913). Sheep were raised primarily for wool, reaching a peak of 7,398 farm sheep in 1910 (U. S. Bureau of the Census, 1913) and the cattle population followed roughly the same trajectory. Virtually every family in the late nineteenth century owned a milk cow, and those who did not were able to purchase or barter for dairy products from those with cows. The forests, of course, provided the primary rangeland for all livestock, with an abundance of nut-bearing hardwoods producing the most nutritious fodder possible for ranging animals. This practice was institutionalized as farmers notched the ears of livestock with identifying marks (much like branding cattle) which were then registered at the local court house (Bowman, 1965: p. 163; Rice, 1970: pp. 157–62).

The residents of preindustrial Wyoming County also relied heavily on the forests for sustenance and raw materials. A variety of hardwoods provided durable timber for housing and furniture, and skilled woodworkers could build a cabin entirely without nails, using flexible wooden pegs. Before extractive industries moved in during the early twentieth century, wild game was abundant and was often relied upon more heavily than domesticated livestock for meat. And a vast lexicon of plants provided food, medicine, and even cash. It might be argued, in fact, that ginseng was the most consistent cash crop in the mountains in preindustrial times, and even into the present. Ginseng roots were small enough to transport to distant exchange points where merchants paid high prices for them, and the roots then yielded even higher prices through the Chinese trade (Rice, 1970: p. 163). For many in Wyoming County, ginseng was the primary means of obtaining cash for tax payments (Bowman, 1965: p. 165). Even today, local residents harvest ginseng for prices that often exceed a hundred dollars per pound.

What emerged, then, in Wyoming County prior to the twentieth century was an extremely localized and self-sufficient economy with minimal ties to distant markets. As late as the 1920s, local residents relied heavily on local seamstresses and other artisans for goods that they did not produce themselves (Bowman, 1965: p. 165). This was at a time when surrounding counties and other parts of Appalachia had become increasingly dependent on external economic forces. The physiographic isolation of Wyoming County initially inhibited the invading extractive industries but this isolation, however, also contributed to a historical framework of peripheralization.

Early Political Institutions and Relations

Salstrom (1994) has suggested that parts of the Appalachian Plateau still qualified as frontier areas as late as the Civil War. If this is true, then Wyoming County was at the heart of the late Appalachian frontier, and yet it was integrated politically, if not socially, into the larger sociopolitical matrix of Virginia and the Unites States as such. Before the Civil War what became West Virginia was part of Virginia, and uneasy relations between the western highlands and the eastern districts had more to do with West Virginians' aspiration to independent statehood than did anything else. At the heart of the split was the fact that Virginia's Assembly was controlled by and catered to the plantation aristocracy of the Tidewater and eastern Piedmont who were determined to maintain hierarchical economic structures from which they derived their power. West Virginia, lacking both an industrial base and the type of land suitable for plantations (and hence for widespread slavery), and being sparsely populated and isolated from major markets, was essentially viewed as unworthy of public investment. Thus, the area that became West Virginia was peripheralized from the outset.

One area of public service in which West Virginia suffered critically was transportation. For the provision of good roads that could link western counties to larger markets, West Virginians had to rely mainly on the federal government. Most of these endeavors, such as the National Road, which traversed the Northern panhandle in 1818, were confined to more northerly portions of the future state where industry was beginning to develop along the Ohio River. The most notable of these was the Kanawha and James Turnpike, a sister project of the Kanawha Canal. Both of these were actually state projects. The turnpike began in 1785 and reached the Big Sandy on the

Kentucky border in 1829 (Rice, 1970: pp. 331–33). Passing through present-day Charleston, this was western Virginia's southernmost major road, but it bypassed Wyoming County by at least eighty miles. Road improvements in Wyoming County, in fact, did not occur to any significant degree until the decade of 1850 to 1860, when the newly formed county passed an ordinance requiring all adult males to contribute two days of labor per year toward road construction (Bowman, 1965: p. 199). Perhaps the Tidewater aristocracy's most blatant act of quasi-disenfranchisement toward western Virginians where transportation was concerned came when the Virginia Assembly refused to approve the extension of the Baltimore and Ohio Railroad through the central part of what is now West Virginia. Western Virginians hoped that the railroad would connect the fledgling salt and mineral industries of the Kanawha Valley with northern markets, but the Tidewater aristocracy was determined to keep western Virginia tributary to Richmond and Norfolk. The Assembly finally agreed to allow the railroad to cross only the northern rim of the state and to exit at Wheeling (Rice, 1970: p. 339). Meanwhile, Wyoming County saw no railroad until after 1910.

Education was another area in which mountaineers received little or no support from the state of Virginia prior to the Civil War. There was no public education in Virginia until 1810 when the General Assembly reluctantly established the Literary Fund for the education of indigent people. This law merely provided partial funding for common schools, which were private endeavors usually directed out of churches or homes. It was not liberally applied to western Virginia, nor was it popular there, for in order for mountaineers to qualify for public education they had to admit to poverty, which most were not willing to do. In 1829 the Virginia Assembly provided for free school districts across the state, but because there was no uniform system yet established for public education, Tidewater politicians found a convenient excuse to avoid educating people whom they believed were "parsimonious and niggardly" (Rice, 1970: pp. 218–24). Although the Virginia Assembly finally approved a uniform public education system in 1846, it was not until after the Civil

War, when West Virginia established its own public education system, that Wyoming County received public schools.

Indeed, residents of western Virginia experienced political exploitation prior to the Civil War insofar as they were putting more into the state political infrastructure than they were receiving in return. The state constitution, as amended in 1830, provided that slaves (as property) should be taxed less than the animals of farmers. Whether they supported the institution of slavery or not, residents of western Virginia saw this as a clear act of discrimination, since they rarely received a fair share of revenues (Bowman, 1965: p. 43). The General Assembly concomitantly inhibited the flow of capital into the region by refusing to charter banks in extreme western Virginia or to allow the expansion of existing banks. The closest *chartered* bank prior to the Civil War was in Winchester, Virginia, which was closer to Richmond than it was to southern West Virginia. Thus, a number of unincorporated banks emerged in West Virginia, primarily in areas of fledgling industrial development, such as the Kanawha and Ohio River Valleys (Rice, 1970: pp. 326–27).

Of course, the sparsely populated western counties were not well represented in the state legislature, which is one of the main reasons why Wyoming filed for recognition as a separate county in 1850. Even so, only two Wyoming County residents served in the state legislature between 1850 and 1861. Significantly, these were both slaveholders and Democrats, which calls into question the degree to which they represented the interests of their constituents. At that time, the county was evenly split between Democrats and old-party Whigs, though the Democrats seem to have been the real power brokers. The first courthouse, in fact, was the living room of a prominent Democratic citizen (Bowman, 1965: pp. 27, 38, 46).

The coming of the Civil War made political representation in the Virginia state government a moot point in Wyoming County. Actually, Wyoming County assumed an enigmatic position regarding secession and wartime allegiance. James Ferguson, a Wyoming representative in the House of Delegates, was a slave owner and stalwart

Democrat, but voted against secession. Other Wyoming planters, however, backed secession and raised Confederate units. Yet later, in 1861, Wyoming joined the other counties of West Virginia at the Wheeling Convention to reject the Virginia Ordinance of Secession. Still, there were sufficient sympathies toward the state of Virginia to allow for the raising of a formidable number of Confederate recruits. The numbers of Confederate and Union recruits were about equal, but frequently fluctuated. Many enlisted according to family loyalties, and several Confederates quickly deserted and joined Union regiments when they found that the Confederate government was unreliable in providing provisions. Significantly, many men opted to join partisan or home guard units rather than serve on distant battlefields for the larger "cause" (Bowman, 1965: pp. 38–52, 87–91).

All of this suggests that the Civil War was not an ideological conflict for most of the residents of Wyoming County, but an assertion of family loyalties in which the local political system became the ultimate testing ground. Indeed, after the 1860 election, the county government was forced to shut down, and Wyoming County experienced a state of virtual anarchy. Wartime skirmishes in the area usually took the form of raids on rivals' crops, and rarely were related to engagements in larger theaters of the war. The net result of the war economically was significant, but not irreparable devastation. Census figures show that agricultural production dropped significantly between 1860 and 1870 but in some interesting ways. For example, tobacco production (a cash crop) dropped by roughly 80 percent, but corn (a staple) production fell by only 5 percent (U. S. Bureau of the Census, 1872: pp. 791–92).

And yet the county rebounded relatively quickly after the war. It was now part of the newly formed state of West Virginia, which had backed away from rebellion against the Union and therefore was not subjected to the programs of reconstruction. However, independent statehood would ultimately invite the intrusion of *other* external forces.

West Virginia: A Tragic Dream

The decision of the delegates to the Second Wheeling Convention of 1861 to form a separate state had little to do with wartime ideologies (abolitionist sentiments, preservation of the Union, etc.) and had more to do with local resentment vis-à-vis the government of Virginia. As noted previously, western Virginia had always been alienated from the state political structure, and proposals to form a separate state had emerged periodically since the inception of the American Republic (Rice, 1970: pp. 118–22). The advent of the Civil War provided a convenient segue for such aspirations on the part of western Virginia politicians.

Unfortunately, independent statehood ultimately served to catalyze the precarious circumstances under which the residents of West Virginia lived—circumstances such as ambiguous land claims, unimproved absentee holdings, and a wealth of natural resources that were just being catalogued after the Civil War. Post–Civil War politics in West Virginia was a complicated affair and has been the subject of a litany of independent works. While this study can provide only a cursory examination of West Virginia politics following statehood, the emphasis here will be on how the emergent system laid groundwork for, and encouraged, the development of a colonial political economy in which outside industrial interests siphoned resources and labor from the state through the manipulation of local elites. This has been the subject of two works by John Alexander Williams (1972; 1976), which warrant special attention here.

Williams points out that the greatest drive for independent statehood in West Virginia came from the growing industrial centers along the Ohio River in the North. The new state's main founders were powerful mercantilists with ties to distant markets, and their actual association with most of the new state was limited. Their prowess as lobbyists and merchants allowed them to formulate and put into action in West Virginia a "modern" political system, while they "subdued or co-opted lower competitors for power, adopted the state's political representation along with its fuels and raw materials

to the use of metropolitan industrialism, and trained their less powerful collaborators and successors to the work of a *comprador* middle
class" (Williams, 1976: p. 4).

The leading statemakers were Republicans. However, state politics were far more complex than a simple two-party confrontation
in which the Republicans were dominant. The Democratic party was
split at least four ways—the most conservative, Redeemers or old-
school Democrats being those most opposed to statehood and ideologically akin to the old Tidewater Democrats. At the other end of
the spectrum were those whom Williams calls the Regulars, who
had much in common ideologically with Republican industrialists.
In between were the Agrarian Democrats, who tended to have more
in common with the Redeemers, but who were also flexible enough
to adapt to industrial forms of political mobilization; and finally the
so-called Kanawha Ring—a clique of middle-of-the-road political
bosses primarily in the Charleston–Kanawha County area (Williams, 1972: pp. 363–64). What is important to note is that after the
Civil War, the salient political leaders in the state, whether old-
guard Democrat or Republican, were power brokers and large property holders. None wanted to abolish statehood, but rather they
wanted to gain control of and form in their own image the fledgling
political system. And in this endeavor, metropolitan-oriented "Captains of Industry" ultimately prevailed and gained control of both
parties.

After the Civil War, the nationally implemented "test Oath" prohibited former Confederates from holding public office for fifteen
years, so it is not surprising that Republicans dominated West Virginia until the 1870s (Bowman, 1965: p. 140). This gave Republicans
sufficient time to stifle old-guard Democrats while a new line of industrialist Democrats came to the fore. Indeed, the founders of the
modern state political system were frequently men from other states
who had recently moved to West Virginia as railroaders and speculators. For example, Johnson N. Camden (1828–1908) was a native
of Wheeling, but his family had intimate business ties with out-of-
state industries. Notably, he became John D. Rockefeller's "right

hand man" in developing West Virginia's oil industry. Camden was a Democrat who had supported the Union during the Civil War and who served as governor and United States senator for the state during his career. Henry G. Davis (1823–1916), also a pro-Union Democrat during the Civil War, was born in Baltimore and gradually migrated to West Virginia as an employee of the Baltimore and Ohio Railroad. He started his own lumber business in conjunction with the railroad, expanded into coal, and accumulated over seventy thousand acres of West Virginia real estate between 1865 and 1880. Elected as the state's first Democratic United States senator in 1871, Davis was also one of the most powerful leaders in postbellum West Virginia politics, and ultimately shifted his informal allegiance to support his Republican son-in-law Stephen B. Elkins (1841–1911). Elkins was a salient figure in the national Republican Party and had traveled the country in search of his own territorial claim to power, finally establishing residence in West Virginia after an extended venture in New Mexico Territory. Through the medium of railroads, Elkins became one of the most prominent coal producers in the state. With Davis backing him, Elkins defeated Camden for the 1895 United States senatorial seat; and Republican domination of West Virginia politics would then last until the Great Depression (Williams, 1972: pp. 358–62, 1976: p. 3).

These were but three of the scores of industrialists who seized control of West Virginia politics in the postbellum era. From the very birth of its statehood, the political system in West Virginia was dominated by and catered to industrialists.

How were these "modern" men able to establish hegemony in a land where metropolitan values were scarce, if not frowned upon? This question must be considered in the context of two competing cultural systems in West Virginia after the Civil War, which in turn determined the character of state and local political systems. The preindustrial political system in most of West Virginia was based on kinship, face to face relations, and "represented a blend of Virginia political institutions and practices modified by the circumstances . . . of the Appalachian wilderness" (Williams, 1972: p. 322). It was a system in which information was disseminated through the medium of oral communication and family or church ties. Itinerant ministers rather than newspapers were often the most important source of news from outside the region. The modern political system—what the founders sought to implant in West Virginia after the Civil War—was based on a "need to marshal votes from a literate mass electorate. It was based in the commercial, manufacturing, and mining districts . . . [and] depended as much on interest groups as upon kinship, on printed communications as upon oral communications" (Williams, 1972: p. 322). Unlike the preindustrial system, the modern system was impersonal and bureaucratic.

The emergent modern political system in West Virginia literally diffused from the industrialized northern panhandle into the plateau. As industrialists-turned-politicians expanded their land and resource holdings into the interior, they opened new lines of communications through railroads, mines, and lumber camps, effectively manipulating information. Local elites were either placated as subordinates or subdued through displays of power (Williams, 1976: pp. 11–12). In the latter case, industrialists often recruited their own company-employed police to impose their will (as shall be discussed later). Although this was not a uniform or consistent process throughout the state, it did define the parameters within which the state government was prone to deal with people at the local level.

Meanwhile, itinerant Methodist and Baptist ministers remained primary figures for people in the remote interior of the state and were pivotal disseminators of political ideology and information. Although their ties with industrialists were indirect, their influence in favor of the emergent status quo was profound, particularly for Republicans. Several counties, including Wyoming, had been represented by minister delegates at the state's first constitutional convention, and the Baptists, who boasted a slight majority in Wyoming County, easily embraced the ideology of emancipation embodied in the early Republican party. These ministers were skilled at face to face communications with the people of the interior, talking to them in their own language. Although their impact on postbellum West Virginia politics cannot accurately be measured, they undoubtedly played a significant role in turning the electorate toward Republicanism as the 1800s ended (Williams, 1972: pp. 344–45).

What ultimately allowed "Captains of Industry" to seize control of West Virginia politics was their near monopoly over capital and resources. In 1865, Congress had provided for the standardization of American currency and in effect prohibited the circulation of local banknotes, which meant that people in remote areas such as Plateau Appalachia who lacked sufficient collateral and proximity to financial centers found it extremely difficult to gain access to capital (Salstrom, 1994: pp. 29–31). Thus, the only people in West Virginia with significant access to capital were industrialists located primarily in the North, who used this power to manipulate state politics in their own interest. Their access to metropolitan capital also allowed them to gain control and ownership of countless acres of West Virginia real estate to which they adhered conflicting or nebulous titles.

The primary legal mechanism facilitating the usurpation of West Virginia lands by political elites and absentee financiers was the state constitution, as revised in 1871. Ironically, the constitutional convention that year was dominated by Democrats who had in mind realigning the state's political system to resemble that of Virginia and who also wished to bring about agrarian reforms. Article XIII of the amended constitution provided for litigative procedures to settle, once and for all, many landholders' tenuous titles that West Virginia had inherited through statehood. As previously noted, Virginia land records had been poorly managed, often resulting in conflicting titles in the western portion of the state. The 1871 West Virginia constitution, though it was probably intended to protect land titles, actually led to the dispossession of thousands of small property owners through endless litigation—thus earning it the nickname "the lawyer's constitution" (Williams, 1972: p. 367). Quite simply, industrial speculators, having access to abundant capital, could purchase questionable titles to lands and then instigate a suit against the yeoman farmer who occupied the land or held a conflicting title. The farmers, unable to afford the costly legal fees necessary to defend their titles, almost always lost.

Related to the new West Virginia land laws were new tax laws by which speculators found easy access to new lands. Under Virginia law, people in the mountains had sometimes managed to evade the burdens of state and county taxation, as local assessors were also their relatives, and Virginia tax delinquency laws were not successfully enforced. When West Virginia became a state, a new set of taxes fell upon its residents. These were more strenuously exacted, notably the property tax imposed to support the state's public school system. Many large landholders found that they could not cope with this new tax burden and were forced to sell their lands (Tams, 1963: p. 16). The new wave of industrialist speculators took full advantage of these laws and forced many previous owners into relinquishing their titles through the enforcement of tax delinquency laws (Williams, 1972: p. 330).

In this manner, the founders of West Virginia and their successors systematically crafted a political system nurtured by industrial interests, a system that became firmly entrenched throughout the state by 1900 (Williams, 1972: p. 115). By that time, many of the industrialist-Democrats had shifted their allegiance to the Republican Party and managed to sway the majority of voters statewide in the same direction. Of the fifty-five West Virginia counties, only two defied these prevalent patterns in political party allegiance. Logan County had always been a Democratic stronghold, and so it remained, never having more than a 30 percent Republican electorate. It was largely for this reason that the county of Mingo was partitioned from Logan when the Norfolk and Western Railway was extended into the vast coal reserves of that western segment of Logan County, where voters had moved increasingly toward the Republican ticket (Williams, 1972: p. 115). Even though Logan remained a Democratic stronghold, it gained infamy in the early twentieth century for its local political system and police force financed almost entirely by coal operators (Lee, 1969; Savage, 1986).

Directly southeast of Logan County lay the other exception to prevailing late-nineteenth-century voting patterns in West Virginia—Wyoming County. Since the Civil War, the proportion of Republicans in Wyoming County had remained consistent, usually maintaining a slight majority, while in other counties (excepting Logan) their number fluctuated widely and/or rose rapidly in the 1890s.[3] The Republican leaders in Wyoming County were not omnipotent. They were held in check by a formidable Democratic electorate who tended to support old-guard Democrats, as will be discussed in the following chapter. However, to the advantage of Republican leaders, Wyoming County had a large Baptist population, which almost universally embraced Republicanism, while most Methodists were Democrats. Moreover, Republican leaders used their slight edge while in power to manipulate the local voting population to maintain the status quo. In 1875, for example, county officials (who all happened to be Republican) ceded a portion of the county along Winding Gulf Creek to neighboring Raleigh County. This cession was evidently made because residents along the Winding Gulf were primarily Democrats, and since Republicans then had a slight majority in Wyoming County, and Democrats a slight majority in Raleigh, the move was politically advantageous to the status quo in both counties (Bowman, 1965: p. 23).

From the outset, the government of West Virginia worked for the benefit of industrial interests, many of them based out-of-state. It is not possible to explain the economic fate of any of West Virginia's counties separate from the rest of the state. The state government served as a catalyst and conduit for extractive industries to enter each of the counties of the state, and bilk them of resources and labor while offering very little in return. However, Wyoming County would be one of the last sections of West Virginia to experience the harsh realities of exploitative industries.

* * *

Wyoming County, West Virginia, was one of the most geographically isolated portions of Appalachia from the inception of Euro-American settlement. This isolation proved to be a double-edged sword over time. On one hand, it allowed settlers and their progeny, whether out of necessity or desire, to pursue a lifeway of economic self-sufficiency. It also afforded them some degree of political autonomy insofar as state and federal institutions had a hand in local affairs only infrequently. On the other hand, due to the remoteness of the area from economic and political centers, Wyoming County and most of what became West Virginia were peripheralized from the beginning of Euro-American settlement. The people of the region were able to engage in trade with external markets only infrequently, and while under the jurisdiction of the state of Virginia their political interests were subordinated by those of the controlling Tidewater aristocracy. When the Civil War provided a convenient segue for the creation of an independent state of West Virginia, the physical isolation of the region from political centers and markets (and hence from sources of capital) allowed a privileged few to develop a political system that would act as a conduit for the region's exploitation by external economic interests. However, because of its extreme isolation within the interior of the plateau, Wyoming County would be among the last of West Virginia's counties to feel the impact of the colonial thrust.

The relatively late entry of industry into Wyoming County due to physical isolation initially left local residents' lives markedly different from the lives of many people in other parts of plateau West Virginia, though the resulting conditions of dependency would ultimately be the same.

5 OPENING THE
GUYANDOTTE VALLEY

The Coming of Industry to Wyoming County

Although southern West Virginia was spared the devastation wrought in the main theaters of the Civil War, the war had
other profound implications for the area. First of all, the war provided a timely opportunity for western Virginia political leaders to
successfully aspire toward independent statehood, and in the process
to establish a political system that facilitated the wholesale invasion
of the state by metropolitan-based extractive industries. Yet another
consequence of the war was the discovery of the vast timber and
mineral resources of West Virginia. Numerous military scouts and
surveyors, both Union and Confederate, entered the region during
the war and made covetous note of seemingly endless stands of virgin timber, and ubiquitous outcroppings of superior quality coal.
Many of these men forged ties with out-of-state financiers to whom
they disclosed their wartime discoveries. Turning their attention to
West Virginia, these early tycoons found a political system that they
could shape in their own image, and mineral-rich lands with tenuous
ownership titles ripe for the picking.

This chapter examines the processes by which timber and mineral
development was inhibited, but slowly came to dominate the Wyoming County economy as an inevitable consequence of the larger
state political system. Wyoming County was anomalous insofar as

its physiographic isolation delayed the advance of industrial forces much longer than in other counties and allowed forms of resistance to keep early developers in check. Nonetheless, the mere fact that Wyoming County was part of the state of West Virginia made it susceptible to a state political system that sustained a colonial political economy. This system, into which Wyoming County has become fully absorbed, has endured to the present.

Post–Civil War Land Speculation

The opening of southern West Virginia and parts of southwestern Virginia to extractive industries can mostly be traced to the single-handed efforts of one man. Major Jedidiah Hotchkiss had served as a topographical engineer for Robert E. Lee during the Civil War. In the course of his wartime service, he had occasion to travel near Flat Top Mountain, an area that extends from Tazewell County in Virginia, northward to Fayette County, West Virginia. He discovered significant outcroppings of bituminous coal in that region. After the war Hotchkiss tried to rally interest in these coal deposits among northern and British financiers but had little initial success in the midst of a postwar economic crisis (Eller, 1982: p. 50; Tams, 1963; p. 19). However, as the Chesapeake and Ohio (C&O) Railroad penetrated the New River coal fields to the north, prospective mineral developers began to take Hotchkiss more seriously, and in 1873 the owners of the Wilson Cary Nichols Grant (a Revolutionary War grant of five hundred thousand acres) hired Hotchkiss to survey these holdings. His assistant, Captain Isaiah Welch, followed a thirteen foot thick coal seam for over fifty miles from Tazewell County, Virginia, into the West Virginia counties of Mercer, McDowell, Wyoming, and Raleigh (Eller, 1982: pp. 50–51).

Hotchkiss's report on this vast mineral reserve embracing the headwaters of the Bluestone, Elkhorn, Guyandotte, and Big Sandy Rivers (in other words, the bulk of the nine southernmost counties of West Virginia) sparked an immediate reaction from a group of Philadelphia financiers headed by Thomas Graham. They began purchasing as much land as they could in the area, although the de-

Wyoming County, West Virginia

pression of the 1870s delayed development (Eller, 1982: p. 51). These industrialists found easy access especially to the larger tracts of land such as the Nichols grant, since the owners of these large holdings could not afford to pay newly imposed taxes. The industrialists had only to request that the state enforce tax delinquency sanctions, confiscate the land, and sell it to the eager developers (Tams, 1963: p. 16).

The most critical investors in the Flat Top coal lands were railroad companies. The post–Civil War recession invited the consolidation of railways, almost uniformly financed by northern investors and thus enhanced the absentee grasp on the economy of Appalachia (Striplin, 1981: p. 42). In 1881, Frederick Kimball, a Philadelphia banker who had intimate ties with the railroad industry, visited the Flat Top region at the site of the future town of Pocahontas. As vice-president of the newly formed Norfolk and Western Railway (N&W), Kimball devised plans to extend that Roanoke-based line to the Pocahontas field and to establish ties with European coal markets. In 1883, Kimball became president of N&W and formed a partnership with E. W. Clark and Company (a Philadelphia financial firm). The partners formed the Southwest Virginia Improvement Company and purchased over a hundred thousand acres of Flat Top coal land (Striplin, 1981: pp. 71, 80–82). Fearing that Hotchkiss would sell the remaining Flat Top lands to the C&O Railroad (Kimball's key competitor), Kimball bid for the remaining lands in 1888, and the two controlling interests in the region merged to form the Flat Top Land Association (Gillenwater, 1977: p. 136; Lambie, 1954: pp. 37–58; Eller, 1982: pp. 71–72).

This merger assured the N&W a firm monopoly over Flat Top Coal interests for years to come, a monopoly cinched by the extension of a major N&W branch line to the Ohio River, thus opening trade with the industrial Midwest. The quantity of coal shipped out of the region shot up. Whereas in 1882 the N&W transported only 4,735 tons of coal, that tonnage skyrocketed to 2,869,215 by 1893 (Striplin, 1981: p. 113). In the early years of southern West Virginia coal development, coal operators rarely owned the land but more frequently leased it from holding companies (which were mainly subsidiaries of railroads) at an average royalty rate of ten cents per ton. Trains being the only practicable means of shipping coal to markets, operators were at the mercy of the railroads when it came to freight rates. "In fact," wrote one operator, "the mines might be said to be in peonage to the railway" (Tams, 1963: p. 26).

Wyoming County was situated squarely within the interior of the Pocahontas–Flat Top region. Absentee speculation was not a new endeavor in Wyoming County. For example, the Robert Morris Grant (originally a Revolutionary War grant issued in 1795) of 480,000 acres spanning parts of Wyoming (near Oceana), McDowell, and Logan Counties, was purchased by New York real estate broker Jesse Irwin, then by Thomas D. Williams of Camden, New Jersey, who in turn sold the land to Philadelphia timber merchant Phillip A. Trimble in 1874. Next J. C. Maben of Philadelphia joined Jed Hotchkiss in the 1880s in purchasing the 90,000-acre James Welch grant at the headwaters of the Guyandotte (Bowman, 1965: p. 218; Tams, 1963: p. 19). As early as 1865, James Freeman of Ohio acquired from fifteen different resident landowners "the exclusive right to mine for petroleum, iron, and all other mineral substances, with necessary rights of removal" (Bowman, 1965: p. 218). The landowners included members of the prominent Cook, McDonald, and Lusk families, who were to receive one-eighth share of any minerals extracted. Similar mineral leases were made in the same year, though there is no record to show that the contractors pursued their extractive endeavors to any large degree.

Thus, absentee speculation for mineral development was well underway in Wyoming County by the 1880s, although far from complete. In an effort to promote speculation in the county, C. D. Wells, editor of the *Wyoming News*, issued a promotional pamphlet to northern financiers in which he boasted of the county's endless natural resources, "as yet undeveloped, [which] await only the approach of the railroad and the application of mind, means and muscle to transfer the same into innumerable mints of wealth to the fortunate

owners" (Wells, 1889: p. 3). Wells undoubtedly had a fair stake in local resources, and a close reading of this passage reveals his primary
concern—namely, the lack of a railroad in or even near the county.
Indeed, the isolation of the county delayed the arrival of any rail system until nearly 1910 when the Virginian Railway entered the area.
Thus, coal development was delayed for thirty years after most surrounding counties began producing large yields of coal by the early
1880s. The absence of a railroad did not, however, impede timber development.

The Timber Industry

According to some estimates, at least 10 million acres (out of a total
of 16,640,000) in West Virginia in 1870 were still covered by origi-
nal-growth forest. By 1920, only a few isolated patches of virgin forest would remain in the state. Timber production peaked in 1909,
when 1,524 mills produced 1,472,942,000 board feet of lumber. By
1920, there were only 398 mills producing 647,055,000 board feet
(Clarkson, 1964: pp. 38–39).

Lacking rail transportation, the postbellum speculators who invaded the region found alternative means of transporting timber.
Commercial timber production began along navigable waterways,
and when these areas were exhausted, lumbermen found ways to
make use of less navigable waterways through the use of splash
dams. The idea behind a splash dam was simply to dam up a creek or
small river, place cut timber in a holding pool behind the dam and
when the water was sufficiently high, tear down the dam. This process essentially created an artificial and highly erosive flash flood that
would carry timber to connecting points along more navigable waterways, if not directly to lumber mills. Such destructive practices
characterized the methods and legacy of the early Appalachian
timber operators, whose pursuit of quick profit led to the stripping
of entire mountains throughout the Appalachian region, which were
then left to erode. Thus, the timber industry, which temporarily
boosted local economies through the provision of jobs, died as

quickly as it had developed. After World War I, timber operations began to vanish rapidly from the region, leaving behind a trail of destruction (Eller, 1982: pp. 90, 110; R. Lewis, 1998).

The isolation of Wyoming County impeded timber development only slightly. Speculators were drawn to the vast stands of superior quality poplar, hemlock, cucumber trees, basswood, chestnut, maple, black walnut, beech, birch, black gum, and pitch pines in the county. The Flat Top Land Association served as a vital agent through which many speculators gained access to local timber reserves (Bowman, 1965: 225; Eller, 1982: p. 96). According to the West Virginia State Board of Agriculture, by 1900, 75 percent of the salable timber in Wyoming County was controlled by "alien owners" (Cubby, 1962: p. 139).

Speculation initially began with numerous conveyances of timber rights by local landowners to outside contractors, either for specific types of trees or for all timber on a given tract of land. One of the earliest of such contracts in the county was a conveyance by A. J. Ellis to the Chicago Lumber Company of rights to cut all poplar, oak, and cucumber trees along his Huff Creek property and to build splash dams as necessary. In 1890, Foster Brothers Company set up a mill on Little Huff Creek that produced two million board feet of lumber in two years, and paid employees three dollars per thousand board feet individually cut, but only after employees transported the cut lumber to the railway in neighboring McDowell County. Between 1898 and 1908, the R. E. Wood Lumber Company timbered another five thousand acres along Little Huff Creek, producing seventy-two million board feet of lumber, all of which was exported (Bowman, 1965: pp. 226, 241). These are merely examples of some of the early operations.

As the above figures suggest, timber production in Wyoming County gained momentum in the 1890s. After the turn of the twentieth century, Wyoming County's timber industry (and much of it in other Appalachian counties) became dominated by the W. M. Ritter Lumber Company of Philadelphia. W. M. Ritter began his operation with a small mill in Mercer County but soon expanded into most of southern West Virginia. In 1909, six years after the entry of the Virginian Railway, Ritter purchased 31,630 acres of the former James Welch grant in the northern part of the county—land that Jed Hotchkiss and J. C. Maben had purchased after the Civil War. At the settlement of Maben, Ritter built a double band sawmill, a narrow gauge railroad to satellite operations, and a large company-owned town for employees (Bowman, 1965: pp. 96, 120, 223; Clarkson, 1964: pp. 96–97). Ritter became a dominating force throughout southern West Virginia, if not the entire southern Appalachian region, ultimately earning him distinction as the "dean of lumbermen in America" (Eller, 1982: p. 104).

Ritter can also be credited with introducing the prototype of the company town system to Wyoming County. The town of Maben developed into a self-contained community, with three rows of four-room houses, larger houses for company officials, two boarding houses, a clubhouse for employee recreation (complete with a movie theater), and a well-stocked company store where employees could purchase anything they needed. The community also contained a Methodist church and a school for grades one through twelve, both built and financed by the company. The camp was divided into a black section and a white section—a division common among most company towns in West Virginia, but nonetheless notable in a state that had no Jim Crow Laws (Bowman, 1965: pp. 245–46; Clarkson, 1964: pp. 96–97).

Ritter had a reputation for treating his employees fairly, providing company families with running water (which was not true with many West Virginia company towns at the time), free electricity and firewood, and reasonable rents—from three to four dollars, depending on the size of the house (Bowman, 1965: pp. 96, 245–46; Clarkson, 1964: p. 97). However, company officials were found guilty of peonage on at least one occasion when foreign employees were harassed and kept from assembling with American workers (Bowman, 1965: pp. 243–45).

Ritter's Maben operation ran until 1946, when timber reserves in the county were virtually exhausted. Most other Appalachian timber reserves had become exhausted by the end of World War I, and by the time the Maben operation closed, sustained-yield practices were being implemented in the timber industry. In 1960 the Ritter Company sold all of its holdings in Wyoming County to Georgia Pacific, which at that time was operating a mill in the community of New Richmond—a mill that produced twenty million board feet of lumber annually throughout the 1960s (Bowman, 1965: pp. 247–48). This suggests that Wyoming County, in part due to its isolation, but also due to the hostility of some local landowners toward timber and mineral development, was able to evade much of the wholesale destruction that the timber industry had wrought in other parts of the mountains.

Nonetheless, the timber industry was responsible for considerable environmental damage in Wyoming County. Most logging occurred in the northern and western portions of the county, while more southerly portions were spared total deforestation (as sustained-yield timbering was implemented by the time these were logged). Thus, hillsides in the vicinity of Mullens, Maben, and Oceana were totally denuded and left to erode, as evidenced by turn-of-the-twentieth-century photographs. Perhaps equally destructive were the numerous splash dams built before the railroad reached the upper Guyandotte River and its tributaries. The C. Crane Company in particular was known for the use of these devices to create flash floods for carrying timber down the Guyandotte to the Ohio River. One such dam was so massive that it required the approval of the Army Corps of Engineers (Bowman, 1965: pp. 227–35). Although it is difficult to measure the impact of deforestation and splash dams in the wake of other destructive industries that entered the county, there is no question that the timber industry contributed significantly to the erosion of local soils and the silting of streams. This created serious impediments to wildlife and to agricultural production and caused severe flooding in narrow valleys. Early timber development impacted the entire upper Guyandotte Valley through a chain reaction of erosion and silting, for most of the denuding took place along the headwaters and tributaries of the river, forcing debris miles downstream.

Development of Coal

Timber development was the vanguard of the industrialization of Wyoming County. After the turn of the twentieth century, coal development would come to dominate the local economy, and its domination would be so profound that virtually every commercial activity in the county was linked to the coal industry. Because of the profound and seemingly permanent impact of coal on the Wyoming County economy, the remainder of this chapter focuses on the development of that industry in detail, not only with regard to the county itself but in the larger contexts of West Virginia and the United States.

Since the inception of European settlement, West Virginians had drawn coal out of seams to burn at home or to fuel blacksmith forges. Even today, a few Wyoming County residents heat their homes with coal from coal banks (small mines) near their houses (Cook, 1996c). Commercial coal production was pursued on a limited basis prior to the Civil War in some parts of the state. In 1840, 7 million bushels (then the standard unit of measurement) of coal were extracted statewide, 870,930 bushels of that in Logan County, of which Wyoming was then a part (Rice, 1970: p. 315; U.S. Bureau of the Census, 1841: p. 167). Yet the rugged topography, physical isolation, relative ignorance of the state's mineral wealth by outsiders, and lack of capital in the region inhibited massive development prior to the Civil War.

After the war, as absentee industrialists became increasingly aware of the vast coal reserves in West Virginia, a number of factors converged to make the wholesale extractive development of the state possible—and in the eyes of industrial entrepreneurs, desirable. First, the quality of coal, particularly in southern West Virginia, was unsurpassed; most of the coal was high-quality "smokeless" bituminous, meaning that it contained very little additional volatile material. Second, because of the topography of the mountains, coal could usually be more easily extracted through horizontal drift mines, without having to dig deep (and costly) vertical shafts. Likewise, it was cheaper per mile to deliver, as railroads usually charged lower freight rates for longer hauls to market. Additionally, labor was cheaper. Remoteness from metropolitan centers meant that those who were beholden to the coal industry for a living had few if any other options for employment, and wages could be kept low. Concomitantly, mining required a small capital investment. In the early days of the Appalachian mining industry, employees provided and maintained their own tools, and were paid only for the number of tons they extracted—not with a daily or hourly wage. The latter two factors gave the southern West Virginia operators a vital advantage over other coalfields in the nation, particularly in the older Pennsylvania and Midwest fields where miners had successfully unionized by 1897 (Eller, 1982: p. 129).

Major coal development in southern West Virginia began first in more northerly counties such as Fayette, Raleigh, and Kanawha, where in the 1870s the C&O Railroad opened corridors to the market along major river systems. By the 1880s, Mercer and McDowell counties were opened to coal extraction by the N&W Railway, which began to compete against the C&O by the 1890s in Logan and Mingo Counties with the building of the N&W's Ohio River branch line. This expedited trade ties with the Midwest and its Great Lakes industrial belt. In 1898, only forty thousand tons of West Virginia coal were shipped to the Great Lakes (less than 1 percent of the state's total output), but by 1913, that amount had risen to over six million tons (or 23 percent of West Virginia's total output). Between 1900 and 1920, coal production in the nine southernmost West Virginia counties (including Wyoming) increased by over 300 percent. By 1925, these nine counties accounted for over 66 percent of the state's total coal production, boosted by the artificial demands for coal created by World War I, as well as by postwar labor troubles in other markets (Eller, 1982: pp. 129–34, 140, 154).

In the early days of coal development in southern West Virginia, most mines were run by small, independent operators and not by large conglomerates. These mines could be opened with a capital investment as small as twenty thousand dollars and a labor force consisting of ten to three hundred men. At least 90 percent of the coal produced at the turn of the twentieth century in southern West Virginia was on land leased by independent operators from holding companies such as the Flat Top Land Association, which received an average royalty rate of ten cents per ton. Thus, most operators found themselves at the mercy of holding companies that were almost always associated with railroads (Tams, 1963: pp. 24–29; Eller, 1982: p. 134). Some operators complained that railroad executives "regarded the operators as hardly more than milk cows" (Tams, 1963: p. 27). The biggest problem, in addition to their control of freight rates, was that railroad executives also functioned as sales agents, effectively controlling the price of coal. Finally, many disgruntled operators began to curtail the railroad monopoly on coal sales by forming their own associations within given fields (such as the Pocahontas Field), as was the case in 1910 when the Pocahontas Consolidated Coal Company formed Pocahontas Fuel Company to sell its own coal (Tams, 1963: p. 27).

The formation of coal operators' associations in specific fields (usually based on county boundaries and proximity of individual mines) coincided with and influenced a growing trend toward consolidation and monopolization of the southern West Virginia coal industry after the turn of the twentieth century. Larger landholding companies and railroads sought to crush competition and maximize profits by buying and consolidating smaller mines under a "parent" firm and by gaining ownership of more coal lands. Eventually, U.S. Steel Corporation and the Pennsylvania Railroad, with the backing of the New York banking firm of J. P. Morgan and Co., gained controlling interest in both the C&O and the N&W railroads, and hence gained control of most of the Flat Top-Pocahontas coalfield by 1910. In 1923, the U.S. Coal Commission reported that Morgan and his affiliates controlled over 750,000 acres of Appalachian coal (Eller, 1982: p. 134–36; Hunt, Tryon, and Willitts, 1925: p. 95).

There was one portion of the Flat Top region into which the Morgan–Pennsylvania Railroad monopoly did not extend: the extreme interior that included Wyoming County and portions of Raleigh County (Eller, 1982: p. 139). At the turn of the twentieth century, southern West Virginia was divided into six major coalfields: the Kanawha Field (surrounding Charleston), the Logan Field (primarily Logan County), the New River Field (to the northeast along the New River), the Williamson Field (the extreme western portion of southern West Virginia), the Pocahontas Field (the first portion of the Flat Top region to be developed—chiefly Mercer and McDowell Counties), and the Winding Gulf Field (essentially a subdivision of the Pocahontas Field in Raleigh and Wyoming Counties). The latter two were extremely coveted by speculators, as the coal in these fields was low-volatile, or smokeless (Tams, 1963: p. 15). Wyoming County lay on the dividing line between these two fields and was situated in the most remote portion of each. Rail access had been the key to opening other counties but it was comparatively late coming to Wyoming. A number of other factors also contributed to this delay of major coal development. First, although absentee ownership of coal lands was well established in the county, it was fragmentary, and there were a significant number of moderately large local landowners who managed to retain all rights to their lands. Second, local political alliances were solidly divided between agrarian Democrats and Republicans, thus complicating the possibility of gaining total control of local power structures in favor of industry (Cook, 1996c; 1996d). And finally, the most cherished coal deposit known at the time in the county—the Pocahontas Number 3 Seam— lay deep beneath the valley floor, and required methods of shaft mining to extract (Gillenwater, 1977: p. 139).

Thus, while the coming of the N&W Railway to neighboring McDowell County in the 1880s had promoted significant coal production there three decades earlier, by the time Wyoming County began to produce any significant amount of coal in 1913 (1,650 long tons), McDowell was recorded as producing 14,913,342 long tons that year (West Virginia Geological Survey, 1915: p. xxi).

In 1907, Henry H. Rogers, with support from John D. Rockefeller of Standard Oil, began constructing the Virginian Railway. Following the Guyandotte Valley, the Virginian gradually moved through the heart of Wyoming County. By 1923, the railway reached the county seat of Pineville in the center of the county, and by the end of the decade reached Gilbert in Mingo County (Tams, 1963: pp. 20–23; Bowman, 1965: pp. 230–31). With the railroad came development of the coal industry.

Still, coal mining did not develop overnight in Wyoming County. By the time coal production in the county exceeded a million tons (1,424,068 tons) in 1920, neighboring McDowell and Raleigh Counties were producing 17,715,824 tons and 7,748,634 tons respectively. And despite the fact that Wyoming County had at least as much (if not more) smokeless coal beneath its surface as any county in the state, annual production did not exceed 10 million tons until 1960, whereas all other southern counties had surpassed that figure by 1930 (Tams, 1963: p. 107).

The first commercial operator in the county was J. C. Sullivan, who set up a small operation near Mullens in 1912. Sullivan gained control of the Bank of Wyoming (the first and only bank in the county at the time) and established a newspaper, the *Mullens Advocate* (Bowman, 1965: p. 255). Numerous small operators followed in the county—despite the concurrent move among holding companies to consolidate lands and operations. The earliest operations were established in the northern part of the county in the Winding Gulf Field, following the route of the Virginian Railway. Between 1910 and 1920, most of these sprouted along the Laurel Fork of the Guyandotte, along Barkers Creek, and along Winding Gulf Creek in Raleigh County. In all, forty-seven operations and twenty-one mining towns were established by 1930 in the Winding Gulf Field (some of which was in Raleigh County), and nine mining settlements were established in that portion of the Pocahontas Field that lay within the county (Gillenwater, 1977: pp. 133, 139).

The Wyoming Land Company and the Pocahontas Fuel and Coke Company were the two primary holding companies leasing out land in the Winding Gulf and Pocahontas fields, respectively, in Wyoming County. A glimpse at the earliest large coal operations opened in the county reveals the growing pattern of monopolization of the southern West Virginia coal market, as well as the hand of the state in facilitating such consolidation. In 1914, the Wyoming Land Company chartered the Wyoming Coal Company for operations along Allen's Creek, four miles from Mullens, with veteran Winding Gulf operator W. P. Tams and West Virginia's secretary of state John Wilson as directors. Tams established Wyco, perhaps the first mining boomtown in the county. Tams's interests ultimately spilled over into the Pocahontas Field when in 1919 he became part owner of the Covel Smokeless Coal Company, a subsidiary of Pocahontas Coal and Coke ("New Mining Town," 1914: p.1; Tams, 1963: pp. 68–69; Bowman, 1965: p. 256). In 1919, Greenbrier County banker Isaac T. Mann, a key investor in the Pocahontas Consolidated Coal Company, opened a large mine at Itman (an abbreviation of the founder's name). While this was established as an independent operation, it was too closely affiliated with the Pocahontas Company to be disconnected (Tams, 1963: pp. 93–94; Bowman, 1965: p. 238). Finally, in 1921 Boston financier G. W. Hyman—also an associate in the Pocahontas Consolidated Coal Company—built one of the most monumental mines and boomtowns in the county at Glen Rogers, aptly named for the founder of the Virginian Railway. Glen Rogers boasted several modern brick houses for employees, and the construction of a 650-foot vertical shaft to tap into the Pocahontas Number 3 Seam alone cost over two million dollars ("Glen Rogers," 1921: p. 1; Bowman, 1965: pp. 256–58).[1]

The Coal Industry and Capitalist Integration

Although local residents did not all take to the miner's occupation, the mere presence of the industry generated new concerns and the need for new services, which in turn drew formerly self-sufficient people into the clutches of the national and world capitalist economy. This process was accompanied by and related to profound changes in local demography and the physical landscape.

Local residents who did seek employment in the mines at an early date did so mainly out of an increased need for cash. The primary reason for this need was the establishment of new state tax laws after the Civil War and the fact that these laws were more rigorously enforced than those under the old Virginia system. Many of the older participants in this study who came from mining families recall that their fathers or grandfathers entered the mines in an effort to generate enough money to pay property taxes (Cook, 1995; 1996c).

By and large, the number of county natives initially willing to work in the mines was not nearly enough to provide a sufficient labor force. Thus, coal operators brought in scores of employees from other parts of the nation and the world. Blacks were most frequently recruited from the Deep South with the (often false) enticement of finding greater economic opportunities in the coalfields, and many companies sent propaganda abroad to coax Italians, Hungarians, and other impoverished Europeans into the Appalachian coal industry. With funds from coal operators, the state of West Virginia even established a Commission for Immigration to encourage the movement of foreign immigrants into the state to provide cheap labor (Eller, 1982: pp. 169–73). The net result of immigration into the southern coalfields was a complicated challenge to the preexisting family and community networks and cultural systems that had developed in the area, resulting in the fractionalization of earlier social homogeneity in the region as a whole. Indeed, this was one of the key intentions of coal operators who, in addition to seeing black and foreign immigrants as a cheap source of labor, believed that injecting a "judicious mixture" of alien peoples into the region would curtail the social solidarity necessary to form labor unions (Bailey, 1973; Barnum, 1970; Laing, 1936). By 1907, 79 percent of the coal workers in the Pocahontas Field were black or foreign immigrants (Gillenwater, 1977: p. 141). While the black population alone ultimately exceeded the white population in neighboring McDowell County, the in-migration of foreign and black miners to Wyoming was not as profound. By 1933, there were 1,019 white miners in the county, 128 of them foreign born (including 37 Italians), and there were 485 black miners (Bowman, 1965: p. 264).

Whites from other parts of the state and the nation also came to work in the Wyoming County mines. Many of the newcomers brought their families, resulting in a drastic increase in the county population. Between 1850—when the county population was 1,645 —and 1880 (population 4,322) the population in Wyoming County increased by roughly one thousand people per decade. Between 1880 and 1910 (population 10,392), presumably due to the development of the timber industry, the population increased by roughly two thousand per decade. The greatest population expansion followed coal industrialization between 1910 and 1920, by which time the population rose to 15,180. The number peaked at 37,590 in 1950 (Bowman, 1965: p. 52). Still, this increase in the population was not nearly as drastic as in other southern West Virginia counties, particularly in McDowell (which had been more or less equal to Wyoming before the 1880s) where the population increased nine-fold between 1890 and 1920 (Eller, 1982: p. 133).

The growing population had profound but contradictory implications for agricultural production in Wyoming County. Salstrom (1994) has shown that in most of Appalachia, per capita agricultural production was declining by the time of the Civil War, primarily due to population increases. In Wyoming County, however, per capita agricultural production almost held steady until 1910. Whereas in 1850 there were 188 farms in the county containing 5,930 improved acres, those numbers peaked in 1910, with 1,462 farms containing 41,680 improved acres. The greatest increase came between 1890 and 1910 (accompanying the rise of timbering in the county), when the amount of improved farm acreage rose from 36,631 acres to 41,680. During the longer period, corn—the staple crop in the county—rose from 47,506 bushels produced on farms in 1850 to 195,698 bushels produced on farms in 1910 (U.S. Bureau of the Census, 1851; 1913).

Subsistence agriculture was still very important in the local economy, but these noteworthy rises in agricultural production were also a sign of increasing capitalist integration. It is difficult to ascertain the precise degree to which local farmers were becoming more involved in commercial agriculture, but many certainly saw it as a preferable alternative to mining as a way to earn cash for paying taxes. The increasing population created a local market for farm goods, as the new labor force needed food. This increased farming trend was more prevalent in the southern part of the county, as the earliest alienated lands were mostly in the northern portion. Older residents of the southern portion of the county recall taking crops over Davy Mountain into McDowell County, where a population explosion had created a market for their products (Cook, 1996c). Some farmers were affluent enough to hire less fortunate neighbors. One man in the Hanover area, whose family raised crops for its own subsistence, recalled working for other farmers to earn cash in the 1920s and 1930s, "I've worked since I was a little ol' boy, about twelve. Picked blackberries and hoed corn. . . . I hoed corn for a dollar a day from daylight to dark." Remembering the 1940s, one man recalled, "When I was a boy, you could go around them farmers and they'd give you—you know, I've hoed corn all day for a dollar, and that was a lot."

An increasing population, however, also resulted in a decline of land for farming, particularly of bottomlands where most coal companies began to build their towns and camps. As the railroad carved its way deeper into the county along riverbanks, prime land became scarcer. Older residents in the southern portion of the county recall the gradual transition from an agrarian lifeway. One man born in 1908 recalled trying to farm marginal land near Baileysville: "Gosh dog, buddy, you raised it on these old hillsides. . . . Land in this territory, when I was young, just a boy, if you couldn't raise corn and beans, taters and molasses and stuff on it, it wasn't no good. Then they [his family] was stupid enough to sell it so cheap." This man's family ultimately sold a portion of their land in order to pay taxes, without realizing its value in mineral wealth. The same man, like many other residents of that part of the county, told of how they took jobs on railroad construction crews for twenty-five cents an hour when the railroad moved into that area (Cook, 1996c; 1996d).

Virtually every family in the county, save affluent merchants and coal operators, depended on subsistence agriculture well after the coal industry became firmly entrenched. One man who grew up on remote Indian Creek recalled how in the 1930s and early 1940s his family lived primarily on what they raised, "Of course, we had a garden. And my mother used to make soap and all them things. . . . We had chickens. We used to sell eggs. Carry them eggs down to the store. 'Bout the only thing you had to go to the store for was kerosene, and sugar, things like that. Things you couldn't produce yourself." However, where Indian Creek emptied into the Guyandotte near Baileysville, the Virginian had extended its main line in the late 1920s, and with it came mines. The same man related how his father had worked in the mines and then sold his land to open a restaurant in Baileysville.

The entry of industry into the county brought about a slow but steady integration of almost all county residents into the national capitalist economy. While for many a subsistence economy was still possible, it could rarely stand alone as the sole means of survival. Industrial forces penetrated the county through the mechanism of new tax laws, enacted by a state political system controlled primarily by industrialists. With industry came a growing population, which had the dual effect of creating a local market for farm produce while placing a growing strain on existing agricultural lands. Native residents met new tax burdens by engaging ever more in commercial agriculture or wage labor. Either way, they became more deeply integrated into the capitalist system. The critical question at this point is, were these trends part of a colonial process, and if so, how oppressive was the situation? In order to answer this, it is necessary to look at the various changes the coal industry brought to the county, the ways in which representatives of the industry consciously sought to influence employees and local officials, and the ways in which various county residents reacted to these situations.

Land Alienation

According to Robert Blauner, one of the first hallmarks of a colonial process is the forced entry of the colonizers into the territory of the colonized (1969: p. 395). Several scholars, notably Helen Lewis, have argued that this occurred in central Appalachia through the questionable means by which absentee speculators gained access to local lands (1983: p. 183). Lewis uses the example of the "broad form deed," a legal document that conveyed upon speculators "all mineral substances" and the arbitrary right to remove these by any means "deemed necessary and convenient" (1983: p. 183). Often these agreements were presented to farmers who were illiterate or unaware of the fine print, and the latter provision essentially gave speculators license to remove people from their homes and property. In a study of land ownership and taxation patterns in selected West Virginia counties, the Appalachian Land Ownership Task Force found in the late 1970s that similar practices had occurred in the state, and that speculators had often used coercive measures by invoking post–Civil War land laws and/or earlier land grants for settling title disputes. Notably, speculators researched original land grants which had subsequently become fragmented, had "quit claim" deeds issued to them without the knowledge the local landowners, and then presented local landowners with an essentially bogus legal document to intimidate them into a quick and unfair sale. In some cases, legal records of land titles mysteriously disappeared from courthouses (ALOTF, 1980: p. 4).[2]

It is difficult to ascertain the degree to which such practices occurred in Wyoming County because few records exist. During my field research I attempted to answer this question through the medium of interviews. Many people had heard of practices such as the broad form deed but could not relate direct experience with such deeds on their part or that of their ancestors. However, existing records and oral histories do reveal that although the legal structure was in place on the *state* level for the systematic and inequitable dispossession of resident landowners by around 1900, many Wyoming

County residents managed to hold onto their lands well into the twentieth century. This was particularly true of small holders in more southerly portions of the county with titles to less than five hundred acres (Cook, 1996; 1996d), and this was probably due to at least two reasons. First, since Wyoming County was in the remotest reaches of the plateau and contained some of the plateau's most rugged terrain, it was relatively uninviting to early industrialists who prior to the construction of the Virginian Railway would have had to spend more capital per ton of coal mined than the coal would have been worth. Thus, local farmers were not as pressured to sell their lands immediately.

Second, local political alliances were sufficiently divided to prevent industrialists from dominating the local system to facilitate their encroachment on local lands and resources. Though the Republicans had a slight edge in the county, Democrats maintained enough of a power base to create formidable obstacles to industrial domination.

The evidence collected here suggests that the main reason local landowners sold their lands and/or mineral rights was to pay taxes. As previously noted, many minimized this burden by engaging in wage labor in the mines or related sectors of the economy. But when the Great Depression struck, wage labor became scarce. It was probably during this period that the greatest number of local landowners sold out. One man who grew up in the southern part of the county recalled that his grandfather worked hard to pay the property tax on his 288 acres, which totaled $2.88 annually (or one cent per acre), an amount a miner's wage could cover under normal circumstances. When the Depression hit, he was forced to sell (Cook, 1995). Another man who grew up along Indian Creek in the 1930s made the following statement, "I've often heard the way [W. M.] Ritter got that land [along Indian Creek]. . . . That land was all heirship, down through the years. So during the Depression old man Ritter come in there and a lot of them people that was heirship was real poor people. So he'd give them a few dollars for their part of that land, which they didn't know it was theirs anyhow, or didn't have no way to get it. So he got enough heirship pieces bought up to where he just took it over." At that time (in the 1930s), W. M. Ritter was beginning to expand into the coal industry, purchasing the Red Jacket Coal Company in Mingo County and expanding its operations into southern Wyoming County. The Depression provided a timely opportunity for Ritter, and probably others, to take advantage of economically disadvantaged landowners who, due to lack of finances or knowledge of the subject, could be pressured into selling their land for a fraction of its worth. The average price paid to local landowners in the days of industrial entry in southern West Virginia was anywhere from ten cents to one dollar per acre, a pittance compared to the actual resource wealth of these lands (Lee, 1969: p. 7).

The above quote speaks of "heirship," which evokes the issue of certain peculiar land tenure titles seen frequently in the county. The practice of maintaining title to lands where several relatives lived in a quasi-patrilineal, single extended family (under one surname) was a double-edged sword when it came to alienating lands. An elderly resident of the Hanover area in the southwestern portion of the county recalled, "We lived right up that holler there. My granddaddy owned all that, head of it. Just about two miles long, the creek is. He owned it all at one time and parceled it out to his family, so many acres, more or less. And one of the girls, she bought all of 'em except my mother's. My mother wouldn't sell. And well, I saw where she sold that property for a hundred and thirty seven thousand dollars. She wouldn't tell anyone, but I saw it in the paper." A single owner, then, could either *prevent* the fragmentation or alienation of family lands, or could *facilitate* the wholesale liquidation of such lands. One Indian Creek family managed to hold onto several hundred acres of land well into the twentieth century because only a single recalcitrant family member held the title. When he died he divided the title among his children, who then agreed to sell their titles to one brother. The brother in turn, agreed verbally to maintain the land for family use (farming and grazing) and further agreed not to sell without the consent of his siblings. However, facing financial troubles, he did sell out in the 1960s without their consent (Cook, 1996c).

The alienation of lands in Wyoming County during the formative years of industrialization was not necessarily as rapid or blatantly oppressive as in other parts of central Appalachia, but it was nonetheless guided by a colonial legal structure set up by the industry-controlled state government. However, it would be an exaggeration to say that the dispossession of the residents of their lands was an entirely coercive process. Other factors, most notably the economic crisis that swept the entire nation during the Great Depression, were at play as well. Yet the legal mechanism for land alienation was in place in West Virginia long before the Depression. As lands became alienated, more local residents turned to the mines not only for work but to fulfill the need for a space to live.

The Miner's Life

Another hallmark of colonialism is the exploitation of natural and human resources (Blauner, 1969: p. 395), which has often served as the starting point for colonial analyses of the Appalachian coalfields (Lewis, 1983; Nyden, 1979). When asked if he thought most people made their living by mining in the 1930s and 1940s in Wyoming County, a retired miner remarked, "That's just about all it was." If people did not work in the mines by the close of the Depression, their occupation was likely *related* to the mining economy. Perhaps 5 percent of the local male population was engaged in managerial or mercantile occupations. Almost all the rest were either miners or railroad workers, or engaged in some other form of manual labor related to the coal industry. Nearly every family that was not of the elite class of merchants or mine operators had at least one miner in the family. Coal miners were the backbone of the coal industry. They were the principal means by which the rich resources of the county were extracted for removal to distant markets.

In the early days mining machines were virtually nonexistent, and almost all coal mining was done by hand. The early operators relied first on a local labor force often comprising farmers who did not need full-time employment but were interested in earning enough cash to pay taxes or purchase goods that they could not produce themselves. Rather than paying miners an hourly or daily wage, operators found it more profitable to pay each individual miner for the actual amount of coal he produced. Hence the tonnage system became standard practice across the coalfields. A miner was paid a certain amount for each ton of coal he produced.

Before the introduction of cutting machines, the miner first had to undercut a specific section of a coal seam with a pick while laying on his side. Then he used a breast auger (a long, manually operated drill) to drill a deep hole above the undercut, placed blasting powder in the hole, tamped it in, and placed a fuse of just the right length. If the fuse was too short he might be blown up along with the coal; if too long, it would likely burn out before reaching the charge. After the coal was blasted, the miner had to collect the pieces and place them in a nearby car, taking care to separate impurities for which he might be docked a large percentage of his pay (Dix, 1977; pp. 4–6, 1988: p. 14; Eller, 1982: pp. 175–81).[3] While some Wyoming County mines were at least partially mechanized from an early date, many smaller mines engaged in hand-loading well into the 1930s. One man recalled with a mixture of enthusiasm and bitterness the task of hand-loading in the 1920s, "You actually got in there and you had to dig that shit, buddy. Well, you got some powder, and you dig a cut out that had to be drawed with a pick. And then you'd bore some holes, put some powder in there, and you'd shoot that down. . . . But you couldn't go but just so fur under there. Hell, you didn't have no supports for the roofs."

The tonnage system was a mixed blessing during the hand-loading days. On the one hand, miners could generally come and go as they pleased, and a skilled and industrious man at the turn of the twentieth century could earn an average of $2.00 per day, which was a decent wage at that time (Eller, 1982: p. 178). The liberty of the tonnage system also meant that farmers who were not dependent on the company for housing could, and often did, put in a minimal amount of work, thus adversely affecting production and irritating operators (Dix, 1977: p. 4). On the other hand, the tonnage system was also subject to abuses by operators, particularly where miners were entirely dependent on them for employment and housing. In remote southern West Virginia, pick miners in 1912 were paid an average of 38.5 cents per ton. Yet in other parts of the state they received an average of 48 cents per ton, and in Ohio and Pennsylvania, $1.27 per ton (Eller, 1982: p. 178). In Wyoming County, fair wages ewere not quite as problematic in the early days, particularly in the Winding Gulf, where the operators' association in the 1920s adopted the practice of implementing shorter work days (eight to nine hours, as opposed to ten or more hours in other coal fields) and higher wages than did unionized mines in the state (Tams, 1963: pp. 40–43). In 1919, the average pick miner's wage in Wyoming County was 63 cents per ton or $1.08 per car, depending on the system of measurement used by a particular mine. Unfortunately, by 1933 the Great Depression brought the average wage down to 45 cents per ton (Bowman, 1965: pp. 263–64). Nonetheless, some participants in this study reported that their fathers or other relatives moved to Wyoming County from neighboring counties because the tonnage rate was higher. One man said that his father made over 50 cents per day more than he had while mining in McDowell County in the 1920s (Cook, 1996c).

So the tonnage rate was plausibly fair, but the burden of guaranteeing the quality or quantity of coal lay on the miner. Other methods of depriving miners of a fair price for their labor were practiced through shortweighing with rigged scales, through docking miners for impurities in the coal they mined, or through docking them for not producing a full ton. From the mine, the carloads of coal that each miner produced went to a tipple, where a company checkweighman weighed each car and checked it for impurities. As a company employee, he was often ordered to use his discretion in favor of company profits, and many miners were unfairly docked a portion of their pay or were arbitrarily singled out for scrutiny (Dix, 1977: pp. 52–53). One retired Wyoming County miner recalled, "Sometimes they'd set your car off. And two men would get a shovel and they'd load that into another empty, and if they got as much as four or five pounds of rock in that, you lost that car of coal."

Another means of short-changing miners for their labor and production was the practice of "cribbing," or placing boards on the sides of coal cars so that they would haul more than a ton of coal. In some cases miners were still paid only for mining a ton; in other cases they were paid by the carload, which could average three tons (Dix, 1977: pp. 53–55, 1988: p. 14). In Wyoming County, a very crude method of cribbing, which was referred to as "humping," seems to have been commonly practiced, as described in the following statements by elderly miners, "At the drift mouth they had a board up there, and if you didn't put a hump on that car where it would drag that board? They'd dock you that whole car. They'd fill up 'til it would drag that board." Similarly another miner remarked, "They'd take it [the coal] to the tipple, and they'd check your coal, and if it didn't have—make a hump over, they'd dock you. It 'us a big ol' board stretched across the track where the coal car went in the tipple. And if it didn't drag that damn board they'd dock you about a third of the car. And then they finally put them scales in, when the Union come in."

Were miners paid a fair wage when they *did* get full credit on a carload of coal? As noted, the average pick miner's wage in 1919 was 63 cents per ton or $1.08 per car (Bowman, 1965: p. 263). This meant that miners who were paid by the carload (at least two, and usually three tons) were making much less than the going tonnage rate. One miner even reported making only 25 to 50 cents per car in the 1920s (Cook, 1996d: p. 105). So whether miners received a fair wage or not, the same structures were in place in Wyoming County that were in place in other coalfields (prior to unionization), which allowed operators to arbitrarily manipulate miners' wages in their own favor, and hence to exercise a disproportionate degree of control over the economic lives of miners and their families.

Even in the most "advanced" mines, working conditions were among the most hazardous in the world, and without a successful union, the miners found little recourse or compensation for putting their lives in danger. Mine accidents came in many forms. Explosions caused by natural gases or clouds of fine coal dust ignited by miners' carbide lights, or even by the striking of a match, were a frequent cause of fatalities and injuries. The incidence of coal dust igniting increased significantly with the introduction of cutting machines, which stirred up more dust. Explosions in the mines could be, and ultimately were, significantly reduced by improving the ventilation of mines to draw flammable gases out, and by rock dusting (coating walls with nonflammable lime dust) or by spraying mine walls with water to keep coal dust down. However, operators were reluctant to pursue such improvements, and state and national laws tended to reflect their reluctance (Dix, 1977: pp. 70–74).

The most common cause of accidents and fatalities in the mines was (and remains) roof fall-ins. Quite simply, the removal of coal from its underground beds deprives the strata of rock overhead of their support. Until well into the twentieth century, mines used only hardwood timbers to support the roof of a mine, and the skilled miner learned exactly where to place a timber to prevent (or at least delay) the collapse of the roof. But even the earliest hydraulic jacks that were used to support sagging roofs were seen by some miners as more of a consolation than as a practical innovation (Dix, 1977: p. 71). As one retired miner recalled of his days at the Red Jacket Mine in the community of Wyoming: "Used to have them ol' spool jacks set up. Those ol' spool jacks. Just a joke. I bet you they's a thousand of 'em layin' in the Red Jacket mine up there."

Between 1903 and 1930, West Virginia led the nation in both mine fatalities and injuries (Dix, 1977: pp. 70–71). Prior to the standardization of national mine safety and inspection laws after World War II, records on mine accidents were often filled with gaps and misinformation. But based on the information available for this study, between 1919 and 1933 there were at least 55 fatalities in Wyoming County mines, and at least 158 injuries. The most serious of these was a gas explosion at the Glen Rogers mine in 1923, in which 27 men died (Bowman, 1965: pp. 258–66). Glen Rogers, in fact, with its 650-foot vertical shaft, had the county's largest record of fatalities and injuries over the years.

Coal operators hesitated to improve mine safety conditions during the hand-loading days and well into the 1930s, simply because they did not have to. Even if an operator was concerned for his workers' safety, the costs of making such improvements would have put many small operators out of business and would have affected the profits of larger operators adversely. It was in the area of mine safety, in fact, that the coal operators' control over West Virginia politics manifested itself most blatantly. Rather than take responsibility for mine safety, most operators preferred to place it on the miners themselves, frequently attributing accidents to the carelessness of workers. State policy-makers tended to concur (Dix, 1977: pp. 73–77, 1988: p. 93). As early as 1886, the West Virginia Department of Mines—which drew its information primarily from coal company managers—reported that "the great carelessness of miners in keeping their work places securely propped is well known" (West Virginia State Department of Mines, 1886: p. 3). Again, in 1910, the Department of Mines attributed 66 percent of all roof fall accidents to "negligence on the part of the parties killed or injured, or some other person" (West Virginia State Department of Mines, 1910: p. 18).

State mining laws in West Virginia codified this "victim blaming" approach to mine safety. The state legislature was dominated by coal interests, and either as a result of direct lobbying or out of a fear of affecting the state's economy adversely if legislation imposed strenuous safety regulations on operators, the West Virginia mine laws from 1883 to the 1930s protected owners from liability (Dix, 1977: p. 87). Typical of such laws was the Mine Code of 1931, in which liability was placed almost entirely on the heads of miners: "Every miner shall thoroughly examine the roof and general conditions of his working place before commencing work and . . . he shall not commence work in such place until it has been made safe, or unless it be for the purpose of making such place safe" (Dix, 1977: pp. 86–87). As Howard B. Lee, a former Attorney General of the State of West Virginia pointed out in reference to mine explosions, "in no case was the coal company ever censured for its willful neglect or refusal to take necessary safety precautions to prevent the slaughter" (Lee, 1969: p. 83). Not surprisingly, of the 1,455 mine safety violations prosecuted in West Virginia between 1908 and 1929, only 3 of those prosecuted were against owners (Dix, 1977: p. 92).

Nor could miners look to the federal government to exert pressure on coal companies to improve safety standards. National mine safety legislation was very slow in coming for two reasons. First, prior to the 1930s, mining was viewed as an intrastate industry and therefore not subject to federal regulations governing interstate affairs. Second, coal operators were able to exert a great deal of lobbying pressure on Congress, especially through national officials from coal states such as West Virginia, where political campaigns were heavily financed by coal money (Dix, 1977: p. 80). Although the United States Bureau of Mines was established in 1910 in part due to complaints about mine safety, it functioned only in an advisory capacity, and until the law was changed in 1941, its officials could not enter coal company property without the consent of owners (Dix, 1977: p. 81; Eller, 1982: p. 181). And until the 1920s, the Bureau of Mines tended to endorse the notion that mine workers alone were liable for their own safety.

In short, miners were seen as a source of labor to be used in a manner that would yield maximum productivity and profits. Although relations between smaller operators and employees were sometimes very personal, mines associated with larger conglomerates tended to be interested in labor only as a commodity. This was true even in Wyoming County, where operators (as will be elaborated in the next section) tended to be more progressive in some respects in dealing with their employees. One man recalled seeing a slogan probably painted by union sympathizers, but reportedly echoed by the proprietors) on the walls of an office at one of the Wyoming County mines held by Pocahontas Fuel Company, which read "KILL A MULE, BUY ANOTHER; KILL A MAN, HIRE ANOTHER" (Cook, 1996d: p. 94). But maintaining a cheap labor force was not merely a matter of manipulating wages and cutting corners on safety. It was also a matter of controlling fundamental aspects of the lives of miners and their families.

Coal Camps and the Company System

Yet another hallmark of colonialism is the institutionalization of unequal power relations between colonizer and colonized. Blauner states that "a formal recognition is given to the difference in power, autonomy, and political status, and various agencies are set up to maintain this subordination" (1969: p. 395). Scholars have placed emphasis on this configuration of power relations in the central Appalachian coalfields (Lewis, 1983; Gaventa, 1980). The main argument is that coal companies in the past and even the present have coopted state and local officials to control the lives of local nonelites, thus allowing elites to control the political behavior of their subordinates and the very space in which the latter lived.

In West Virginia prior to the Depression, coal barons unquestionably controlled state politics. This control gave them legal sanction to impose certain power structures at the local level. As local residents and immigrants grew ever more dependent on the coal industry, coal operators often used their money and power to force workers to live on company property, to shop exclusively at company stores, and to abide by certain rules governing their behavior. These rules were enforced by local law officers who were often on the company payroll, or by mine guards hired by the company directly. The remainder of this chapter examines restrictions imposed on workers through company policies and life in company towns, and the ways in which the state and local power structures supported (or challenged) these unequal relations that were the defining character of the company system in West Virginia.

In the late nineteenth and early twentieth centuries, hundreds of coal towns (towns owned and controlled entirely by coal companies) and smaller, unincorporated coal camps emerged in central Appalachia. In some respects, these communities were autonomous, as they provided miners with all the essential requirements for living, including company stores stocked with the fundamentals for survival, tool repair shops, and in more progressive company communities hospitals and even recreation facilities. The latter amenities, however, were uncommon in West Virginia prior to the 1930s. Nor were these services complementary. Miners had to pay rent on their houses, and any services that were conducted through company agents (tool sharpening, health care, etc.) were deducted from their paychecks.

In the average coal camp, houses were crude "board and batten" structures and seldom contained more than four (and often no more than two) rooms. Those houses close to coal tipples received a thick showering of coal dust every day (Eller, 1982: p. 182–83). Several members of mining families reported having to scrub floors and change sheets, which had become black with coal dust, at least once a day in the 1930s and 1940s (Cook, 1995, 1996c).

Very few camps had running water. In 1925, the U.S. Coal Commission reported that while 90 percent of the coal communities in Ohio had indoor plumbing, only 14 percent in West Virginia could boast the same (U.S. Senate, 1925: pt. 3, p. 1473). While many camps had outside running water, only 2 percent of those in West Virginia in the 1920s had any kind of sewage system. Indeed, sewage ran directly into nearby streams, already clogged with coal silt and litter, inviting diseases such as hookworm and typhoid (Eller, 1982: p. 186).

Because most coal camps and towns were isolated from centers of commerce, the company store provided the main source of food, clothing, and general goods that mining families did not produce themselves. But the company store was also a key mechanism—along with other services for which miners were charged—for increasing company profits. Prior to the 1930s, mining was often seasonal work, and when it was not, mines often overproduced, causing declines in coal prices. Fluctuations in the market meant temporary layoffs. In 1904, for example, the average cost of producing a ton of coal in southern West Virginia was seventy-six cents, while the average selling price at the mine site was only eighty cents (Tams, 1963: p. 25). Ordinarily, good business sense would dictate that mines should shut down in slack seasons, but many stayed open because they made their greatest profits from what Dix calls the "system of company owned subsistence" (1988: p. 25). Many coal companies more than made up for lost profits through rents and store profits, as veteran coal operator W. P. Tams freely admitted (Tams, 1963: p. 25).

Company stores often abused their monopoly on goods by charging disproportionately high prices. The U.S. Coal Commission found in 1925 that the average prices of goods in stores in isolated coal camps were 5 to 12 percent higher than in the nearest independent stores (U.S. Senate, 1925: pt. 3, p. 1457). Not infrequently a company required its employees to shop exclusively at the company store. One McDowell County miner recalled mine guards confiscating groceries that his family bought at a non–company store in the 1920s (Cook, 1995). When miners were short of cash to pay for needed commodities the company issued scrip, or tokens redeemable for credit only at the company store. Even if mining families could ordinarily pay their debts, they were drawn into debt during bust cycles when mines were closed but company stores continued to do business. In this manner, thousands of West Virginia miners were drawn into debt peonage, and companies were assured a cheap source of labor (Dix, 1988: pp. 22–26).

Even in the coal camps, families still relied heavily on subsistence agriculture to survive. This has been well documented in other parts of the central Appalachian coalfields (Salstrom, 1994; LaLone, 1996) and was true in Wyoming County as well. The words of one retired Wyoming County miner, when asked if his family engaged in agriculture to any extent while living in coal camps, reflect a common response: "Yeah. You just about had to to eat." In other words, mine wages were not enough to allow a family to survive. In the earliest days, in fact, when many miners still lived on their own farms, they relied almost exclusively on subsistence, and the company store was less patronized. As they grew more dependent on the company store, many continued to rely on subsistence agriculture to make ends meet. Thus, as Salstrom points out (and as also was true of the

Monacans engaged in tenant farming and orchard labor in the early part of the twentieth century) a "subsistence reproduction of labor power" was at work (1994: p. 82). In other words, the miners and their families actually subsidized the mining industry through their personal subsistence practices. If coal operators were not aware of this at first, they were quick to catch on. Many companies, including some in Wyoming County, encouraged the planting of gardens, even holding contests to determine which family had raised the best garden (Bowman, 1965: pp. 259–62; Cook, 1996c).

In coal camps and towns, companies owned or controlled everything from houses to stores, the intended end being to promote maximum productive efficiency and to "give stability to the labor supply" (Eller, 1982: p. 193). The coal operators did this through control of local politics and law enforcement. In many southern West Virginia counties, local political elites were easily coopted and made a part of a comprador (i.e., indigenous intermediary) class in the overall colonial scheme, and it was not uncommon for local law enforcement officers to be on the company payroll. The main objective of this system was to stifle the threat of unionism. A 1919 state investigation, for example, revealed that the Logan County Coal Operators Association had paid the local sheriff $32,700 for twenty-five extra deputies who worked exclusively for coal companies (Eller, 1982: p. 215). Most often, operators simply hired their own mine guards, primarily from the Baldwin-Felts Detective Agency in Bluefield. These guards were little more than mercenaries. As former state Attorney General Howard B. Lee fittingly described these men and their duties, "In reality ... they were fearless mountain gunmen, many with criminal records, whose chief duties were to keep the miners intimidated, beat up, arrest, jail, and even kill if necessary, any worker or visitor suspected of union activities " (Lee, 1969: p. 11). Those who were found guilty, or who were even suspected of union organizing, were at the very least "blacklisted"; that is, their names were reported to local coal operators' associations to ensure that they would not secure mine employment anywhere in the area (Lee, 1969: p. 9).

With employees' futures in their hands, coal operators frequently attempted to secure their power by instructing employees whom to vote for in state and local elections. Some simply handed completed ballots to employees, while others paid workers at the polls to check each ballot as it was passed to them (Hall, 1933: p. 137; Lee, 1969: p. 9). Thus, in much of central Appalachia, Howard B. Lee was not exaggerating when he wrote that "every phase of the people's lives [was] dominated by a super oligarchy of coal operators" (1969: p. 65).

The bleak picture painted above of life and power relations in pre–Depression Appalachian coalfields was typical of most of southern West Virginia. In Wyoming County, however, the situation was somewhat different. As noted, commercial coal mining did not begin to any significant degree until 1913, and by the 1920s, when larger companies were moving into the county, many coal operators were realizing that meeting the needs of workers could be good business. Some of the larger operators were subscribing to ideas of "scientific management," which held that miners and their tools and equipment should function as a well-oiled machine, fostering optimum efficiency and maximum production (Dix, 1977: pp. 59–65). This meant that some operators saw benefits in taking care of miners. A few operators took care of their employees out of benign interest, such as W. P. Tams, a pioneer operator of the Winding Gulf Field, who established the Wyoming Coal Company town of Wyco in 1915. Tams prided himself in knowing each of his employees personally, and he set a standard for most of the Winding Gulf when, in 1910, he built the first bath house in the West Virginia coalfields long before it was required by law. Tams also constructed the first movie theater in the southern coalfields (Tams, 1963: pp. 62–74; Dix; 1977: pp. 40–41).

Tams evidently set a standard for the larger operations in the county. In 1921, the Raleigh Wyoming Coal Company opened the mine and town at Glen Rogers, which boasted six hundred "modern brick houses," each with steam heat and hot-and-cold running water ("Glen Rogers," 1921: p. 1). By the end of the 1920s most of the larger companies in Wyoming County provided recreational facilities such as movie theaters and clubhouses for employees. The town of Kopperston, associated with Eastern Gas and Fuel Company, operated a summer camp for the children of its miners and sponsored several civic organizations for workers (Bowman, 1965: p. 262).

Nearly every large coal operation in the county provided families living in their facilities with some form of running water. However, many smaller coal camps did not have indoor plumbing as late as the 1960s (Cook, 1996c). One notable exception to the provision of an adequate water supply was Isaac T. Mann's Pocahontas affiliated mine at Itman. While Mann constructed impressive stone buildings for his offices and employee living spaces, there was no bathhouse for years. This may explain in part why the Itman mine was forced to close after World War I and did not reopen until 1958 (Bowman, 1965: p. 258). Bowman also points out that the mine at Itman and other companies dumped waste into the Guyandotte River, all but annihilating its wildlife and making it unfit for human contact (1965: p. 258). In fact, there was no sewage system in the county until the 1930s, and until the 1960s these were restricted to larger municipalities such as Pineville and Oceana (Bowman, 1965: pp. 159–60).

Most of the participants in this study who lived in various coal camps in Wyoming County over the years spoke highly of the manner in which the companies maintained their homes and the services they provided. A retired miner who worked at the Red Jacket mine and lived in the community of Wyoming in the 1940s and 1950s recalled, "If you got a house back then, you didn't pay but about ten or fifteen dollars a month. Two dollars for a ton of coal. And it was right close to work. They'd [the company] put windows in it and stuff." Another man recalled of even earlier camps in the northern (Winding Gulf) section of the county, "I guess Wyco was one of the top. They had a poolroom, they had their own theater, they had recreation for the men, they had their own skeet trap ranges, archery, and whatever. Swimming pools. . . . They didn't have to leave the community for anything. And they kept 'em up good. At Kopperston they had a beautiful community. . . . They kept all the camps up pretty good."

The operators of the Winding Gulf Field, which constituted the largest portion of the Wyoming County fields, are reputed to have treated employees much more equitably than operators in many other fields. Although Bowman (1965: p. 263) reports that the average miners' wage in the county in 1919 was $1.08 per car (two to three tons) and 63 cents per ton, some participants in this study reported wages ranging from 25 to 50 cents a ton in the 1920s (Cook, 1996c; 1996d). Wages were subject to market fluctuations, as there were no minimum wage laws as yet, and regardless of what miners made, the costs of living mounted. For example, Tams reported that in the 1920s, miners paid an average of 50 cents per month for blacksmith and tool sharpening services, $1.50 per month for the rental of a simple board and bratten house, or $2.00 per month for a weather-boarded home, 50 cents per month for doctor's service ($1.00 if a man was married), and $5.00 for baby delivery (Tams, 1964: pp. 34, 51–53). The latter figures point to a trend throughout the coalfields—the absence of a medical plan. Even after the passage of workman's compensation laws in 1910, the operators contracted with private hospitals and deducted medical expenses from miners' paychecks. "In this way," writes Eller, "the workers were made to pay a part of the cost of their own hospitalization for industrial accidents which otherwise would have been free to them under the compensation law" (1982: p. 189).

The portion of miners' wages that did not go toward other services generally got siphoned into the company store. In his semi-autobiographical account of the smokeless coalfields, W. P. Tams condemned the abuses many companies exercised through their company store monopolies, and he boasted that most company stores in the Winding Gulf operated at profit margins that were even lower than local non–company stores. Yet he also admitted that salaried employees were sold goods at cost, while miners had to pay higher prices (Tams, 1964: pp. 28, 52). A lifelong resident of Mullens, who worked for a period in the mines in that area in the 1920s recalled how some companies (notably in the Winding Gulf Field) took advantage of employees through the company store:

"They [miners] needed black powder to blast the coal out, they'd pay for that. They'd pay for the tools. They'd pay for the can of beans, they were ten cents a can. But if they come here in town, they may buy them for seven cents, see. They was cheatin' people. But if you didn't trade at the company store, they would fire you. . . . You've heard the Tennessee Ernie Ford song, 'I Owe My Soul to the Company Store'? Pretty good song."

Urban centers such as Mullens and Oceana in particular depended on coal miners' money to sustain their blossoming business districts. Mine operators had a heavy hand in controlling these business districts, as evidenced by the activities of J. C. Sullivan, one of the earliest commercial coal operators in the county. Soon after establishing his mine near the growing railroad hub of Mullens, Sullivan gained a controlling interest in the Bank of Wyoming and established the newspaper, the *Mullens Advocate*, thereby gaining a formidable influence over local business ventures through the control of capital and the local media (Bowman, 1965: p. 255).

Although coal barons controlled the bulk of capital available in the county prior to the 1930s, their success in controlling the local political structure was only limited. The mine guard system was in use from a very early date. In fact, Baldwin-Felts agents were employed in Wyoming County as early as 1907, when Ritter Lumber Company officials (including Baldwin agents) were indicted for peonage (Bowman, 1965: p. 243; Bailey, 1973: p. 196). There is very little information, however, about the *extent* to which mine guards were employed in Wyoming County.

It is unlikely that coal operators were able to gain total control over local law enforcement officers, and they certainly did not wield unlimited power over the county political system. Republicans had always been strong in Wyoming County, but even with a slight majority they found formidable opposition from local Democrats. While coal operators had been able to gain control of Democratic strongholds such as Logan County simply by coopting local leaders, they found that much more difficult to do so in Wyoming County, where the electorate and leaders were solidly divided between parties. The Republican party was almost uniformly the party of coal operators, and in Wyoming County, operators were known to pressure employees to vote for Republican candidates or else lose their jobs. An elderly man in the Baileysville area described such practices as they occurred in the 1920s: "Way back there sat this little ol' schoolhouse, and they put two men in the winder of the schoolhouse. One Republican, one Democrat. And they walked up and wanted to know which one to vote for, and then they'd mark the ballots. And then they got so the coal companies, they'd fill out a ballot, just the way they wanted it."

The same man, however, was from a prominent Democratic family. He told a lengthy story of how he and his relatives were often able to counter the coal-controlled Republican vote by offering miners money and even alternative employment if they voted the Democratic ticket. "I never called that stealing," he added. "If you can't use your vote to better yourself, why use it?" In other words, the Democrats fought fire with fire, and although their ethics might seem questionable, the practice of buying votes predated the onslaught of industry and was tied to the old kin-oriented political system.

Among the Wyoming Democrats was Judge R. D. Bailey, an agrarian politician whose blunt charisma gained him support from various factions in the state Democratic Party. Bailey served for several years as a state supreme court judge for the district that included Wyoming County, and he remained a power behind the scenes in that section of the state for several years (Cook, 1996c).

Given the above comparative description of conditions in Wyoming County and other West Virginia counties, it can be said that the experiences of Wyoming County residents vis-à-vis powerful coal companies were, on the whole, not as harsh as in other southern West Virginia counties. This can be attributed to several reasons. First, as previously discussed, the coal operators were not able to gain exclusive control over the local political structure to reinforce the company system. Second, the relative isolation of Wyoming County delayed the entry of industry, and the rugged physiography continued to pose barriers even after the railroad penetrated the county. Quite simply, it was easier to pursue colonial inroads in other counties. Finally—and perhaps as a corollary to the county's inaccessibility—by the time large-scale coal operations became well established, many operators were seeing the wisdom of taking better care of employees to ensure a stable and healthy workforce. As a second generation Mullens businessman succinctly stated, "I think the coal operators saw the handwriting on the wall, that the population voting shifted from the Republican control that the operators had, to the Democratic rank and file of the miners."

The company system did become established in Wyoming County, and with it the same colonial structure that dominated the lives of local residents elsewhere in West Virginia. But it was not as firmly entrenched in Wyoming County. Regardless of how recalcitrant local residents and some of their elected officials were toward the encroachment of coal operators, however, they were still subject to the whims of a more powerful industry-controlled state government.

Labor Relations, State and Federal Politics

The degree to which coal operators controlled state politics in West Virginia prior to the Great Depression cannot be overemphasized. Coal operators provided the foundation for the state's colonial political economy. The coal operators' influence on laws and policies governing labor relations in West Virginia was pivotal to maintaining the local power structures from which they benefited. With the law on their side, those who would impede the maintenance of a quiescent labor force—namely, labor organizations such as the United Mine Workers of America (UMWA)—could be dealt with as violators of justice, bent on destroying the "American" way of life. Meanwhile, the miners and their families who found in labor organizations their only hope for recourse were all but completely alienated from the state (and at times, even the federal) political system.

A prime example of the intimate relationship between coal and state law in West Virginia can be found in the workers' compensation laws and procedures in the state prior to the 1930s. Federal law had made such procedures mandatory in 1913, but the West Virginia legislature found a convenient loophole by appointing a coal operator as head of the Workman's Compensation Commission, a position he held for fourteen years. In 1927, Governor Howard M. Gore boldly replaced this commissioner with a new man who was not connected with the coal industry. The new commissioner found that the compensation fund was insolvent, as several coal companies had not been making the required payments into the fund. Thus, he increased the assessments against all coal companies and filed suit in the state supreme court against a delinquent company owing in excess of three hundred thousand dollars. However, after the general election of 1928, coal operators resumed full control of the governor's office and legislature, and they secured passage of a law that simultaneously eliminated the non–coal industry commissioner and created a new commission, again headed by a coal baron. When the non-industry commissioner refused to leave office, the new governor ordered state police to remove him. The exiled commissioner continued pressing his suit in the state supreme court, further charging that the new law and the governor's actions against him were unconstitutional. Yet the justices—many of whom were major shareholders in coal interests[4]—upheld the constitutionality of the new law and dismissed charges against the delinquent company (Lee, 1969: pp. 9–10).

The greatest threat to the coal barons' power in West Virginia and their control over state politics was the UMWA. Miners' unions had come and gone sporadically in the United States since the Molly McGuires organized in the Pennsylvania coalfields in the 1870s. In 1890, several small unions consolidated to form the UMWA, and thereafter the northern coalfields became solidly organized, and operators there found no choice but to negotiate labor contracts with the union, granting better wages and working conditions (Finley, 1972; Lunt, 192: pp. 12–13). While the union made some inroads into northern West Virginia, the sheer isolation of the southern fields made it difficult for organizers to maintain strong lines of support from union offices and organized mines. As noted, this isolation meant that most miners were completely dependent on the company for their existence and had more to lose if they engaged in union activities. Moreover, southern coal operators were intent on keeping the union out, and they used every measure at their disposal—be it cooptation or sheer coercion—to do so. Cabell Coolidge, president of Island Creek Coal Company, one of the largest in the southern fields, expressed the sentiments of all operators in the region in 1921, "we kept out, and continue to keep out—and propose to keep out, the United Mine Workers of America" (Thurmond, 1964: p. 55).

Howard B. Lee wrote that coal operators in West Virginia prior to the Depression sustained their "feudal proprietorship" and kept unions out through the use of six principle defensive measures: injunctions, martial law, suzerainty over county government, elaborate espionage systems, coercion and intimidation of workers by the use of mine guards, and blacklisting (Lee, 1969: p. 12). While some of these measures have been discussed previously, it is worth mentioning at this point the relationship between blacklisting and court injunctions against strikers. Coal operators in southern West Virginia almost uniformly required their miners to sign individual employment contracts called "yellow dog" contracts, in which each miner agreed not to engage in union activities while employed by the coal company. In 1907 the West Virginia Courts deemed these contracts legitimate grounds for issuing injunctions against the UMWA for conducting activities on coal company property (Lunt, 1992: p. 15). All of the aforementioned tactics used by coal operators meshed to deprive miners and their families of fundamental rights of freedom of speech and assembly. These were among the grievances that the UMWA sought to remedy through political pressure.

In spite of the formidable obstacles to unionization, the UMWA drew strong, albeit sporadic, support in the southern fields. Countless strikes occurred between 1900 and 1933 (when federal law mandated employees' rights to join unions), the most dramatic of which have become known as the West Virginia Mine Wars.[5] The Paint and Cabin Creek War erupted in 1912 when the mines in those communities refused to join other companies in the Kanawha Field in signing union contracts. In 1920, a shoot-out involving miners led by local police chief Sid Hatfield in Matewan (Mingo County) resulted in the death of seven Baldwin-Felts detectives hired by the Stone Mountain Coal Company to evict miners suspected of union activities. The "Matewan Massacre," as it became known, sparked a general state of violence in Mingo County. Evicted miners occupied tent colonies along creek bottoms, and some were subjected to drive-by shootings by mine guards wielding machine guns.

In 1921, motivated by the assassination of Sid Hatfield (who had become a union hero) by Baldwin-Felts detectives, an estimated fifteen thousand miners from the Kanawha Field and other parts of southern West Virginia marched on Logan County with the intent of crushing the coal-controlled government run by Sheriff Don Chafin, known as the "Czar of Logan." From Logan, the miners intended to move into Mingo County and free miners who had been jailed in the insurrection of the previous year. At Blair Mountain, the miners met opposition from well-entrenched mine guards, state police, and vigilantes with machine guns and homemade bombs that were occasionally dropped from airplanes. Two days of fierce fighting ensued along a ten mile front. In the end, the failed march on Logan was suppressed by federal troops, and martial law ensued, as was the case in the earlier mine wars.

During this turbulent period for West Virginia mining families, any sympathy they received from state policy makers was fleeting and virtually ineffectual. Occasionally a reform-minded governor came into office, but he would be overshadowed by a legislature and court system solidly controlled by coal interests. William Glasscock, who served as governor during the outbreak of the Paint and Cabin Creek Strike in 1912, was interested in labor reform primarily because the Socialist Party was beginning to gain formidable popularity in Kanawha County—the site of the strike zone and dangerously close to the state capital. Nonetheless, Glasscock imposed martial law in the strike zone, and scores of miners were jailed without due process and denied writs of habeas corpus while being tried in military courts (Lee, 1969: pp. 30–31). When two victims of this denial of constitutional rights filed suit in the state supreme court, the court held that Glasscock was exercising his legal authority to declare martial law "in the event of invasion, insurrection, rebellion, or riot" (*Mays and Mance v. Brown, Warden*, 71 wv 519 [1913]). Still, Glasscock decided to appoint a committee headed by Catholic bishop P. J. Donahue to investigate conditions in the strike zone. The Donahue Committee reported blatant violations of human rights committed against miners by mine guards and fervently urged the abolition of the mine guard system. Glasscock made feeble efforts to effect such legislation despite coming under fire from coal operators. Finally, the state legislature passed a law that technically outlawed the mine guard system but provided no punishment for offenders (Lee, 1969, pp. 23–24, 139–40; Lunt, 1992: pp. 25–29).

In 1913, Dr. Henry D. Hatfield became governor. Initially gaining support from coal barons on the Republican ticket, he surprised operators and legislators when he decided to make a personal visit to the strike zone and volunteer his skills as a physician while conducting his own investigation. Hatfield sympathized with miners and opted to utilize martial law in the strike zone to stifle the mine guard system. He soon delivered an ultimatum to the state's coal operators, informing them that if they refused to negotiate with miners for fairer wages and hours, he would dictate the terms of such an agreement himself. However, Hatfield's stubborn opposition to coal operators led to the defeat of his reform-minded proposals, and his 1915 proposal for a coal severance tax on out-of-state corporations caused coal operators to shift their support to the industrial Democrat John J. Cornwell in the 1916 gubernatorial race (Lee, 1969: pp. 43–46; Lunt, 1992: 30–33, 57–58).

Cornwell made no attempt to hide his opposition to labor power. In the context of World War I and the Russian Revolution, he cast unionism as a communist plot to "destroy our Government . . . and social system" (Lunt, 1992: p. 64). With the coming of World War I, Cornwell successfully pursued the passage of a number of laws intended to ensure the suppression of organized labor. The first was a compulsory work law, which essentially gave coal operators license to have strikers arrested and jailed for vagrancy. Next, despite UMWA opposition, Cornwell had no trouble getting the state legislature to enact a "red flag" law, which made it illegal to display any flag or emblem, or to speak publicly in any manner expressing, "un-American sentiments." As if the denial of freedom of speech, press, and assembly was not enough, Cornwell also urged and won passage of legislation creating the West Virginia State Police in 1919, arguing that said force was necessary lest the state become "a dumping ground for Bolshevists and anarchists" (Lunt, 1992: pp. 63–63). Perhaps as a measure to appease the labor constituency, Cornwell also argued that the state police force would bring about the end of the mine guard system, though in truth it only supplemented the latter. And finally, when UMWA miners made their first attempt to organize Logan County in 1919, Cornwell borrowed the tactics of coal operators themselves and sent state-employed spies into the county to unveil union plans (Lunt, 1992: pp. 77, 81).

West Virginia coal miners and their families, then, were alienated from state politics prior to the 1930s. At the level of national politics, the situation was only mildly better. The executive branch of the government dealt with miners throughout the nation in a lukewarm manner. President Woodrow Wilson supported various labor reforms early in his administration. However, with the coming of World War I, and the passage of the Lever Act (40 St. 276) in 1917 authorizing the wartime regulation of certain industries through government agencies, Wilson treated all miners' strikes as acts of treason. Unfortunately, this trend continued after the war was over. Martial law ensued in Mingo and Logan counties, enforced by federal troops. Interestingly, the federal presence brought about a sudden acquiescence among many miners, particularly in Logan County when the regular army intervened in the Battle of Blair Mountain in 1921, as many miners were themselves veterans of World War I and did not wish to bear arms against fellow servicemen (Savage, 1990: p. 147; Lunt, 1992: pp. 34, 64). It was President Warren G. Harding who ordered federal troops to intervene in the war in Logan and accordingly he issued a proclamation for all miners to lay down their arms. Harding, who faced constant pressure from John L. Lewis, the powerful and verbose president of the UMWA, was marginally interested in labor reform and initially urged a 1921 congressional committee investigating violence in West Virginia to act as an arbiter between striking miners and coal operators. Unfortunately, the coal operators exerted greater pressure on Harding, and the president ultimately decided to remain silent on the issue (Savage, 1990: ch. 19; Lunt, 1992: p. 149).

The federal judiciary was by far the least sensitive and most destructive branch of the federal government in dealing with the rights of coal miners, especially in West Virginia. When the Central Competitive Coal Field—which encompassed Pennsylvania, the Midwest, and small portions of northern West Virginia—became unionized in 1903, the Hitchman Coal and Coke Company of West Virginia refused to acknowledge the union. Hitchman miners nonetheless opted to join a general strike in that field in 1906, and Hitchman filed in the federal district court for an injunction against the UMWA, arguing that Hitchman employees' participation in the strike violated their yellow dog contracts. In 1907, Judge Alston C. Dayton, himself a major shareholder in West Virginia coal interests, issued an injunction stating that the union was violating Hitchman's labor contracts and attempting to interfere with the company's business through work stoppages. Dayton cited common law, in essence arguing that property rights superseded personal rights (Lunt, 1992: pp. 19–21, 79–80).

Seven years later, the UMWA appealed the case in the U.S. Circuit Court of Appeals. In *Mitchell v. Hitchman Coal and Coke Co., et. al.,* the court unanimously reversed Dayton's injunction, stating that his reasoning was archaic and that property rights should no longer be "recognized as paramount to personal rights" (214 Fed. 685 [1914]: p. 698). Nonetheless, when the case reached the U.S. Supreme Court in 1917, the court ruled in favor of Hitchman, holding that yellow dog contracts were legally binding agreements—thus opening the door for innumerable injunctions against the union (*Hitchman Coal and Coke Co. v. Mitchell, et. al.* 245 U.S. 229 [1917]). Although World War I temporarily halted further litigation, in 1927 the U.S. Circuit Court of Appeals advanced the precedent set in *Hitchman* when it awarded injunctive relief against the UMWA to 315 southern West Virginia coal operators (*United Mine Workers v. Red Jacket Consolidated Coal and Coke Co.*, 18 F2d 839).

During this period, then, the only place miners possibly had to turn for legal recourse was Congress, where a few outspoken advocates of organized labor championed their cause. The net result of this advocacy was a considerable amount of time in the 1910s and 1920s devoted to congressional investigations into labor conditions in West Virginia, but no substantive legislative measures to resolve labor disputes. The most significant of these investigations began in 1922 when bituminous coal miners called a general nationwide strike. Senator William Borah—a staunch advocate of nationalizing the coal industry—successfully petitioned Congress to create the U.S. Coal Commission, which would thoroughly investigate labor relations and living conditions in the nation's coal fields, with the end goal of generating a national coal policy. The investigation turned out to be a double-edged sword. On the one hand, the commission failed to achieve its ultimate goal of producing a national coal policy to regulate the industry (Lunt, 1992: p. 165). Moreover, it endorsed the dehumanizing ideology of "scientific management" in order to bolster cost-effective methods of mining (Dix, 1977: p. 64; U.S. Senate, 1925: pt. 3, p. 1913). On the other hand, the Borah Commission yielded a multivolume comprehensive report containing thousands of pages of raw data detailing deplorable living and working conditions at mines nationwide, especially in West Virginia. Significantly, the commission made a firm stand in opposition to the Supreme Court's *Hitchman* decision regarding yellow dog contracts, labeling such contracts as "a source of economic irritation, and no more justifiable than any other form of contract which debars the individual from employment solely because of membership ... in any organization" (U.S. Senate, 1925: pt. 1, p. 179). Again, Congress did not act immediately on the Coal Commission's meager recommendations. However, the effort and intentions of the commission reflected a growing federal cognizance of the need to protect the rights of miners. Indeed, the 1920s were watershed years for coal miners who sought to secure better living and working conditions and fundamental rights as human beings.

The 1920s, however, also saw a momentary but profound decline in union membership, especially in West Virginia. Many miners were demoralized by their losses in the major drives to bring the union to southern West Virginia. Adding to their burden was the fact that World War I had created an artificial market for coal, resulting in postwar overproduction, which meant that even if mines were unionized it would not be profitable to operate full time. In the midst of a lagging coal economy, and with the legal system against them, miners in southern West Virginia abandoned the union for low-paying employment as nonunion workers. Yellow dog contracts and below average wages abounded. For instance, in 1926 the average West Virginia miner worked 225 days a year while earning an average of $3.75 per day for an annual income of $843.75; the average Illinois miner worked only 162 days per year, earning an average of $7.50 per day for an annual income of $1,215 (Lunt, 1992: pp. 16, 167). Such were the conditions for miners and their families, who consitituted the majority of the population in southern West Virginia in the 1920s. And although New Deal reforms were just around the corner, by that time no less than fifty thousand men, women, and children had been evicted from their homes in West Virginia coal camps as a result of their failure to sign or abide by yellow dog contracts (Lee, 1969: pp. 82–83).

How did Wyoming County figure into this scheme of state and national politics and labor disputes? With the exception of evidence that Isaac T. Mann (owner of the Itman mine) was involved as president of Pocahontas Fuel Company in a conspiracy with United States Steel to monopolize southern West Virginia coal (U.S. Senate, 1922: p. 649), references to Wyoming County are conspicuously lacking in the manifold congressional investigations into the state's coalfields. Very little evidence exists of union activity and labor

strife in Wyoming County prior to the New Deal legislation man-
dating employees' right to join unions. Operators of the Winding
Gulf Field evidently negotiated union contracts prior to World War
I but reneged in the aftermath of the *Hitchman* decision and the
postwar economic crisis (Lunt, 1992: p. 67). I found no one who had
participated in, or remembered relatives participating in, the mine
wars or any major strikes prior to the Depression, with the exception of one man whose father had left Wyoming County to work in
the McDowell County mines (Cook, 1996c). However, there were
vague recollections of labor strife in the 1920s. One man who mined
for a period in the 1920s before securing employment on the railroad
recalled the following peculiar incidents occurring in certain mines
near Mullens when miners expressed opposition to their working
conditions: "They'd cut the men off and hire their wives. They would
pay their wives a cheaper wage. . . . They'd hire the women to work.
Except some wouldn't do it. And sometimes they'd hire the kids—
five, six. . . . Yeah, some places they would get women. A lot of them
wouldn't go. Some miners wouldn't work if women were in the
mines. But they'd pay them a real low wage."

Child labor was no rarity in any of the coalfields nationwide in the
1920s, but nowhere (to my knowledge) is there a record of women
having been recruited for mine labor prior to the 1960s. Indeed, the
coming of industry spawned a sharper gendered division of labor in
Wyoming County, as will be discussed more in the next chapter.
Some women had had prior experience digging coal from small coal
banks for home use (Cook, 1996c), but it is apparent that the operators who sought to employ women intended such measures to be a
means of suppressing labor opposition through emasculation.

Unionism apparently did not find a devoted following in Wyoming County prior to the Depression. Why? First, because coal
mining was a relatively young endeavor in Wyoming County, and
many mining families were at least part-time farmers of their own
land until the 1930s and 1940s. Second, coal operators in the county
actively recruited foreign-born and black miners with the intent of
discouraging solidarity within the labor force (Bailey, 1973). Every

major mine had separate sections and schools for blacks and whites, some even for foreigners (Cook, 1996c; Bowman, 1965). By 1933, when the county's population had reached 20,926, there were 1,019 white miners, 128 foreign-born miners, and 485 black miners in the county (Bowman, 1965: pp. 52, 264). These numbers not only reflect the relatively small percentage of people engaged in mining at the time, but also they suggest that the nonwhite workforce was sufficiently large to deter homogeneity and discourage the solidarity necessary for the miners to form an effective union.[6] Finally, most major mining operations in Wyoming County prior to the Depression took measures to satisfy their workers. Camps were generally cleaner and better-equipped than in other southern parts of the state, and wages were on the whole higher. Yellow dog contracts were undoubtedly in use among county coal operators, but there is evidence that some county operators provided a fallback for miners blackballed elsewhere with no questions asked. One man recalled, "That's how come [my uncle] to have to leave McDowell County. See, he was on that organizing, and they blackballed him, and he couldn't get a job nowhere in McDowell County, and he moved in with us. And we moved off Indian Creek and that whole family moved to Pierpoint with us, and he got a job there at Otsego."

It would seem, then, that Wyoming County miners fared markedly better than miners in other parts of the state vis-à-vis the politics of the coal industry. However, many miners were beholden to company stores and became increasingly dependent on them for their provender during the Depression, and many of those with land were forced to sell to make ends meet. Although the company system was not as firmly entrenched, as coal operators did not have absolute control over the county government, for many—especially foreigners and blacks—the company still controlled their purse strings and required employees to abide by certain rules within and without the mines if they wished to retain their jobs. Most significantly, Wyoming County was still part of West Virginia and subject to a state political system dominated by coal barons. Had miners in the county made a concerted effort to unionize, their drive would surely have been squelched, as in Mingo and Logan Counties, though local officials may not have played an integral role. In short, although Wyoming County was not yet fully integrated into the colonial structure that bound most of the state, it was certainly not isolated from it.

Colonialism and Dependency: Early Stages

This chapter has dealt extensively with the development of a colonial political economy in the state of West Virginia, which was the result of industrial domination over the newly formed state government after the Civil War. Much of the state, and southern West Virginia in particular, became systematically exploited through the manipulation of state law and local politics by industrial magnates— most notably coal operators. I have argued that Wyoming County, due to its physiographic isolation and solidly divided political alliances, was industrialized at a much later date and that the company system that was a cornerstone for the coal operators' colonial control of much of West Virginia did not become as firmly entrenched in Wyoming as in other southern West Virginia counties prior to the Great Depression. Moreover, although agricultural decline came immediately on the heels of the initial industrial thrust into Wyoming County, it occurred much later than in other parts of West Virginia and Appalachia, and complete dependency of many local residents on external markets was slower to develop than in other areas.

This does not mean, however, that colonial processes were not at work in Wyoming County prior to the Depression, nor that the seeds for dependency were not sown and sprouting. Agricultural production was already in decline, complicated by a waxing pattern of environmental destruction and a rising population. Moreover, the industry-controlled state political system was already taking a heavy toll on the county; wage labor became more necessary, partly to meet new tax burdens. Eager entrepreneurs were flooding into the county in search of mineral wealth and labor power, and few legal constraints inhibited their unilateral extraction of these resources. Those residents who still owned land—and a considerable number still did into the 1930s—were in a precarious position. Industrialists already enjoyed a discretionary control over major channels for capital, primarily the local banks, and the law was virtually in their hands. The Great Depression, then, provided an opportunity for industrialists to gain access to unalienated lands, as many residents who still held their lands to raise the cash necessary to pay taxes and to obtain commodities that they could not home-produce.

6 THE EPOCH
OF PERPETUAL DEPENDENCY

The New Deal to the Present

The Great Depression brought drastic changes to Wyoming County. For many coal miners it meant a greater frequency of unemployment in the midst of an already declining coal industry. Ironically, Wyoming County saw a major expansion in coal production in the 1930s, though still not reaching a level of output comparable with neighboring counties. The Depression also marked the beginning of overt federal intervention in the region. Coal miners won major victories with the passage of labor reform legislation, and the Roosevelt administration directed a multitude of federal agencies to provide relief opportunities for displaced workers and farmers. These reforms, however, proved to be a double-edged sword for the Appalachian region. They ultimately reinforced dependency by creating an additional channel for such relations—namely, federal largess. Although economic dependency was delayed in Wyoming County by virtue of the fact that it was slow to be dominated by a single industry in the first place, it was also during the 1930s that the coal industry secured a major footing in the county. This chapter examines developments during the 1930s and how they have affected Wyoming County. I argue that colonial processes are still at work in the county because local residents have no control over the county's land base, and they experience severely limited political efficacy in terms of gaining such control. I also argue that relations of dependency are firmly entrenched and seemingly immutable under the county's current economic and political circumstances.

New Deal Labor Reform

In 1931, of the 112,000 miners in West Virginia, one third were unemployed and another third worked only two days a week (Lunt, 1992: p. 177). UMWA president John L. Lewis (who in spite of allegations of socialist activity was a Republican who believed in laissez-faire economics) was convinced that government intervention was the only hope for saving the coal industry and bolstering the welfare of workers. Beginning in the late 1920s, Lewis had put increasing pressure on a number of pro-labor Democrats in Congress, and ultimately he shifted his own alliance to that party (Dix, 1988: pp. 187–88). As economic conditions grew worse for miners, they found that they had little to lose and much to gain by voting in opposition to their employers' candidates. With Lewis's successes, they began to realize a measure of political efficacy through the Democratic ticket. In 1930, for example, when James Elwood James secured the Republican nomination for West Virginia's open U.S. Senate seat, the Democratic party made public the fact that as a mine operator he had used yellow dog contracts extensively. They rallied miners to successfully defeat James in the election (Lee, 1969: p. 82). In the midst of economic crisis, federal reforms to labor law brought a ray of hope to miners.

Democratic senator George W. Norris, chairman of the Judiciary Committee, sponsored the first reform. In the late 1920s, Norris had become the most outspoken opponent of yellow dog contracts in the Senate. With a progressive Democratic majority seizing both houses in 1932, he secured passage of the Norris-LaGuardia Act (47 St. 70), which prohibited courts from enforcing individual employment contracts. This act presaged the critical reform legislation in the National Industrial Recovery Act (NIRA) of 1933 (48 St. 195). The NIRA made the coal and other industries subject to federal regulation with

the goal of promoting "the fullest use of production power through
. . . reduction of unemployment, improvement of labor standards,
and otherwise to rehabilitate industry and to conserve natural resources" (48 St. 195). Most significantly, the act guaranteed the
right of employees to organize and bargain collectively and sanctioned the negotiation of better wages and working conditions. It
also encouraged the establishment of a national coal code, which in
turn prohibited such practices as blacklisting and requiring employees to do business exclusively at company stores. Ultimately it led to
the abolition of the scrip system. It also gave miners the right to
have a Union checkweighman at each mine to ensure that their tonnage was measured fairly.

Within a week of the passage of the NIRA, a West Virginia union
organizer reported that the job of organizing all the miners in the
state was nearly complete (Dubofsky and Van Tine, 1977: p. 185).
Indeed, by year's end, under government protection almost every
mine in West Virginia was organized (Lee, 1969: p. 12). With their
collective bargaining power protected by law, Union miners in the
Appalachian coalfields saw wages rise from forty-eight cents per ton
in 1933 to ninety-three cents per ton in 1939 (Dix, 1988: p. 200).

The passage of the NIRA paved the way for other legal reforms directed toward the coal industry. In 1935, West Virginia passed a law
explicitly prohibiting the mine guard system for good (Lee, 1969:
pp. 139–40). Federal mine safety laws also became more strictly enforced, especially after 1940 when Congress authorized the Bureau
of Mines to exercise regulatory power over coal operations. For example, between 1930 and 1948 mine fatalities dropped from 2.9 per
million man hours to 1.35 per million man hours (U.S. Bureau of
Mines, 1950: p. 44). The record was not nearly as impressive for
Wyoming County, however, where between 1933 and 1960 there
were at least 40 mine fatalities and 1,375 injuries (Bowman, 1965:
pp. 258, 262–66).

The New Deal labor reforms, though sorely needed, were also
characterized by significant shortcomings. On the one hand, the
company system met its demise. Miners now had collective bargain-

ing power. On the other hand, these reforms came at a time when the coal industry was dwindling, and operators could scarcely afford to pay miners the higher wages they demanded. As will be illustrated in a later section, this would ultimately have crippling effects on the economy of much of central Appalachia. Yet ironically, at a time when the coal industry was experiencing a national decline, it was just beginning to thrive in Wyoming County.

Expansion of the Coal Industry in Wyoming County

Some of the largest mines in Wyoming County were established during the Great Depression. In 1938, for example, Eastern Associated Company opened a state-of-the-art mine and camp at Kopperston, which by 1940 produced more than one-third of the county's coal. In 1933, there were only twelve large coal operations in the county but by 1950, there were forty-four deep mines and four strip mines. With the opening of new mines in Wyoming County, coal production rose steadily while the industry elsewhere was suffering. The county had produced 4,461,428 tons of coal in 1933. That figure rose steadily until it reached a plateau at 9,690,107 in 1962 (Bowman, 1965: pp. 260–67).

It is difficult to ascertain precisely why the coal industry was more successful in Wyoming County than in other portions of the Appalachian coalfields during the Depression, but it probably had to do with the fact that, for the first time, many residents were faced with a real economic crisis from which the safety net of subsistence farming could not fully protect them—and thus they were willing to work for less money than people elsewhere. Miners everywhere found themselves in a situation that required compromise, particularly in Wyoming County. Although union contracts had increased wages in most of central Appalachia, in Wyoming County wages in 1933 averaged forty-three cents per ton and increased only to sixty-two cents by 1940 (Bowman, 1965: pp. 263–64). West Virginia's property taxes did drop during the Depression (in 1933), but the people's need for self-produced goods did not lessen, and facing a decrease in work hours and wages (if not outright unemployment) many families were forced to sell their lands at unreasonably low prices, as indicated by some of the oral testimony in the previous chapter (Cook, 1996c; 1996d). With no home of their own, their only options were federal relief, out-migration, or employment in the mines.

Moreover, enforcement of new federal mining labor standards was not a foregone conclusion, especially in the midst of such a severe economic crisis. There is evidence that in some mines blacklisting of subversive employees continued. And even when miners' wages did increase, coal companies commonly compensated by boosting rents on company-owned houses and prices in company stores, thus allowing mine families' survival at the price of perpetual debt (Dix, 1988: pp. 201, 207). In fact, coal companies found many ways to manipulate employees' wage increases in the company's favor. For example, one Wyoming County woman who worked in the Mariana Smokeless Coal Company store in the late 1940s reported that the company deducted a dollar a month from each employee's paycheck for the maintenance of the company-owned church, whether they attended it or not (Cook, 1996c).

The Depression, then, brought about the complete absorption of many Wyoming County residents into a coal-dominated economy. This was accompanied by further changes in the already altered preindustrial social and economic order. First, it was probably during the Depression that the greatest number of local families lost their lands, often due to an inability to pay taxes. While time did not allow for a thorough examination of the often incomplete land records in Wyoming County, material from informal interviews suggested that this was the case, especially in the southern part of the county. This point has been touched on several times, and bears repeating, as it was the mass alienation of lands that set the stage for rigid relationships of dependency. By 1940, the majority of the county's land base was probably in the hands of absentee owners. Although at that time there were a multitude of such owners, as time progressed most of these lands would fall into the hands of a select few. Presently, about 90 percent of the county's mineral rights are owned by no more than ten absentee corporations (Cook, 1995, 1996c).

With the majority of the county's land controlled by absentees, many of the county's residents became dependent on these absentees for a place to live. For those who were native to the region, life in a coal camp was a radical and not necessarily pleasant change. Those who grew up on large, open family farms where the nearest neighbor might be over a mile away suddenly found themselves in organized, crowded communities where the nearest house might be only a few feet away. This meant that extended families were no longer necessarily associated with specific localities, which complicated cooperative networks. In short, people found themselves akin to industrial workers in a quasi-urban environment, engaged in a cash economy and increasingly dependent on strangers. With a growing nonfarm population, commercial centers in Wyoming County grew into virtual urban centers offering a coal-based service economy. Towns like the three primary commercial centers of Oceana, Mullens, and the county seat of Pineville drew crowds of miners and their families on the weekends to their large department stores, movie theaters, and various saloons and restaurants (Cook, 1996c; Eller, 1982: ch. 5).

While coal camps were intended to be self-contained, they were not homogeneous. Although the practice of separating white, immigrant, and black residencies (and schools) endured for some time in the coalfields, people from diverse backgrounds living in a small space could not help but interact. This often resulted in crime and violence. It should be noted that although West Virginia was not devoid of racial and ethnic tensions in the days of mass industrialization (approximately 1880–1940), such tensions were comparatively mild compared to other states. This was probably due in part to the union policy of encouraging solidarity among its members (Bailey, 1973: p. 161). But in a setting where the intimacy of preindustrial family, church, and community ties had been disrupted, the old mechanisms for social control were lacking. While both civil and criminal cases were heard before state circuit courts in West Virginia in preindustrial times, at the turn of the twentieth century in coal camps crime became so rampant that the state legislature provided for the establishment of separate criminal courts (Lee, 1969: p. 7). In other words, the introduction of people from divergent social backgrounds challenged existing social norms and resulted in a state of what Durkheim called *anomie*—or social disorder due to ill-defined tenets of acceptable behavior in a given society (Durkheim, 1964). Yet due to the late development of the coal industry in Wyoming County, a criminal court was not established there until 1949 (Bowman, 1965: p. 150).

Perhaps the most profound change wrought by the invasion of the coal industry—a change intimately related to land alienation—was the sudden imposition of a rigid class structure. This is not to say that social classes did not exist in preindustrial times. There were certain families in Wyoming County, particularly those who owned plantations worked by slave labor prior to the Civil War, who were regarded as local elites. Yet in preindustrial times, most farm families controlled their own destinies and worked for no one but themselves. However, in a setting where very few residents owned land, and where coal companies owned housing and controlled jobs and store prices, a very pronounced class system came into existence in which socioeconomic mobility was virtually impossible.

Coal operators, in turn, frequently reinforced this class structure by constructing large houses for themselves perched high above the town at some distance from the workers' tiny houses, but in plain view of everyone (Eller, 1982: p. 196). One of the earliest commercial operators in Wyoming County, J. C. Sullivan, built on a hillside an elaborate home with Greek columns (Cook, 1996c). A more subtle but potent means of expressing the prevailing power structure in coal-dominated communities occurred through community naming. This occurred throughout the Appalachian coal belt (Caudill, 1963; Gaventa, 1978: p. 143). In some cases, operators simply built new communities and named them after themselves or family members or prominent financiers, as in the case of Itman and Glen Rogers. In other cases, they replaced earlier place names with names of their choosing, such as the community of Nuriva, which was formerly called Trace Fork (Cook, 1996c).

Summing up these skewed power relations in the era of the coal camps, Eller writes about a miner's life: "Except for his decision to stay or leave, persons other than himself made the decisions affecting his life. Thus, he was individualistic, fatalistic, and present-oriented, and the powerless situation in the company towns augmented these traits" (1982: p. 196). The traits Eller describes have been used to explain forms of mountaineer resistance to industrial domination (Knipe and Lewis, 1971) and to attribute underdevelopment in the coalfields to the "backward" cultural values of mountaineers (e.g., Ball, 1968). While these values did (and continue to) exist among many natives of central Appalachia, miners were certainly not passive victims of industry, as evidenced by their fervent unionism.

All this can help to illuminate how industrialization affected the role of women in Wyoming County. In chapter 4, I suggested that if preindustrial society in the area was not egalitarian, then at least the gendered division of labor was not as sharp as scholars such as Eller suggest. Domination by the coal industry, however, seems to have had a paradoxical influence on gender roles where labor was concerned.

First of all, the development strategies employed by industrialists in the region were clearly guided by classical modernization ideologies, which espoused binary oppositions between the household (female) domain and the public (male) domain (Wallerstein, 1983: pp. 39–51; Scott, 1995; Dunaway, 1997). Included in the public domain was the realm of wage labor, for which there was no place for women in the early days of industrialization in the mountains. Evidence of this lies in the previously noted revelation concerning the way in which certain coal operators near Mullens attempted to deal with labor disputes in the 1920s—that is, by offering to replace disgruntled miners with miners' wives. Most male miners refused to work with women, indicating that they accepted mainstream gender ideology.

Shortly after the onslaught of industry, however, space did develop for women in the wage labor force in the form of domestic work. Women were commonly hired to clean the houses of coal barons, serve as matrons in boarding houses, or do laundry for itinerant workers. In time, clerical positions opened for women in coal company stores. The hiring of women in the workforce outside of the mines was expedited by two conditions: the death of husbands or fathers in the mines and the greater need to pool household incomes—the latter circumstance becoming all the more urgent during the Depression. A number of female participants in this study reported having to go to work at an early age because their fathers had died in mining accidents. One man said his mother supplemented the family's meager compensation income following her husband's death in the late 1920s through gardening and hunting—traditionally regarded as "men's" activities (Cook, 1996c).

Ultimately, women's exclusion from mine labor led to a diversification of occupations and to more time spent outside the household domain. A Mullens woman related that she began working at an early age following the loss of her father, a coal miner, "I babysat and cleaned houses when I was real young, but when I was fourteen I went to the courthouse in Pineville and got a work permit that allowed me to work in G. C. Murphy's [department store]. I started there working as a clerk, and . . . when I was in the ninth grade I went to Wyoming General Hospital as a switchboard operator and a receptionist in the evening after school. And I worked there until they trained me for bookkeeper, and I graduated high school and went there as full time bookkeeper." The same woman eventually became a teller at the local bank. Meanwhile, her brothers entered the mines and the military. Thus, although women were essentially barred from the mines as workers, the employment opportunities available to them brought about a relative equilibrium in many households. For those engaged in part-time subsistence—a household activity—the tasks involved were generally shared equally between men and women (Cook, 1996c; 1996d). Later, beginning in the 1970s, women in southern West Virginia were able to secure employment as coal miners.

For most people in Wyoming County, the aforementioned socio-economic changes occurred in the midst of the Great Depression. They could not have occurred at a more confounding time, for in the wake of a national economic crisis, the federal government sought to soften the blow of the Depression through perhaps the greatest federal thrust into local affairs since the Civil War. But in spite of good intentions underlying the federal relief and reform programs of the 1930s, their ultimate results for central Appalachia were of dubious benefit.

The New Deal and Dependency

The American coal industry was already declining rapidly in the 1920s for manifold reasons. First, the opening of coalfields in central Appalachia had led to overproduction, as the vertical slopes of the mountains allowed easier access to coal veins at lower costs, and transportation and labor costs were also low. Overproduction of Appalachian coal created fierce competition for markets and led to a reduction of coal prices. World War I also contributed to overproduction by creating an artificial market, which would leave a postwar surplus of coal. Second, coal operators tried to compensate for their losses by raising rents on company houses and reducing employees' wages. This led to increased strikes and labor opposition, creating rifts in the industry. Third, by 1928 the overseas market for American coal was diminishing, as European mines were resuming their operations after a long postwar delay. Fourth, railroads and other coal-dependent industries were developing more efficient furnaces and engines that did not require as much coal for energy output. Finally, both consumers and various industries were turning increasingly toward fossil fuels other than coal and toward other forms of energy such as hydroelectric power (Eller, 1982: pp. 156–59; Dix, 1988: p. 126).

Then came the Depression and an unsurpassed national economic crisis that prompted emergency federal intervention. To many people around the nation, the various programs and reforms of the

New Deal seemed like a godsend. Apparently few foresaw their eventual adverse effects.

In his dependency analysis of the Appalachian region, Salstrom suggests that New Deal legislation and programs were ultimately harmful to the region as a whole for four principle reasons (1994: p. xxiv). First, the NIRA and certain federal employment programs hastened wage increases for Appalachian workers at a time when that tended to reduce the market share for their employers. Second, New Deal agricultural programs benefited mainly capital-intensive farms, which were uncommon in Appalachia. Third, the wages offered workers through federal relief programs such as the Work Progress Administration (WPA) often exceeded those affordable by private producers (including some coal producers), thus reinforcing the latter's exclusion from market production. And fourth, the vast amount of federal capital that entered the region through relief programs caused mountaineers to rely more heavily on hard currency. Whereas many transactions had formerly been conducted through bartering, such forms of exchange were often supplanted by a cash system. This, in turn, diminished the amount of industrial labor power subsidized by subsistence activities. These points merit elaboration and critique here in light of what was transpiring in Wyoming County during the Depression.

Salstrom is correct in pointing out the eventual adverse effects of legislation such as the NIRA in sanctioning wage increases. The act was far too late in coming, as it essentially called for an increase in workers' wages and coal prices, in addition to recognizing the right and power of collective bargaining, at a time when coal demands were dropping. Had the miners in Appalachia been able to organize at a much earlier date, Salstrom points out, the coal industry may have developed stability (1994: p. 90). The ill-effects of the NIRA will be discussed in greater detail in a later section, but at this point it is necessary to address Salstrom's assertion that subsistence farming could have continued to compensate for low wages. Salstrom argues that many miners and farmers throughout the region were able to survive through subsistence activities prior to the Depression and could have continued to do so had they simply not adapted to a cash economy. However, circumstances in Wyoming County suggest another possibility. Although it may be true that some subsistence farmers could have continued to sustain themselves without increased cash activity, many farmers had entered the wage labor force to meet state property tax burdens. The Depression forced many Wyoming County farmers to sell their lands to pay taxes. After 1925, coal production in Wyoming County dropped by over 65 percent during a six-year period and did not recover substantially until 1936 (Bowman, 1965: p. 266).[1] This meant that prior to and in the first years of the Depression, jobs in the mines were scarce, which meant that some small landowners who relied on mine wages to pay taxes probably accumulated significant back taxes, as affirmed by some of the participants in this study (Cook, 1995; 1996c).

This warrants a reconsideration of Salstrom's fourth point, which concerns bartering. Bartering continued within coal communities and between friends and neighbors in Wyoming County even after the Depression. It was simply a necessity. But with little or no land of their own, subsistence and bartering were not enough to contend with the burdens of company rentals and store prices, especially when miners' wages in the county were (in spite of union membership) somewhat lower than union averages. Thus, at least in Wyoming County, higher wages were necessary.

Salstrom's assessment of the harmful effects of New Deal agricultural endeavors is more on target, although again not fully applicable to Wyoming County. As he points out, the Agricultural Adjustment Act (AAA) of 1933 and concomitant programs of the Department of Agriculture were aimed at large-scale farming. If any Appalachian farmers hoped to benefit from these programs they had to follow specific federal guidelines dictating precisely how much and what they could produce. Of course, by that time there were few farmers in Wyoming County who might have remotely hoped to benefit from this program. At a time when subsistence agriculture was in high demand in the region, the AAA was of little use to its inhabitants (Salstrom, 1994: ch. 6). Notably, the U.S. Agriculture Department conducted a thorough study of economic and social conditions in the southern Appalachian region from 1929 to 1933, but its director, Lewis C. Gray, was more concerned with the relationship between ecology and economy than with social issues. One key recommendation of the survey was that part of the solution to Appalachia's economic and social problems lay in the "conversion of the land to public ownership and its utilization for public forests, parks, or game preserves" (U.S. Department of Agriculture, 1935: p. 6). As Salstrom and others have pointed out, this basically gave the federal government license to dispossess scores of Appalachian people of their lands while assuming a position alongside private corporations as absentee landowners (Kahn, 1978; Branscome, 1978; Salstrom, 1994: p. 107). Although there was some delay, the federal government finally did assume control of thousands of acres of Wyoming County land in the 1970s when the Army Corps of Engineers began construction of R. D. Bailey Lake and Reservoir.

Finally, Salstrom argues that federal relief programs such as the WPA and other programs—which evolved into what is now welfare—expedited dependency in Appalachia by luring people away from subsistence farming. According to Salstrom, before the New Deal, most of the region's population relied heavily on subsistence farming for survival, but by midcentury a significant portion of the region's people were dependent on welfare. Again, his argument is that many Appalachian farm residents did not need relief money but that they simply adjusted to it. Focusing on West Virginia, Salstrom points out that in 1932 cumulative relief payments were barely over $2 million, but between 1933 and 1940 they totaled $320 million. Specifically, he mentions that the 1940 census of agriculture lists 27 percent of the state's population as farm residents, and he suggests that the percentage of these who were working for the WPA was virtually as high as the percentage of West Virginia's *nonfarm* residents who were working for the WPA (1994: pp. 116–18, 166 n.29).

It is difficult to ascertain the extent to which Wyoming County residents took advantage of New Deal programs, as records for such programs were poorly kept and such programs often required people to leave the place of their residence to go to work. A ccc camp was located near Pineville for a period in the 1930s, but all of its inhabitants were from other states (Bowman, 1965: pp. 453–54). However, what is important here is the structure that was put into place by New Deal welfare programs and how it endured and transformed preexisting alternatives to welfare. As early as 1850, the county had had a "poor farm" where debtors, orphans, and indigent people could find shelter and food. This farm was ultimately managed by the state. But the people who went to the farm had to *work* to earn their keep (Bowman, 1965: pp. 157–58). Although New Deal programs such as the wpa provided work, various others provided channels for payment without labor. In an area where job availability had always been irregular, this distracted people from depending on their own means for survival. One man who grew up during the Depression (and whose father had to sell his land during that period) lamented, "Now the government takes care of everybody. Poor people lines up at the welfare office instead of lining up at the cornfield."

The above statement seems to add weight to Salstrom's argument. In all fairness, however, it should be noted that although Appalachia is often stereotyped as a welfare region—an assertion backed by various statistics—most of what is loosely classified as welfare in Wyoming County comes in the form of social security checks to retired people and pension and black lung checks to retired miners (Cook, 1996c). Moreover, the disproportionate occurrence of absentee land ownership in the county rendered the possibility of extensive subsistence farming problematic. Subsistence, after all, did not pay taxes, and when land was lost as a result of tax burdens, what alternative did people have other than increased wage activity? Thus, one cannot ignore the relationship between colonial processes that took the form of land alienation supported by state legal mechanisms and the development of dependency in Wyoming County.

Whatever criticisms can be leveled at Salstrom's analysis, it must be admitted that the Great Depression and the concomitant New Deal legislation did increase economic dependency on external forces in Wyoming County, even if complete dependency did not seem immediately apparent. By the mid-1930s, Wyoming County began to experience its own coal boom and the opening of new mines was soon hastened by the onset of World War II. Hopes that were fostered by this boom, however, ultimately translated into a false sense of security.

Labor Relations, Resistance, Dependency

The New Deal brought major reforms in the area of labor relations, particularly through provisions of the NIRA, which guaranteed the right of miners to organize in unions and to engage in collective bargaining with coal operators. With the backing of the NIRA and federal Coal Codes, the union quickly negotiated better wages, a pension fund, and a comprehensive health plan into which coal operators made payments, and safer working conditions. Moreover, with the law now on its side, the union became a potent force to be reckoned with—so potent that coal operators soon had to find innovative ways to undermine its efficacy at the expense of thousands of miners.

The provisions of the NIRA that sanctioned collective bargaining and especially wage increases presented an untimely contradiction when the coal industry was facing a serious economic crisis. No longer able to reduce wages, operators sought other means of compensation for their losses in a suffering market. The most immediate solution was rapid mechanization of their operations (Dix, 1988: p. 198). Mining machines for cutting and loading were in use in some mines as early as the 1870s, but were not readily adopted by most American coal operators, in part due to their expense but primarily due to abundant cheap labor. As long as miners could be prohibited from organizing for collective bargaining, hand loading was more profitable, especially when miners spent some of their wages on company rents. But when the NIRA guaranteed the right of miners to bargain collectively, the tables turned. Thus, many coal operators during and after the Depression began to supplant human labor with more sophisticated technology, such as cutting and loading machines, that could mine more coal in a fraction of the time it took miners to do it by hand (Dix, 1977: pp. 25–27, 1988: p. 77–78). Most miners had long opposed mechanization, for they knew that it would mean the loss of many jobs. Moreover, mechanization would mean that the tonnage rate would be supplanted with a standard day wage, which might also mean a reduction in pay. Ironically, John L. Lewis endorsed the idea of mechanization, believing that it would stabilize the coal industry and protect the remaining jobs (Dix, 1988: pp. 164–68). Thus, the systematic mechanization of Appalachian mines began in earnest in the 1930s and became a uniform reality by the 1950s. This meant that thousands of miners lost their jobs, and in areas where coal dominated the local economy, many unemployed miners and their families saw no alternative but to leave home to find work (Dix, 1988: ch. 11; Salstrom, 1994: p. 84).

In Wyoming County, mechanization came with some of the earliest mines, such as Glen Rogers, which required some automation due to its 650–foot vertical shaft, but most mines were not fully mechanized until the 1950s. Nonetheless, the relationship between rapid coal production by machines and unemployment is well illustrated by Wyoming County statistics. In 1930, when the county's population was at 20,926, the county produced 2,238,864 tons of coal. In 1950, when the population peaked at 37,590, coal tonnage was 6,764,143. During the 1950s decade, mines mechanized rapidly in the midst of a postwar recession, and the population dropped to 34,836 in 1960, even though the amount of coal produced in the county that year exceeded 10 million tons (Bowman, 1965: pp. 52, 267). Nearly all of the participants in this study, miners or otherwise, attributed the county's high rate of unemployment and out-migration primarily to the mechanization of the mines (Cook, 1996c; 1996d).

Mechanization would have transpired sooner or later, so it would be unjust to suggest that the UMWA was solely responsible for the loss of miners' jobs to machines. As Salstrom suggests, had the union gained solid legal footing prior to the Depression, the coal industry might have been more stable in the first place. However, the union did eventually constitute a formidable source of dependency for miners, as it was the conduit through which they found legal recourse and through which they hoped to influence the stability and conditions of their jobs.

Unfortunately, by the time all miners gained the legal right to belong to the union, it was no longer a democratic organization. The growing political efficacy of the UMWA in the late 1920s stemmed from the fact that its president, John L. Lewis, had gained autocratic control and managed to stifle internal opposition factions. This meant that the fate of thousands of miners lay in the hands of a few leaders who decided when to strike and what to place on the negotiating table (Finley, 1972; Dubofsky and Van Tine, 1977). If the union leadership called for a general strike, miners in local union districts had to join, regardless of how satisfied they were with their own working conditions. Following World War II, general strikes were almost an annual event as the union exercised its legally sanctioned right to challenge coal operators for more and more amenities. Of course, during strikes miners were not working and thus not receiving pay. They had to rely instead on the union relief fund, which was rarely a dependable source of income. The 1948 general strike, for example, lasted 120 days. Miners nationwide lost $106,274,000 in wages, the union relief fund lost $4,500,000, and the UMWA was fined $1,400,000 in contempt of court charges when Lewis falsely alleged that a strike had not been officially called (Lee, 1969: pp. 165–68). Union losses, of course, had to be made up through increased membership dues.

Strikes had additional adverse effects on the economic welfare of miners. Not only did they encourage further mechanization, but if miners were unemployed for long periods with minimal relief from the union, they often turned to company stores to purchase the necessities on credit, thus placing them in debt (Cook, 1996c). Moreover, while some strikes were well justified, Lewis developed a habit of asking for too much at the negotiating table, which he usually got. In the 1948 union contract, for example, in addition to substantial pay raises, Lewis slipped in provisions requiring miners to work only when they were "willing and able," and allowing him to call miners off work at his discretion for "national days of mourning" (Lee, 1969: p. 168).

While Lewis had achieved much for American miners, his autocratic rule unfortunately set a precedent that would be abused by subsequent union leaders. In the 1950s and 1960s, the union grew increasingly dictatorial. Leaders began to call strikes and cut deals at the negotiating table and behind the scenes to bolster their own interests rather than those of rank and file miners. In 1969, incumbent president Tony Boyle defeated reform candidate Joseph (Jock) Yablonski for the leadership of the union. Yablonski helped to lead a West Virginia based reform movement called Miners for Democracy to change the autocratic character of the union. When Yablonski continued to drive for the restoration of members' rights, Boyle had him and his family assassinated (Gaventa, 1980: ch. 7). Although Boyle was tried and convicted, union leadership continued to ignore the interests of ordinary miners, as evidenced by the conclusion of the 1977 general strike in which union leaders virtually sacrificed the miners' comprehensive health plan at the negotiating table.

In the long run, union activity had a two-pronged effect in southern West Virginia. Critics of the union often point out that high unemployment rates among miners resulted because the miners "struck themselves out of their jobs" by asking for too much, causing coal prices to rise and some mines to shut down (Lee, 1969: p. 174). While there is a degree of truth to this, it is not an adequate explanation. The mining industry is exploitative by nature, and without formidable union opposition it will always opt to place profit before concern for the labor force. The argument is often made that it is now cheaper to buy coal (and other products such as steel that rely on coal for their production) from overseas markets. In truth, however, most major coal corporations are part of multinational conglomerates, which means that they already own overseas interests. While they may find labor costs cheaper in other countries at any given moment, they still hold reserves in West Virginia with the intent of extracting them under favorable economic conditions. Moreover, companies such as U.S. Steel hold their own coal reserves, often called "captive mines." Thus, they have fewer indirect costs to worry about in producing coal for steel production. USX (formerly U.S. Steel) is both the largest producer of coal and employer of miners in Wyoming County, producing over six million tons a year and employing nine hundred people (Wyoming County Chamber of Commerce, n.d.).

Although some mines have closed and others have reduced their labor force as a result of union demands, still others have responded by offering better wages and benefits to nonunion members. They are able to do so because loopholes in the 1935 Wagner Act and related legislation exempt small operations from mandatory unionization. These "truck mines" usually employ no more than fifteen workers and ship coal in large trucks to processing plants in cities such as Huntington, West Virginia, rather than pay railroad freight rates. Unfortunately, these "scab" mines have not compensated for the thousands of jobs lost over the years.

Views on the union have always been mixed in Wyoming County, even among members. In the early years (after the NIRA) miners in the county joined the UMWA with fervor (Feller, n.d.). In 1970, while Tony Boyle was in office, Wyoming County miners rallied with the support of neighboring union subdistricts over Boyle's failure to maintain the disabled miners' pension fund, threatening wildcat strikes if the matter was not corrected. Apparently the threat to Boyle's authority issuing from southern West Virginia was enough, for soon thereafter Boyle began to lobby Congress for legislation to protect disabled miners' federal benefits regardless of union income (*Independent Herald*, 2 Jul. 1970: p. 4; 13 Aug. 1970: p. 13).

Today, local union enthusiasm is lukewarm. "See, everybody don't want to be union anymore," one man stated, " 'cause them guys put them mines in, you see, and they'll pay them better than union wages. . . . Ain't as strong as it used to be." A retired Red Jacket miner reflected on his long association with the union: "The union was pretty good to us. Down here miners—back in the fifties—they built their own hospitals and they had their own hospitals to go to.

It didn't cost you nothing. None of it." On the union in the 1970s, he said, "We had a president there that sold our hospitals, and sold out on us. And the union was messed up in its own wars. Puttin' in presidents that wasn't for the men, you know. Just for the money, and the companies. So they gave all of it away, just about. Just to put money in his own pocket." But he also expressed a renewed faith in the union: "I believe the union is making a slow comeback. . . . Cecil [Roberts—newly elected UMWA president]? He gets out more with the men."

In the 1930s the union was sorely needed, but as it developed into an autocratic machine a profound contradiction became evident. On one hand, the UMWA served to motivate the political consciousness of miners and to mobilize them in the fight for their own rights. Later, the union became yet another and possibly more devastating mechanism for colonial domination of West Virginia miners. Union activities ultimately had adverse effects not only on miners, but also on entire local economies in areas such as Wyoming County, where most economic activities—primarily railroads and services—revolved around the coal industry. But the union was a necessity. Without it, miners would have had no political voice. And today, despite a lagging coal industry, the union appears to be more responsive to the interests of rank and file members. Current president Cecil Roberts spends more time in the field than in the office. In West Virginia in 1996, the successful election of several major state and national political candidates hinged on endorsements not from the union bureaucracy but from the local membership. One can hope that this is a positive sign of a new era of political clout for miners based on their own awareness.

Cooperation, Subsistence, and Poverty

The ascendancy of the UMWA in the 1930s momentarily decentered the political control by coal operators in West Virginia and gave miners a new channel for influencing state and national politics for their own welfare. But the union was not always dependable when miners were unemployed during strikes or periods of industrial bust.

People in the coalfields had to look after themselves to survive the unpredictable cycles of prosperity and depletion so common to the coal industry. Salstrom (1994) argues that the programs of the New Deal propelled many mountaineers into welfare dependency when wage opportunities were bleak. However, subsistence farming and family- and community-based cooperative activities also remained an important and necessary means of survival in Wyoming County long after the Depression.

In her anthropological survey of southwestern Virginia coal communities, LaLone (1996) identified three levels of cooperative practices used by mining families to compensate for the economic pressures of the Depression, slack work periods, and low wages: household cooperation, interhousehold exchange, and community support systems (pp. 53–54). She identifies four primary household strategies: pooling multiple incomes of various household members, gardening, raising livestock, and gathering environmental resources (e.g., hunting; pp. 55–58).

LaLone's structural model—based on Polanyi's (1944) theory of modes of exchange—stresses the importance of *nonmarket* modes of economic activity in post–Depression Appalachia, particularly the mode of reciprocity, which predates more complex, hierarchical forms of exchange. Her model is fully applicable to Wyoming County, where cooperative strategies and activities are still common. The pooling of household incomes is, of course, common anywhere wages are low and the threat of poverty is constant. What is important here are the last three strategies, which are indicative of the degree to which Wyoming County families depended on subsistence after the Depression. Virtually every participant in this study reported relying on gardening, livestock, and/or hunting at some point in their lives, most continuing even into recent years (Cook, 1996c; 1996d). Even a retired railroad worker who lived his entire life in the town of Mullens reported owning milk cows into the 1940s, and he still raises a substantial garden. A Baileysville woman who worked for years in a company store while her husband worked in the mines told of how their subsistence actives kept them out of debt and free from needing welfare: "We had a big garden from 1949 'til 1970. And I canned, and my mother canned a lot. . . . We lived off it quite a bit as far as food was concerned. I remember like when the coal miners had a strike, we always had plenty of canned food, and potatoes, cabbage . . . and when the mines went back to work, we owed very little, just for sugar, or salt and cleaning supplies. And other people may owe thousands of dollars. . . . And we raised chickens, too. We had many a chicken fry at our house."

This quote indicates that some mining families, even though reliant on wage labor, managed to utilize supplemental subsistence activities to avoid the shackles of debt that forced others into greater dependency on nonsubsistence means of survival. This woman and her husband had their own small tract of land and were not as dependent on coal companies or the union as were those who lived on company property. However, even in coal camps most miners had small plots in which they kept kitchen gardens, raised chickens, and sometimes hogs.

Hunting and fishing provided vital dietary staples as well. Miners in camps along the Guyandotte River related how they relied on fish and game well into the 1960s, despite the pollution in the river (Cook, 1996c; 1996d). One Mariana resident boasted of never having to purchase vegetables or meat from the store unless he simply wanted to, "I'm a big deer eater. And rabbit. . . . We eat a lot of game. That's one reason my cholesterol's down. I don't eat any store bought meat."

In the category of interhousehold exchanges, LaLone found three forms of transactions employed: swapping or direct exchanges of goods, such as chickens for tools; cooperative labor- and gift-giving, such as barn raisings and corn huskings; and wheeling and dealing or exchange of services, such as boarding a neighbor's mules in exchange for their use (LaLone, 1996: pp. 58–60). These forms of balanced reciprocity seem to have been most affected by capitalist integration (Sahlins, 1965; Schneider, 1989: p. 99). As Salstrom (1994) would suggest, these forms of bartering have been supplanted (to a large degree) by cash exchanges in Wyoming County. This is particularly true of cooperative labor and mutual gift-giving activities that had served as important social functions in the past. As noted in earlier chapters, gatherings such as corn huskings brought families and neighbors together to share news and company, while aiding households in farming tasks that were not efficient without large amounts of intensive labor. But with a decrease in land for farming, and with a growing reliance on the trappings of modern technology, these networks have eroded significantly. A retired Mullens railroad worker expressed the sentiments of many in assessing these developments: "Young people now . . . they just can't understand it. They take all this here lights, water and gas, television, radios. . . . See, that's all they think. But I was back when there was very few radios. And people was closer together back then than they are now. They didn't have air condition so they could sit in their home and stay there. They got out in the community, visited with each other, and participated in a lot of things together. But now, they don't have time."

"Swapping" and "wheeling and dealing," on the other hand, are still common practices in Wyoming County and throughout southern West Virginia. For example, one family in the southern part of the county still barters dairy and poultry products for rifles, car parts, and until recently government commodities. Both husband and wife ran a scrap metal business for years to make do when the mines were not working. Through various bartering transactions, they managed to obtain building materials to add rooms to the once modest house they had purchased from the Red Jacket Coal Company in the 1970s (Cook, 1996c).

LaLone's third category of community support strategies entails: helping each other out—with no return favor expected, and relief activities—such as pooling food and money for sick neighbors (1996: pp. 60–62). These forms of generalized reciprocity are not *unique* to the coalfields but certainly do remain strong in Wyoming County (Sahlins, 1965; Schneider, 1989: p. 99). They seem to be most frequently conducted through the church to which a needy community member belongs, and less frequently through the physical community. A retired employee of Mariana Smokeless Coal commented on these informal networks in his community: "This is a funny community. You don't visit one another much. But if someone's gotten sick or there's a funeral, everybody will come out."

Clearly, preindustrial cooperative networks and strategies for survival have become modified, adapted to changing circumstances, or diminished significantly in Wyoming County. This can be attributed in part to changing settlement patterns. Moving off the farm, out of old localities associated with one's extended families, native residents found themselves in the restricted confines of coal camps or commercial centers. However, even in the coal camps they quickly established cooperative networks with neighbors out of necessity. What confounded cooperative networks and reliance on subsistence the most was the increasing reliance on the trappings of capitalist society and advanced technology, something that could hardly be avoided in the coal camps or commercial centers. Quite simply, people developed a greater need for cash to sustain the living conditions they had become used to. While Salstrom places blame on New Deal programs for increasing this dependency on cash, it is vital to recognize the role the coal industry played in initiating and perpetuating this need. The industry came to control virtually all of the land, including the houses which people had to rent, thus restricting the space needed for subsistence farming. With the majority of the county's land in absentee hands, it became less feasible for residents to let their livestock range freely in the hills. This diminished the amount of livestock families could maintain. And over the years the industry caused devastating environmental damage, not only complicating agricultural endeavors, but also endangering the wild game population and polluting local streams to the detriment of aquatic life. The natural occurrence of flash floods in these V-shaped valleys was severely augmented by deforestation, wholesale stripping of the earth's surface, and the ensuing erosion of hillsides and stream banks (Gidez, 1973). Bowman (1965) reported that from the 1930s to 1960s the Guyandotte and other streams were "thick with black coal refuse," and "unfit for fishing, swimming, or recreation of any other kind" (pp. 157, 258). Some county residents reported that by the 1940s, certain game species such as turkey had become extinct in the county, remaining so until the state Department of Natural Resources reintroduced them in the 1970s (Cook, 1996c).

Although the structural boundaries for dependency may have been firmly in place in Wyoming County by the end of the Depression, complete capitalist integration was a far more gradual process. Relationships of dependency were not fully manifested until the 1950s, when the county's population began to drop steadily. But what about that long transition period leading to the 1950s?

The popular image of the Appalachian coalfields past and present is one of sheer poverty. This is not, however, the image that Wyoming County residents had of themselves. Most of the workers in the mines and on the railroads, whether they were native residents or foreign born, shared one thing in common: they were accustomed to adapting to the worst that life could offer them. When the participants in this study were asked if they had ever thought of themselves as poor, the universal answer was no. "Everybody seemed to make it," remarked one man who grew up on Indian Creek during the Depression. "I don't ever remember no regrets. We was poor, but everybody else was too, so we didn't think nothin' about it." Similarly, a Baileysville woman who saw the loss of most of her family's land while growing up in the same period recalled, "We didn't realize that we were poor. But I wouldn't count us . . . with today's standards we would have been poor materially. But as far as having both the mother and father, and extended family, aunts, uncles, grandparents, cousins, we had all that." But the most striking statement came from a retired miner of forty years, who worked at various mines until settling with Red Jacket, "I've had it pretty easy. I don't reckon I've drawed unemployment but maybe three times. But I always just depended on myself. . . . If I didn't have it, I didn't have it. Did without."

As with the Monacans, the above statements evoke Precourt's (1983) argument that capitalist society needs a poverty population to define its own standards, and Appalachia has served that purpose due to its contrast with the *values* of metropolitan society. A common theme may be derived from the above statements (which are representative of all participants in this study): no one ever went without food, shelter, or clothing. Be that as it may, Wyoming County was becoming more completely drawn into unequal economic relations with metropolitan society from the time of the Depression onward. Today that relationship appears irreversible.

The Ramifications of Dependency

In a relationship of dependency, the economy of the subordinate region is heavily conditioned by that of the core region or country on which it depends (Dos Santos, 1970: p. 251). And so it is in Wyoming County, where ripples in the national economy create waves of economic turbulence or prosperity. Specifically, as evidenced by local economic and demographic trends of the last half of the 1900s, the *coal industry* determines how fluctuations in the national and global economy affect southern West Virginia.

The coal industry never fully recovered after the Depression; new sources of energy increasingly replaced coal. Nonetheless, coal production continued accelerating, even though coal operators took extreme measures to cut labor costs in the face of union demands. Some mines simply shut down, but most became increasingly mechanized and significantly cut the number of workers needed to produce coal. In 1950, there were 119,568 miners employed in West Virginia; by 1962 there were only 31,734 (Lee, 1969: p. 175). The mass drive to mechanize mines in the 1950s (and in many places earlier) translated into mass migration out of the region.

Beginning in 1950, then, a mass migration out of West Virginia occurred, which continues to date. Between 1950 and 1970, West Virginia was the only state east of the Mississippi to experience a population loss, even among its urban population. The state's overall population dropped from 3,005,552 in 1950 to 1,744,237 in 1970 (Dixon and Singh, 1977: pp. 69–70). To put it into greater perspective, West Virginia had a 6.2 percent population loss between 1960 and 1970, while the rest of the nation experienced a gain of 13.3 percent, and in 1971, the state ranked number one in population de-crease (Monmonier, 1977: p. 81; Adkins, 1977: p. 185). Between 1950 and 1960, Wyoming County's population dropped by 9.4 percent, from 37,590 to 34,836 (Bowman, 1965: p. 52). Moreover, that number has dropped further since 1960, reaching 29,000 in 1990, a 19.4 percent decrease from 1980 (Couto, 1994: p. 268).

The drastic decline in Wyoming County's population during the 1980s is indicative of the relationship between the local economy and the position of the coal industry in the national and global econ-omies. Approximately one-third of the county's workforce was em-ployed by the coal industry in the 1960s, while the other two-thirds were in the service sector (schools, health care, etc.), which depended on the coal industry for its own prosperity (*Independent Herald*, 1 Jul. 1965: p. 1). Meanwhile, in the midst of a national labor shortage, the national unemployment rate was 4.0 percent, lower than it had been in the postwar years, while it was at 6.0 percent and rising in West Virginia as a whole (Joshi, 1977: p. 96). By 1971, the state's unem-ployment rate was 7.2 percent, and West Virginia ranked forty-sixth in the nation in per capita income (U.S. Bureau of the Census, 1974: p. 396). While the rest of the nation appeared to be prospering (at least on paper) in the midst of a labor shortage, West Virginia seem-ingly defied fluctuations in the national economy because of a short-age of *skilled labor*. Specifically, the coal industry was experiencing another cycle of bust, but it continued to mechanize mines to a higher degree than ever. Thus, it required fewer and fewer workers to produce greater amounts of coal, and those who did work re-quired more technical training.

In the 1970s, West Virginia seemingly defied national economic trends once again. In the midst of the energy crisis, the nation expe-rienced an economic recession, with unemployment rates as high as 10 to 15 percent in major cities. In the West Virginia coalfields, however, unemployment was barely 6 percent, as the energy crisis fostered a renewed national dependence on coal. Thus, the state's per capita income rose from 70.7 percent of the national average in 1969 to 80 percent in 1989 (Lieble, 1977: p. 5; Couto, 1995: pp.

105–07). But the tables turned again in the 1980s as the end of the energy crisis sent the coal industry spiraling downward. The inception of the Reagan administration brought drastic budget cuts in federal social and economic development spending as well. By 1989, West Virginia's per capita income ratio had dropped back to 70.7 percent of the national average. Wyoming County was one of the hardest hit counties in the entire Appalachian region. Its per capita income dropped 17.6 percent in that decade to 50.9 percent of the national average in 1989, and the unemployment rate rose to 12.9 percent in 1990 (Couto, 1994: pp. 88, 268; 1995: p. 109).

It is no surprise that the Reagan budget cuts had such a profound impact on Wyoming County, as much of the county's infrastructure was built on federal funds. Most of the major roads in the county had been built or improved with federal funds, as well as the local vocational school and community college. The majority of the county's belated sewage and sanitation systems have been funded with federal moneys, beginning with a project in Pineville in the 1930s. In 1962, the county's first waste treatment facility was built using funds from a $400,000 local bond issue, and $10,000 in Farmers Home Association funds (Bowman, 1965: pp. 160, 452). Many rural coal communities did not receive sewage systems until 1970, when the Farmer's Home Administration allocated $246,000 to the county for such projects (*Independent Herald*, 16 Apr. 1970: p. 1). Federal funding, however, could not save the county's only hospital, located in Mullens, which was forced to close in the 1980s due to a diminishing tax base and population.

Indeed, the neglected physical infrastructure of Wyoming County is a telling sign that the county is locked into a relationship of dependency. The nearest hospital now is in Beckley, at least fifty miles from the remotest reaches of the southern part of the county. Many roads are poorly maintained and it is not uncommon to see local power lines and sidewalks obscured by kudzu. Several buildings are abandoned in the small downtown areas of Mullens and Pineville, formerly thriving commercial centers. Whereas there were once six high schools in the county, a declining population and tax base has forced consolidation, and by the year 2005 there will be only two (Cook, 1996c). The segment of the local infrastructure that is not maintained by federal moneys is funded by the taxpayers. Ironically, Wyoming County's largest landowners are not among the taxpayers who shoulder the bulk of revenues required, as I will discuss shortly.

The relationship between colonialism and dependency becomes most apparent in this situation. As discussed below, absentee mineral corporations own most of Wyoming County's land base, thereby complicating development alternatives. Although they extract millions of tons of coal from the county each year, they give very little in the form of jobs or revenues back in return. Absentee ownership of land is often cited as one of the leading causes of underdevelopment in Appalachia (e.g., ALOTF, 1981). In Wyoming County, the most recent comprehensive figures reported that 86 percent of the local land base (including surface *and* subsurface mineral rights) was owned by the top twenty-five absentee corporations in the state, excluding over six thousand acres owned by the state and federal governments. At that time (1977), Eastern Association Coal Corporation was listed as the single largest controller of coal land—surface and subsurface—in the county, holding 29.4 percent (Zimolzak, 1977: pp. 164, 169). Since then, several of the former landholdings have been consolidated under larger multinational conglomerates. Island Creek Coal Company, for example, is now part of the Fairchild Corporation, and Pocahontas Fuel has merged with Consolidation Coal. This means that fewer corporations own more land; the majority of the county's land base (as with much of West Virginia) is controlled by an oligopoly. Although data has not been compiled, recent estimates suggest that about 90 percent of Wyoming County's mineral land is absentee owned. It is quite possible that more land in Wyoming County is absentee owned than in any other Appalachian county.

The implications of this oligopoly are many. First, mineral corporations that control the land thereby control the types of development that will occur in the county. Coal corporations are hesitant to free any of their holdings for any type of permanent development even when the coal industry is lagging, as they anticipate a day when they will again extract coal. Second, the concentration of the industry in the hands of a few corporations diminishes competition *within* the industry. As oligopolies become a global trend in the form of multinational corporations, they are increasingly able to exert power over local labor forces. Not only can the corporations determine the degree of mechanization, thereby further reducing the labor force required, but unionized workers now face the growing reality of capital flight to other regions or countries where labor opposition is not as strong or as organized (Gaventa, 1994).

Perhaps the most harmful aspect of excessive absenteeism in Wyoming County is the damage it inflicts on the local tax base. West Virginia tax laws are based on the agricultural productivity of lands, a system abandoned by most states years ago (Rasmussen, 1996: p. 141). Under this system, land is taxed primarily on the number of "improvements" the owner has made. Mineral corporations in the state hold vast reserves of coal land but have made very few "improvements." Thus, coal corporations in the state receive major tax breaks while extracting millions of tons of coal each year. Meanwhile, citizens end up compensating for lost revenues by paying a disproportionate share of taxes on personal property and improved land. Yet in an environment where employment and population are constantly fluctuating, citizens can scarcely sustain the revenue base to maintain quality public services. Local school systems, for example, are heavily dependent on property revenues, and when these are low, they are often forced to compromise on staff and teacher salaries and even on curriculum (ALOTF, 1981: pp. 91–97). In most cases, property taxes on corporations are disproportionately low in West Virginia counties. A 1980 study on state taxation patterns suggested that over 75 percent of the state's mineral owners paid under twenty-five cents per acre in annual property taxes (ALOTF, 1981: p. 78).

The inequity of this system has been apparent for years, but the state did not take any measures to begin reform until pressures mounted from numerous citizens' groups and county tax assessors in the late 1960s. In Wyoming County a coalition of citizens, local officials, and merchants united to petition the state legislature for equitable tax reforms and more stringent environmental quality regulations (*Independent Herald*, 12 Mar. 1970: p. 1). Thus, in 1971 the state legislature passed a tax on coal reserves that provided for an annual tax on coal lands in each county based on their assessed mineral value. The law gave county assessors some discretionary power in determining the tax value of coal lands and in the actual percentage to be collected from mineral corporations. In 1980, the average tax per mineral acre in West Virginia was still only $1.09 per year (ALOTF, 1981: p. 80). In Wyoming County, coal land was assessed at $135 per acre, one of the highest in the state (ALOTF, 1980: pp. 7–9). However, the state government has not rigidly enforced the coal tax. Coal operators continue to lobby the state legislature relentlessly for tax breaks—exemptions from paying the full value of mineral assessments—and as long as their lands remain "unimproved" they still enjoy substantial tax breaks (Rasmussen, 1996: p. 144).

People in Wyoming County are painfully aware of the skewed tax structure. A Mullens man who owns less than an acre remarked, "On this mountain behind me here, they say it isn't any good and they don't pay much taxes on it. I pay more on this place than they pay on the mountain. But if you go up there and try to buy part of that mountain, it's got an awful steep price on it." A former member of the county commission recalled constant disputes with corporations over local tax assessments: "I don't think they pay their fair share of taxes. . . . I think they have lobbyists. Because I know when we would get in a dispute with them, they would come with eight or nine lawyers."

How much has the state political system changed since the Depression? In some other counties, coal corporations simply coopted local assessors and sheriffs to reduce the severance tax in their favor, but such has not been the case in Wyoming County, where the coal industry has never gained full control over the county government. Yet although reform legislation has waxed and waned at the state and national level, coal operators still seem to hold the controlling interest in the state government. The colonial political economy that matured with the state government after the Civil War has remained intact until the present.

State and National Government, Political Integration

Since the 1930s, West Virginia has been solidly Democratic, in large part because the Democratic party is associated with the New Deal reforms and concomitantly is viewed as the party of the underprivileged. "The GOP will not be represented on the ballot for any of the major posts," reported a Wyoming County newspaper in 1970, and nearly identical reports can be found in the county in any given year (*Independent Herald* 12 Feb. 1970: p. 1). But coal operators in the state have simply responded by shifting their own political alliances. It can hardly be said, then, that the colonial structure of the state government, which developed in the post–Civil War years has been dissembled. Moreover, federal programs in West Virginia since the 1960s have benefited the region only in a two-edged way, and in some instances have added to the colonial situation and regional dependency.

Space does not allow a thorough examination of the still intimate relationship between mineral corporations and the state government in West Virginia; a few examples will have to suffice, beginning with the office of the governor. Virtually every governor has been either from a family of coal barons or closely associated with the industry. As a result, very few governors have challenged the exploitative practices of the industry directly, and those who did so generally brought about the demise of their political careers. In the previous chapter, for example, I pointed out that Republican governor Henry Hatfield prompted coal operators to shift their alliance temporarily to the Democratic party when he proposed a coal severance tax on out-of-state operators. The same thing happened when Governor William C. Marland—himself a former miner from Glen Rogers—proposed a severance tax in 1954 (ARDF, 1978: p. 278).[2]

Most governors, however, have avoided such sensitive issues, which comes as no surprise given their ties with coal and other industries. Governor Arch Moore, for example, who had held executive positions in various chemical corporations, was the premier apologist for the coal industry in the 1970s. In 1972, an illegal coal sludge dam built by Pittston Coal Company broke and sent a thirty-foot wall of sludge down the narrow valley of Buffalo Creek in Logan County, killing 150 people and destroying sixteen communities. When Pittston dismissed the disaster as an "act of God," Moore summarily agreed and asserted that the biggest tragedy of all was the unflattering coverage West Virginia received from the press (Bethell and McAteer, 1978). Moore also pardoned certain Wyoming County operators for reneging on union contracts and refusing to pay into the Black Lung fund (Cook, 1996c). His catering to the industry in exchange for bribes ultimately led to his conviction and imprisonment. Other governors have not been as daring as Moore, but their ties to and standoffish attitudes concerning the coal industry are clear. Gaston W. Caperton, who completed his final term in 1997, came from a family whose fortune was made in Winding Gulf Coal. Rather than addressing the serious barriers the industry poses to development, Caperton sought to encourage the development of another potentially exploitative industry—tourism—with the hope that West Virginia would become "the playground of the east" (West Virginia Department of Transportation, n.d.). And current Republican governor Cecil Underwood had served a term as governor in the 1960s and became vice-president of Island Creek Coal in the interim (ARDF, 1978: p. 277).[3]

The state legislature is equally reluctant to address the problems the coal industry has created with alternative development possibilities. Not all members of the state legislature cater to the industry, but most fear the economic consequences that might confront the state if the industry is alienated. Although the legislature did give in to pressures from citizens' groups and enact a coal reserves tax in 1971, the law had significant loopholes. Corporations are not beholden to the decisions of county assessors. If they believe they are being overtaxed, they can circumvent the authority of county governments and appeal to higher officials in the state government.

Rather than focusing on reforms in mineral laws, the state legislature now has a tendency to emphasize the development of tourism. While this is not unusual in any state, what *is* peculiar is the fact that every year numerous proposals emerge in the state legislature to transfer state parks to private lessors. The rationale behind this proposal is that the state would be relieved of millions of dollars in maintenance costs while simultaneously using its taxing power to raise revenues through the taxation of these private endeavors. This is a novel and dangerous idea, for at best tourism offers mostly seasonal employment. Moreover, privatization could open a formidable Pandora's box of overdevelopment and consequently the commercial exploitation of local culture and environment (Salstrom and Hollenhorst, 1994).

It is worth pointing out that Wyoming County benefits very little from tourism. There are two primary attractions. The first, Twin Falls State Park, is a four-thousand-acre resort that employs seventy seasonal workers at its peak and generates very little income for other businesses in the county, as most visitors eat in the park's restaurant. The second, R. D. Bailey Lake, is the result of a reservoir initially justified as a means of flood control on the Guyandotte. Built and maintained by the Army Corps of Engineers, the project ultimately forced the removal of twenty-four hundred people, six hundred homes, and the relocation of the entire town of Baileysville (*Independent Herald* 20 Feb. 1970: p. 7). Both of these facilities are government-owned, which means that nearly ten thousand acres of Wyoming County are absolutely exempt from taxation. Meanwhile, Wyoming County can boast of two golf courses and no hospital.

Twin Falls Park was made possible through federal funds allocated under the provisions of the 1961 Area Redevelopment Act (ARA, 75 St. 47). While the ARA grant programs were intended to address national job shortages, in West Virginia over 68 percent of the ARA grants received were poured into tourism development (Whisnant, 1994: p. 74). In the same period, however, more profound federal programs were being developed and applied to the region, which had the dual effect of drawing more federal funds for infrastructural development while imposing development strategies framed within the dogmatic ideologies of modernization theory. Born out of the New Frontier and Great Society programs of the Kennedy and Johnson administrations, these programs were (and remain), as Whisnant puts it, "above all the intellectual and political progeny of exploitative private development in the mountains, and the condescending middle-class missionary attitudes and activities that accompaniy it" (1994: p. xv).

John F. Kennedy had visited West Virginia during the 1960 primaries, hoping to gain the support of the Democratic majority there. Kennedy's visit brought the entire Appalachian coal belt into the national limelight as a region of profound poverty, and various New Frontier programs of his administration were arguably inspired by this visit. The ARA was at the vanguard of the renewed wave of federal intervention into the region. Then came the Economic Opportunity Act of 1964 (78 St. 508), which established the Office of Economic Opportunity (OEO) to coordinate the funding of several community development programs for impoverished areas. The OEO programs were a mixed blessing for Appalachia. On the one hand, they provided funds for job training, Head Start, and numerous other community-based services that were previously lacking. They also provided for the establishment of Community Action Programs (CAPS), which in theory were to become instruments of grassroots empowerment. The overall plan for CAPS, however, was designed to address the needs of metropolitan ghettos and was ill-suited to many Appalachian communities (Whisnant, 1994: p. xxi). The results of these programs varied from county to county. In some cases, oppressive county governments seized control of CAPS to advance their own agendas. In others, CAPS did serve as conduits for grassroots political opposition to corrupt county governments, only to be shut down by the latter (Perry, 1972). In some counties, CAPS provided a channel through which young political ideologues from outside the region attempted to dictate the terms of "grassroots" political and economic development as "overnight experts" determined to "uplift" the poor mountaineers (Branscome, 1983: pp. 251–53; Batteau, 1990: ch. 9; Whisnant, 1994: ch. 4). Such was the case in Wyoming County.

The county did gain some benefits from OEO programs. In 1965 alone the county received $108,000 for seven Head Start programs, $65,600 for job training and counseling, and $26,078 for an agricultural field marketing program (*Independent Herald*, 17 Jan. 1965: p. 1; 28 Jan. 1965: p. 1; 17 Feb. 1966: p. 1). In the same year, county citizens organized Community Action Groups, and by 1965 three community centers were under construction or renovation. The OEO also provided for a corps of volunteer workers known as Volunteers in Service to America (VISTAS), who were sent to various communities included in OEO programs to help facilitate community activities. These were usually politically active youths from as far away as California, riding on the wave of radicalism in the late 1960s. In some communities they were welcomed; in others they were banished by county officials who feared VISTA's opposition to the status quo.[4]

In Wyoming County, they were almost uniformly resented by county officials and local community members alike for their condescending efforts to shape local consciousness in their own image. A retired Pineville power line worker recalled: "People felt like, you know, 'they comin' in here tellin' us how to live! And we don't need nobody to tell us how to live.' Some people got plum hostile about it." "They were hippie kids," recalled a Mullens woman, "and that's what they were called. The hippie kids. And they came in to help people—low income, elderly—to fix up their homes, do things like that. But I don't think they were very well thought of." In the southern part of the county, VISTA volunteers established a community center at the old Marianna company store, and purported to run a youth program. A former employee of that company, who lived directly beside the center in the camp, was less restrained in his opinions of the VISTAS: "Bunch a hippies. Raisin' cain, smokin' pot, and carryin' on. Start raisin' cain every night." By the end of the decade, the VISTAS were just a sore memory in Wyoming County.

In the meantime, the Council of Appalachian Governors (CAG) became dissatisfied with federal programs in the region and began to petition the administration for special consideration. President Johnson responded by opening a special niche under the Great Society programs, the President's Appalachian Regional Commission (PARC). The PARC was basically an advisory committee consisting of the governors of the eastern mountain states, who soon petitioned Congress for legislative sanction (Bradshaw, 1993: p. 33). Thus, in 1965 Congress established the Appalachian Regional Commission (ARC) as a medium to produce a comprehensive regional economic development strategy through collaborative efforts of the federal and state governments (79 St. 5). Since that time, the ARC has received endless criticism. The most common complaint is that the commission's peculiar delineation of the region (comprising 397 counties in thirteen states) is too broad to allow effective coordinating of economic planning, and thus precludes the possibility of effectively treating the region as a homogeneous entity (Ergood, 1983; Watts, 1983; Whisnant, 1994: p. 134). Mississippi and New York were among those in the ARC, because they had powerful senators who promised support if their states were included (Couto, 1995: p. 100).

The creation of the ARC brought about a fragmentation of federal programs in the region, as the commission was primarily concerned with infrastructural development and the OEO with social issues. While the OEO ideally purported to promote grassroots initiatives, state governors controlled the ARC and treated its funds like any other federal bloc grant. The OEO was phased out by 1970, and as early as 1967 the ARC had virtually full control over federal expenditures in the region. Outside of the controlling interests of state governments, the full-time staff of the ARC has rarely comprised natives of the region, which translates into cultural and political biases. Over the past thirty years the ARC has consistently ignored the roots of regional underdevelopment, such as unemployment, exploitation of untaxed mineral wealth, and lack of social support, and has focused on "infrastructural development." Specifically, the commission has focused on projects—most notably roads—that will boost those industries it believes will regenerate local economies. In short, the ARC espouses a philosophy of "trickle-down" economics; rather than giving grants directly to poor citizens to finance their own development strategies (including self-employment), the commission caters to industrialists and businesspeople whom it assumes will provide jobs for the needy (Whisnant, 1994: ch. 5). In essence, the federal government—through the medium of the ARC—is subsidizing the coal industry, not only through infrastructural improvements but also by providing it with a shelter from local taxes (ALOTF, 1981: v. 1, p. 93).

One of the most disturbing strategies generated by the ARC in its early years was its emphasis on demographic growth centers. The idea was that commerce and jobs could be generated either by stimulating the growth of urban centers in the region, or by encouraging residents to migrate to distant growth centers—that is, by depopulating the region (ARC, 1968; Davis, 1977; Whisnant, 1994: p. 136). At one point, ARC planners actually proposed the complete depopulation of the central Appalachian coalfields and the construction of urban complexes on the periphery, from which workers would be shuttled into the coalfields, which would then be opened to mass mining and stripping operations (Egerton, 1983: p. 240). Fortunately, this proposal never came to fruition. The commission has become milder over the years, though it remains unresponsive to real needs of the region's residents.

The residents of Wyoming County do not expect a great deal from the ARC. For most it is just a conduit for obtaining federal money in whatever form they can get it. The commission can be credited with providing funds for such infrastructural improvements as sewage systems and road construction and repair in the county (Cook, 1996c). The most notable road funded by the ARC is Route 99, which passes through Wyoming County while connecting Logan with Beckley. The initial 10.016-mile stretch of the road cost $5,200,000 to construct in the 1970s, but interestingly, it did not attract enough traffic to pay for itself through the state gasoline tax. Instead, it connected several coal mines from Raleigh to Boone Counties and served as an artery for the trucking of coal and for employees to commute to work (ARDF, 1978).

The ARC was nearly eliminated during the Reagan administration. This is ironic given its mutual embrace of "trickle-down" economics. But having survived the Reagan budget cuts, the commission continues to control federal funds moving into the region with the same contorted logic it always has: the proposition that Appalachia's problems are a result of its lack of integration into the national economy, rather than acknowledging that the real problem is the *manner* in which it has been integrated (Whisnant, 1994: p. 129). What is equally disturbing is the way the ARC represents Appalachia to the American mainstream—as a homogenous region of poor people. Whisnant points out that the commission's publications— most notably its monthly magazine *Appalachia*—consistently cast a romantic image of "backward" mountain folk experiencing positive changes in their lives as a result of ARC intervention (Whisnant, 1994: p. 279). The 1995 thirtieth anniversary edition of *Appalachia*, for example, featured a color photograph of a swinging bridge spanning a creek and providing the only means of access to a log cabin. The caption reads: "Throughout Central Appalachia, isolation from the political and economic mainstream of American life was the *natural* result of geography and the fierce independence of the Region's settler" (ARC, 1995: p. 62, emphasis added). Such an appropriation of cultural nostalgia illustrates the middle-class values, which Whisnant argues motivate endeavors such as the ARC, and it also resembles the colonial rhetoric that saturated the reports of the U.S. Commissioner of Indian Affairs well into the twentieth century. Such a representation of the Appalachian "other" is a contradiction; the ARC presents both a static image of culture and one of sweeping change. Like the Bureau of Indian Affairs, the ARC perpetually juxtaposes images of backwardness and "progress" to justify its own existence.

Thus, the residents of Wyoming County are integrated into state and federal political systems that hesitate to address the real issues behind chronic economic problems in the area. While the state government overall has maintained its intimacy with industrial interests since the turn of the twentieth century, the federal government in the last half of the century lost the reform-orientation of the New

Deal in favor of a federalist approach. Interestingly, West Virginia Senator Robert C. Byrd, as head of the Senate Appropriations Committee, is one of the most powerful men in Congress. The people of West Virginia know this and continually reelect Byrd in return for generous appropriations for the state, most often channeled through the ARC.

Living In Wyoming County

On paper, the current economic situation in Wyoming County looks bleak. The below-poverty-level population is listed at 27.9 percent, the unemployment rate is 12.9 percent, and the county's population has dropped another 2.7 percent since 1990 (Couto, 1994: p. 268; ARC *Annual Report*, 1995: p. 57). According to the ARC's system of measuring the severity of economic crises from county to county, Wyoming County is classified as "very distressed," the worst possible ranking on the ARC scale (Couto, 1994: p. 263). Feeble efforts at alternative development have emerged, including an ammunition disassembly plant in Herndon that employs about forty people. State and local officials continue to search for ways to boost the tourist industry, the most recent proposal being the Hatfield-McCoy Recreational Area—an extensive trail system that is to span southern West Virginia and eastern Kentucky (*Independent Herald*, 30 Dec. 1996: p. 1).

Meanwhile, extractive industries continue to dominate the local economy despite a prolonged cycle of bust in the coal industry. Most mining now is done by small operators contracting from large holding companies. The contractors, although they may be affiliated with the larger companies as subsidiaries, employ so few workers at each mine that they need not unionize. They ship their coal in trucks that tear up the roads, which they contribute little or nothing to maintain. Moreover, the increased use of trucks over the past three decades has crippled the rail industry, thereby eliminating many jobs. The large mines in Wyoming County that are still in operation have mechanized to the point that fewer and fewer workers are needed each year. The U.S. Steel mine at Pinnacle Creek, for example, which until recently employed nine hundred workers and continues to pro-

duce over six million tons of coal annually, has become so automated
through computer technology that it could theoretically operate
without a single worker underground (Cook, 1996c).

County residents are well aware of the implications of a coal-
dominated economy. A Baileysville woman succinctly expressed the
county's dependency on external market forces: "We kind of laugh
and say that we have all this timber up here that, you know, they
timber it, and saw it and cut it, and ship it to North Carolina. And
they make furniture and we buy it back. Which is true." She thought
that a furniture factory would provide a lucrative economic boost for
the county, but said that she doubted it could ever be realized, as past
efforts to bring in a pulp mill were vetoed by the Environmental
Protection Agency—despite the environmental destruction inflicted
by the coal industry. For many people in the county, prospects for a
revitalized economy seem grim. "Not unless we get some more
roads," remarked a retired miner, expressing the sentiments of many
county residents. When asked if he thought there were any feasible
alternatives to lucrative development other than the coal industry, a
former Mullens railroad worker could only say, "Well, that's what
we thought we had before. With the railroad and the coal mines and
everything thriving. But I don't believe that you could plan on having jobs like that now."

There are, however, subtle but steady changes occurring in the
county that might have an impact on the local economy. "Well, I
think Wyoming County has stabilized as far as development is concerned," said a Mullens businessman. "And it will be a rural suburb
of Beckley. As a matter of fact a large number of people live in
Mullens and do work in Beckley." Mullens is approximately thirty
miles from Beckley, the nearest major commercial center. Most
county residents now go to Beckley for medical care, and a growing
number are finding jobs there and commuting to work, even those
from distant sections. Moreover, Beckley residents are beginning to
move into Wyoming County to escape Beckley's developing metropolitan atmosphere. If Wyoming County does become a suburb of
Beckley, which seems probable, it will certainly provide a substantial

boost to the service sector economy. On the other hand, it may bring about new social ills and contribute to the erosion of many relatively close-knit communities.

The question that inevitably arises when dealing with an area that looks so economically grim on paper, at least by metropolitan standards, is why people continue to live in Wyoming County? A Mullens man provided a partial answer, "Economically, we've slumped to a certain point, and we're accustomed to our standard of living right now. Which isn't bad. . . . Things are not that bad, really, as far as the standard of living in this area. It all depends on how high on the hog you want to live, or how many silk stockings you can afford to buy, or how many pairs of shoes you think you ought to have."

Many people commute to distant towns or leave the area altogether (at least temporarily) to find work. There are many, however, who refuse to leave. One remote community in the southwestern part of the county is reputed to be the poorest in the county. Many homes are without electricity, some without running water. But people remain there and live in "poverty" by choice. In a sense they reflect to the extreme the sentiments of other county residents who may be more affluent in varying degrees. What seems most important to those who remain in Wyoming County is a sense of home and community.

It would be difficult to classify the residents, or even specific communities, of Wyoming County as *a People* in the rigid sense in which Spicer (1980; 1994) and Thomas (1990) characterize groups such as Indian tribes and the Jews. People from divergent ethnic backgrounds are still represented in the county despite significant outmigration. And culture is not a static entity; if homogeneity can erode over time, it can also develop among given populations. At the very least, people in Wyoming County—immigrants included—adhere to a common *cultural system* insofar as there is a "mutual degree of coherence" concerning shared symbols that give meaning to experience among the people in the area (Geertz, 1973: pp. 17, 45). This is particularly true at the community level, where kinship remains a vital element of identity. It is their relationship to community, family, and the land that keeps people from leaving Wyoming County.

Although a few of the participants in this study said they might move as far away as Beckley to have better hospital access, most said they would never leave the county. "You know, people in this county still speaks and associates with each other," said a Pineville man. "I'd rather stay around people I know. Our crime rate's not so bad. You still feel safe to go out." Indeed, few people in the county bother locking their doors when they leave their houses unattended. The land is just as important. "This is home," said a Mariana man. "Around here, you know, you got your ridges and your hollers and rivers. I get paranoid if I don't see a mountain." And a retired miner expressed the meaning of his relationship with the land and his family and community with a blunt eloquence: "I'd just like to be around my people. This is home to me. Anywhere I walk here, why, I'm steppin' in my younguns' footsteps. They was raised up here. And anywhere I'm in this holler, why, I know that wherever I step I'm steppin' in their tracks."

Such reluctance to leave the area itself constitutes a form of resistance. People can and do leave the area in search of jobs or better economic opportunities but many return. Current statistics suggest a declining population, but there is evidence that the decline has halted as people choose to commute to jobs as far as eighty miles away each day. Moreover, although the remaining three high schools in the county are in the process of consolidating, enrollment at some of the elementary schools is rising rapidly (Cook, 1996c). It should be noted, however, that the ties to the land, community, and family that keep people at home or returning home are not peculiar to Wyoming County. Many of these ties transcend county lines, and the cultural system described here can be found throughout much of southern West Virginia. What makes Wyoming County worth studying as an isolated entity is its anomalous place in the history of mineral development in southern West Virginia, which has been a recurring theme throughout these chapters.

* * *

Several scholars have argued that the internal colonialism model is not appropriate for explaining the subordination of Appalachia in the national and world political economies, suggesting instead that the world-systems (Walls, 1976) and dependency (Salstrom, 1994) analyses are more appropriate. What I have attempted to show here, however, is that no *single* theoretical construction can adequately explain such conditions. Moreover, I have attempted to illustrate that in certain parts of the region at least, dependency *is* a consequence of colonial activities. Power relations in West Virginia are unquestionably skewed in favor of extractive industries. In Wyoming County, citizens have little if any say in local development strategies because absentee holding companies control the majority of the land on which such developments would take place. The future of Wyoming County is uncertain, but one thing is clear. Before any meaningful, sustainable development can take place that reflects the interests and impetus of local residents, major land reforms will have to be effected. But before such reforms can be possible, there is an even more formidable *cultural* barrier to transcend: the mainstream middle-class values that have defined Appalachia—and West Virginia in particular—as a land of chronically backward people with whom the "conscientious" outsider can only interact in a missionary capacity. Allen Batteau (1990) has proposed that the very concept of Appalachia is an ever-developing *invention* of mainstream America, beginning with local color writers in the 1870s and continuing into the present through media and public policy. At any given time, the "Appalachia" of mainstream America reflects the fears and/or aspirations of the middle-class by creating an image of a place and a people either reminiscent of a proud past or typical of what America ought not to be (i.e., poor, ignorant, backward). This externally generated image of Appalachia is the image that informs public policy. As long as this is the case, public policy cannot truly reflect the interests of the residents of Wyoming County.

7 CONCLUSION

Diversity, Power, and Development

"It is ironic that a region for so long characterized by a single stereotype is actually almost too diverse to generalize about at all," wrote David Whisnant, referring to the mainstream perception of Appalachia as a region of poor, backward people (1994: p. xix). This study has provided ample support for that assertion. The foregoing analyses have dealt with two very different communities in divergent environments within the Appalachian region. The Monacan Nation is a group of people indigenous to this continent who relate to one another as a single *People* with a shared sacred history and a relationship to their homeland that predates the European presence on this continent. The residents of Wyoming County are not indigenous to the continent. Although they may interact with each other within the parameters of a common cultural system peculiar to time and space, they cannot admit to the sociocultural solidarity of Peoplehood in the sense that Barth (1969) and Spicer (1971; 1980) used the term to distinguish ethnic nations. Moreover, although both communities inhabit the mountainous reaches of Appalachia, their respective physical environments are considerably different, and these differences have significantly influenced the manner in which external political, economic, and social forces have influenced and interacted with them.

However, some generalizations can be drawn. Both groups observed a strong sense of family and community prior to the entry of external forces and continue to do so. Both were subjected to externally generated exploitative forces that entered their respective territories in search of land, resources, and labor. In the process of relations with outside forces, both groups became subordinate parties in colonial situations that evolved into relationships of dependency on external economic forces.

Many scholars of Appalachian underdevelopment seem to have repudiated the internal colonialism model because they perceive it as implying that the region's economic problems stem from its exclusion from the capitalist system (Walls, 1976; Salstrom, 1994). Specifically, Marxist scholars have argued, "The colonial analogy makes dominated consciousness smack too loudly of a conspiracy foisted upon the unsuspecting Appalachians instead of an inevitable consequence of capitalism. Eliminate the conspiracy and eliminate the problem" (Foster, Robinson, and Fisher, 1978: p. 302). These scholars are correct in asserting that the internal colonial model alone cannot adequately account for unequal economic relations in the region, and between parts of the region, and national and world metropoles. This is the main reason why I have chosen to supplement the internal colonial model with a dependency analysis. However, the colonial model should still be retained in the analysis. The birth of capitalism was contingent upon the colonization of distant lands—the Americas in particular—by European nation-states. Yet capitalist integration or colonization do not necessarily spawn a condition of dominated consciousness among those who are subordinate within such processes. This argument merely reflects an effort to repudiate capitalism outright while ignoring the existence of such groups as the Amish, who have managed to coexist with capitalism while holding steadfastly to communal values. Although capitalism has always been an exploitative system, it is not my intention here to condemn it outright, for it is also a constantly changing system. Before anyone can hope to achieve its elimination or its reform, it must be dealt with in the present.

What I have attempted to illustrate here, then, is that colonial processes have played a significant role in determining the manner in which certain parts of the Appalachian region have been integrated into the national and world economies, and that colonial processes are still at work in the region. I have analyzed how these processes affected and became manifest among both the Monacans and the residents of Wyoming County. The following sections constitute a binary analysis to compare and contrast the experiences of the respective communities vis-à-vis exploitative forces. I am interested not only in generalizations concerning the existence and implications of colonial relations in each case, but also in how the divergent experiences of these communities illuminate the present conditions each faces. I am especially intrigued by the fact that the Monacan Nation seems to have made formidable strides in breaking the bonds of colonialism. What implications does the Monacan experience have for Wyoming County, for Appalachia in general, and for other communities positioned as subordinates in unequal power relations?

A Comparative Synthesis

In the first chapter, I posed ten broad research questions to guide the application of the internal colonial model and dependency analysis. Having applied these to each community individually, I will now consider each of these questions separately in a comparative light.

---

1. What were the salient cultural and economic features of the respective communities before the entry of colonial forces, and how have they changed over time?

As a tribal entity indigenous to this continent, the Monacans enjoyed—and continue to enjoy—a fluid sense of *Peoplehood* in that to varying degrees they distinguished themselves from all other people through a process of ethnogenesis, and from a political standpoint they might now be considered a nation in the purest sense of the term. By contrast, the settlers of Wyoming County and their progeny were of European origin and did not distinguish themselves as a nation or a people. They did, however, interact with each other within a common cultural system insofar as they shared common meanings and symbols. Relations in both groups were interpersonal and kin-oriented. In precolonial times, of course, a cash economy was unknown to the Monacans, although they apparently controlled much of the copper trade in the Virginia interior. Although the residents of Wyoming County were engaged somewhat in a cash economy, most relied primarily on subsistence for survival prior to the entry of industrial forces. In both communities, subsistence farming and household and community cooperative activities endured out of necessity after colonization. In both cases these have eroded considerably with the loss of lands for agricultural endeavors, depletion of game, and the increased involvement of community members in the capitalist exchange system. But within the Monacan Nation some of these practices seem to have endured much longer and have become institutionalized as part of the contemporary tribal government. This is a critical point, as the Monacans' identity as a People—that is, a distinctive ethnic and political entity—has served as a rallying point for the preservation of these communal networks. Although they have lost many of the tangible aspects of their aboriginal culture (e.g., language, certain ceremonies, particular customs) the bonds of community have endured. Indeed, while residents of Wyoming County were drawn into dependence on wages from the outset, that was not as true for the Monacans. Under the semifeudal economy that existed in Amherst County until well into the twentieth century, the Monacans did not always receive wages for their labor.

---

2. Who were the initial colonizers, and what were their initial responses to each group? What was the initial impact on each group?

The Virginia Company, then later the British Crown, through the medium of the colonial government of Virginia was the initial colonizer of the Monacans. Although the Monacans in the area that became Amherst County probably had little contact with early colonial agents, their confederates to the East and the South were engaged in tense and often violent relations with the colonial Virginia government. At various times Virginia pursued policies of extermination toward Indians, and later sought to engage in treaty relations when it was realized that western tribes were a formidable military threat. At that time, some of Virginia's Monacan confederates were established at Fort Christanna to serve as a buffer between "hostile" tribes and white settlements. The Monacans in Amherst County, however, seem to have had their most extensive contact with traders, many of whom settled in the area and married Indians. For them, the initial impact of colonial forces was an increased dependency on European trade goods, accompanied by a loss of thousands of square miles of aboriginal territory by the time of the Revolutionary War.

In Wyoming County the initial colonizers were absentee industrial speculators who worked in conjunction with West Virginia's newly formed state government. The industrialists viewed farmers as a cheap source of labor. Their initial impact on the county was to expedite newly imposed tax burdens in the late nineteenth and early twentieth centuries with the hope that they might gain legal access to mineral and timber lands. If the alienation of some of the lands in the county was delayed, the enforcement of taxes was not, and many residents became increasingly dependent on cash incomes, whereas previously they had sustained themselves through subsistence and bartering, with minimal cash to acquire commodities they could not produce themselves.

---

3. What resources did the prospective colonizers seek to exploit from each group in their respective regions?

The British initially sent explorers up the James River in search of precious minerals. They were disappointed, however, and by the time colonial forces made their strongest thrust into the area of Amherst County, the British and their progeny sought land for agriculture. Later, Euro-American settlers of the county sought to exploit the Monacans for labor power after the institution of slavery was abolished. In Wyoming County, the industrial invaders sought land only for the coal and timber reserves contained thereon, and although labor was recruited from other parts of the nation and world, from the outset they attempted to exploit the local population for a cheap source of labor as well. Thus, while the exploitation of the local population was immediate in Wyoming County, it was delayed for over one hundred years among the Monacan population, as African slave labor was preferred until it was outlawed.

---

4. To what degree did the colonizers engage in doctrines of racism or cultural superiority?

The colonial Virginia Assembly's passage of laws sanctioning the extermination of Indians reveals that doctrines of racism permeated colonial policies toward the Monacans. Direct relations between the early trader/settlers and Indians in Amherst County were relatively peaceful, yet Virginia law quickly excluded the Monacans from the privileges of citizenship by requiring them to register as "people of color" and by withholding rights to property and the franchise. As these policies evolved after the Civil War through the imposition of more elaborate miscegenation laws, the Monacans filled the lowest category of a virtual caste system. State and local officials interpreted these laws to sanction the chastisement and continued disfranchisement of those perceived to be of mixed race, and through Walter Plecker's "scientific" system of determining race, the Monacans were denied the legal right to assert their Indian identity. Local officials and owners of agribusinesses interpreted these laws as sanctioning the exploitation of Monacans as virtual slaves, as the meager wages they received were frequently irregular.

The situation in Wyoming County was not nearly as pronounced, but ideologies of cultural superiority certainly motivated the early industrialists, who saw local residents mainly as a source of cheap labor. This was evidenced by the reluctance of coal operators to provide adequate safety conditions for their miners. Complicating the situation is the fact that, in order to avoid unionism, coal operators tried to encourage racial tensions by recruiting miners from other races and nationalities. Today one finds that development strategies applied to Wyoming County are informed by nostalgic, ethnocentric mainstream perceptions of Appalachian natives as "backward, chronically poor hillbillies." This is evidenced by the static images presented in publications of the Appalachian Regional Commission.

One clear parallel between the experiences of the Monacans and the residents of Wyoming County can be drawn in this category. Even those outsiders with the most benign intentions have often approached the respective groups through a cultural screen of mainstream middle-class values. For the Monacans, it was the early missionaries; for the residents of Wyoming County, it was the numerous government volunteers who often accompanied OEO programs.

5. At what point did internal colonial structures emerge and how have they changed over time? Have the initial colonizers been supplanted/augmented by other agents?

For the Monacans, *colonial* structures were in place by the 1670s when the colonial Virginia government began to send explorers into the western extremes of the colony. However, these structures did not become firmly entrenched until the early 1700s when many of the Monacan confederates were resident at Fort Christanna. At that point, it is likely that some of the ancestors of the present-day Monacans were enclaved in Amherst County, which was still unpopulated by whites. Their colonial experience began to grow after traders moved in during the mid-1700s, followed by land-hungry colonists. At that point the Monacans were not even acknowledged by Virginia as constituting an independent tribe, much less as having any substantive political authority. By the close of the Revolutionary War, it was assumed that most Indians had been exterminated or removed from the state, and the situation evolved toward *internal colonialism*, for the Monacans were categorized legally as "free people of color." Although they enjoyed a status higher than slaves, only the select few who passed themselves off as whites could own property or vote. The primary colonial agent through all those years was the state of Virginia, which continued to elaborate miscegenation laws and to chastise those believed to have violated them. The situation reached its zenith in the early part of the twentieth century with the ascent of Walter Plecker to head the Office of Vital Statistics. At the local level, county officials reinforced Plecker's eugenic plan, and counter to the U.S. Constitution prohibited Indians from voting while protecting the semifeudal structure in which the Monacans served as subordinate laborers. In many instances, orchard owners and farmers did not merely exploit Indians for their labor with no guarantee of a steady wage, but required Indians to relinquish a major portion of the crops they grew themselves. This situation changed drastically after minimum wage laws were instituted along with the mandatory desegregation of public schools in the 1960s. These and other changes converged, prompting the Monacans to reassert themselves as a distinct people and as a nation.

In West Virginia an internal colonial structure was in place shortly after the Civil War, as industrial magnates seized control of the nascent state government. However, effects on Wyoming County were delayed due to the county's isolation, as well as the recalcitrance of some of its citizens and local officials. Ironically, the internal colonial structure became firmly entrenched during the Depression when, despite federal reforms that allowed miners to challenge the state-industrial partnership through unionization, many local residents were forced by tax burdens to sell their lands. This is when absentees came to control the majority of the county's lands, milking the vast timber and mineral resources while contributing virtually nothing to the local revenue base. The situation has changed very little over the past fifty years. Despite tax reforms intended to make corporations pay their fair share of local taxes, absentee businessmen still have powerful lobbyists in the state's capital—if they themselves are not state officials.

While the situation confronting Wyoming County may not seem

as intense as that which once faced the Monacans, it has been less susceptible to positive change, a situation that will be discussed shortly.

---

6. What roles did members of each community play in facilitating or challenging colonial processes?

The Monacans did not passively accept the colonial situation confronting them. Although the situation was upon them before they might have realized it, they continued to assert their Indian identity over the years, whether through their refusal to attend "Negro" schools, their continual attempts to be classified as "Indian" on legal documents (notwithstanding the threat of prosecution under the scrutinous eye of Walter Plecker), or by resisting the draft during World War II when Selective Service attempted to place them in black units. A more subtle form of resistance was found in their maintenance of subsistence patterns and cooperative networks. But just as important is the fact that although many left the area to escape persecution, many refused to leave their homeland. Their emergent sense of Peoplehood provided them with a solidarity that was ultimately reinforced by a shared sense of powerlessness. This solidarity enabled the Monacans, as a collective entity, to rebound toward the positive changes and aspirations of the present.

The residents of Wyoming County, on the other had, never expressed such solidarity. Ironically, it was this *lack* of solidarity that spawned some of the more overt forms of resistance to industrial domination in the county. While the coal operators attempted to coopt local Republicans or to force their employees to vote the Republican ticket prior to the 1930s, the agrarian Democrats were strong enough to counter these tactics and to sway the vote away from operators' candidates. This early opposition by local officials to the coal oligopoly became a permanent phenomenon. County officials and local citizens worked together in the 1970s to lobby for tax reforms, and current county officials continually challenge corporations on their anemic tax payments, whereas in some neighboring counties local officials cater to coal operators. Beginning in the 1930s, local miners began to realize a degree of political efficacy through the United Mine Workers. When the union became corrupt and dictatorial in the 1960s and 1970s, local miners presented formidable opposition to union leaders and successfully petitioned for pension reforms. Unfortunately, the union ultimately contributed to the loss of jobs, and the efficacy of its local impact is questionable in the long run. But as with the Monacans, the sheer refusal of many local residents to leave the area—despite declining employment opportunities and occasional federal efforts to encourage depopulation—is one form of resistance.

---

7. At what point can a structural relationship of dependency be said to have emerged between colonizer and colonized, and how entrenched did it become in each community? Are such relations permanent?

Relations of dependency certainly emerged for the Monacans of Amherst County when Euro-American traders moved up the James River, though I would argue that they merely *adapted* to a reliance on European goods and technologies rather than becoming fully dependent on them. In truth, most of the Monacans remained relatively autonomous in economic terms until after the Civil War. They were able to survive almost entirely through indigenous and new subsistence practices and cooperative networks, many living as squatters on unimproved lands in the mountains. But with the abolition of slavery after the Civil War, local farmers and orchard owners turned to the Indians for a cheap source of labor. Because Virginia's miscegenation laws essentially sanctioned the chastisement of those claiming to be Indians, local commercial farmers found a quasi-legal justification for exploiting the Monacans. Simultaneously, the orchard industry began to expand into previously undeveloped lands, forcing many Monacans off the lands they had once occupied as squatters. The Indians were presented with only two choices: leave the area, or move onto the orchards and farms and work under the conditions dictated by the landowners. There were simply no other alternatives, as these were the only jobs available to Indians in the county. Under the post–Civil War capitalist-feudal economy, labor costs of Monacans were probably cheaper than slave labor, as the Monacans subsidized the industry through their own subsistence practices out of necessity, and all that orchard owners provided was a living space and irregular wages. This situation worsened as miscegenation laws became more elaborate, and the state Office of Vital Statistics adopted more stringent measures to penalize "people of color" who claimed to be anything other than "Negro." What is most impressive about the case of the Monacans is the fact that changing social and economic conditions beginning in the 1960s—racial integration, growing metropolitan sympathies toward Indians, and so forth—allowed individual Indians to become more equitably integrated into the cash economy close to home. Although this higher degree of capitalist integration has taken a toll on cooperative networks in the Monacan community by prompting tribal members to devote more time to individual wage-earning activities, these networks still endure and have become institutionalized in the nascent tribal government. There is still a very strong sense of community and Peoplehood within the tribe, and the possibility of breaking from the grasp of dependency as a collective entity is high.

The picture in Wyoming County is not so promising. The structural framework for dependency was established as soon as the state government was established during the Civil War by the guiding hand of industrialists. As I have reiterated throughout this study, the postwar land and tax laws implemented by the new state forced many formerly self-sufficient, subsistence-oriented farm families into a greater dependence on cash to meet new tax burdens. The coal industry added substance to this structure through the company system. Most miners were dependent on the company for housing, and even those who managed to evade life in the coal camps at first were often required to do business at the company store exclusively. Coal companies took advantage of this monopoly by charging excessive rents and prices at the company store, thus forcing miners into perpetual debt. Low wages also meant that mining families had to continue to rely partly on subsistence to survive, thereby subsidizing the industry. This structure became firmly entrenched in Wyoming County during the Depression, when a momentary paucity of employment opportunities forced many people to sell their lands when they were unable to pay taxes. At the same time, the New Deal's legal protection for labor unions through the NIRA served to quicken automation of the mines, setting the stage for dependence on federal largess in the area. As will be discussed under question 8, the coal industry still dominates the local economy. The state government does little to ameliorate problems caused by this domination, and the federal government, while providing a significant amount of funding for local infrastructural improvements, basically subsidizes the coal industry through such infrastructure.

---

8. Are local economies diversified, and to what degree do they hinge on fluctuations in the national and world economies?

This is where the Monacans have been fortunate in recent years. At the peak of dependency for the Monacans, Amherst County was dominated by an agricultural economy that was sustained by a semifeudal system based heavily on Monacan labor. But as minimum wage laws and integration brought an end to this system, and as the nearby metropolis of Lynchburg began to provide more diversified service-oriented jobs within the county, opportunities expanded for the Monacans. Lynchburg boasts a diversified industrial base and lies at the crossroads of several major transportation arteries. Because of this diversification, the Monacans have not only found better and more equitable employment opportunities, but as a tribe have been in a better position to organize and to buy back large tracts of land, as the local land base is not dominated by single-industry absentee owners.

In Wyoming County, however, coal is still king. About 90 percent of the local mineral land base is held by absentee corporations. State tax laws, though purporting to provide for the equitable taxation of mineral lands, are laced with loopholes, and the industry still holds the controlling interest in state government. When the coal industry suffers, so do the other components of the local economy. The once thriving railroad industry, for example, has shrunk with the coal industry. So has the service sector, which depends on the paychecks of miners, many of whom have lost their jobs to machines. Thus, the local economy is very sensitive to fluctuations in the national and world economies, though often in seemingly contradictory ways. For example, in the midst of the 1960s national labor shortage, the coal industry was experiencing a period of bust, and unemployment rates were high in Wyoming County. But during the national recession of the 1970s, when unemployment was as high as 15 percent in some metropolitan areas, the energy crisis momentarily revived the coal industry, and unemployment stood barely at 6 percent in southern West Virginia.

9. What is the relationship between the respective communities and state, national, and local governing entities, and how have each of these governing entities functioned to facilitate or ameliorate colonial processes and conditions of dependency? Which, if any of these seem most representative of the communities in question?

The Monacans have always had a tenuous, if not turbulent relationship with the state government of Virginia. It was the state that elaborated miscegenation laws, and under the direction of Walter Plecker on behalf of the state, these laws were used to justify a virtual witch hunt. Local officials were partners in this process, using state policies toward perceived "mixed-race" people to sustain and justify the county's semifeudal economy in which the Monacans were situated at the bottom. The most powerful constituents at the local level were large agribusiness owners who depended on cheap Monacan labor. The federal government did very little to ameliorate the conditions of colonialism and dependency under which the Monacans lived until World War II, when the federal judiciary ruled that Monacan draftees had the right to classify themselves as "Indians" in military records rather than as "blacks." With the landmark *Brown* decision and the federally mandated abolition of miscegenation laws, new doors began opening for the Monacans. Even after the Supreme Court mandated public school integration, the state and local governments generated a myriad of excuses and tactics to prevent the Monacans—though not blacks—from integrating into white schools. It can be said, however, that *federal* policies that have had a direct impact on the Monacans in recent years have addressed the real issues behind the oppressive conditions they have faced. Yet this is subject to change if the Bureau of Indian Affairs rejects the Monacan Nation's petition for federal recognition. Although many Monacans are skeptical of federal largess, if they are denied federal recognition then they will also be denied the right to political autonomy as an indigenous nation, which may be the key to their final break from dependency.

Meanwhile, it seems that the local government has become quite supportive, as local officials now recognize the tribe's political efficacy as a potential voting bloc. This is largely attributable to public school integration, as the generation of Indian and non-Indian students who went to school together at an early age became accustomed to one another and bridged many racial barriers. The Virginia Office of Vital Statistics, on the other hand, still denies that it previously altered racial classification on Monacan birth certificates, despite incontrovertible evidence to the contrary.

Similarly, most residents of Wyoming County have rarely been well represented in the state government. Instead, the government caters to industry and continues to provide tax shelters for absentee landowners, which allows them to avoid contributing their fair share to the local revenue base. As pointed out, many state officials, notably governors, have themselves served as industrial executives. The federal government has been little better. The reforms of the New Deal were a double-edged sword. On the one hand, the NIRA guaranteed the constitutional right of miners to unionize and bargain collectively with employers. On the other hand, these reforms set the stage for unilateral federal interventions in the region, which commonly ignored the actual roots of regional social and economic ills. The programs of the OEO, for example, though born of benign sentiments, brought an army of naive middle-class idealists to the county who purported to promote grassroots development initiatives while actually attempting to impose their own views on local residents. The ARC, on the other hand, has virtually ignored social issues altogether and has implemented "trickle-down" strategies of infrastructural development, which have essentially subsidized exploitative industries. The local government, it seems, has always been the most representative of the citizenry in the county. From the very beginning, agrarian Democrats used their clout to hinder control by industrialists over the county government while guaranteeing some form of employment to those miners who voted against the operators' candidates. In the 1970s a coalition of citizens and local officials worked together to lobby for tax reforms, and even today county officials battle ceaselessly with corporations over their failure to pay assessed taxes. Unfortunately, the Wyoming County government is an anomaly in southern West Virginia, and its political efficacy in the state is limited.

10. Are there any cultural factors of each community, which may have served to facilitate relations of dependency, or are such features reactions to the unequal distribution of power and wealth? What environmental features may have served to aggravate conditions of dependency and colonialism?

The very assertion of their tribal identity served to aggravate the colonial situation confronting the Monacans, particularly after the Civil War, and continued to do so well into the twentieth century. Chastisement of Indians for claiming to be Indians is the epitome of colonial oppression. But less overt cultural features also had an impact on the intensity of the conditions of dependency and colonialism with which they had to contend—notably, their cooperative subsistence practices. These practices were, paradoxically, both an adaptation to and an expedient of the unequal distribution of power and wealth, as they essentially subsidized the reproduction of cheap labor power for local agribusinesses and at the same time were a necessity for survival. These practices became increasingly difficult, however, as the orchard industry began to flourish. Whereas more level lands in the county at the foot of the Tobacco Row Mountains had long been alienated for tobacco plantations, in the late nineteenth century, farmers found that the more marginal lands in the mountains were highly desirable for cultivating fruit trees, and this led to the displacement of most Indians into tenancy on the orchards.

Similarly, the cooperative subsistence practices of many of the residents of Wyoming County were carried over as both a necessary adaptation to hard times and as a means of subsidizing the coal industry. It should be noted, however, that those who engaged in such practices had no other option besides leaving the area to find work elsewhere. Related to these cooperative networks was the peculiar practice in southern West Virginia of deeding the title to hundreds of acres of extended family land to a single relative. While this may have lessened tax burdens in preindustrial times, with the mass entry of industrial speculators into the county it often facilitated the dispossession of families of the lands they had once relied on for self-sufficiency. Alienated from their homes and fields, these mountaineers had to move into commercial centers or coal camps, and place their welfare in the hands of coal-dominated institutions. The lands they lost were marginal in terms of agricultural desirability, but their rich mineral reserves were easily extracted due to the rugged topography of the mountains. Rather than digging expensive vertical shafts, most operators could reach coal veins with simple horizontal drift tunnels. This easy physical accessibility, in turn, contributed to the overproduction of coal in southern West Virginia, which affected the national coal market adversely and caused a severe lag in mine employment, while forcing families into greater debt with company stores. The rugged topography coupled with the erosive stripping and deforestation of lands by extractive industries has also aggravated the frequency of flash floods, which have never been uncommon in the region. Floods can destroy crops that families grow to supplement their incomes, demolish homes, and expedite the need for federal relief in the area. Flood control projects such as the R. D. Bailey Reservoir have only partially alleviated this problem.

* * *

In sum, from a political economy perspective, the present situation confronting the Monacans appears more promising than that facing the residents of Wyoming County. Nonetheless, the above comparison of variables illustrates that at specific points in time and space both communities qualified as internal colonies if measured by conventional standards. If, for example, one applies Blauner's (1969) famous list of criteria for determining the occurrence of colonialism, then both communities have fit squarely at some point in their respective histories. Both became politically and economically dominated by external forces; in both communities the colonizers exploited the land and natural and human resources; in both cases differences in power and autonomy were maintained through special laws and agencies. In the case of the Monacans, for example, miscegenation laws were ultimately enforced through the Virginia Office of Vital Statistics, while in Wyoming County the state government was (and to a significant degree remains) the colonial intermediary of absentee mineral corporations. And in both cases, doctrines of racism and ethnocentrism have played a key role in maintaining colonial structures.

But again, the situation facing the Monacans has notably changed for the better, while that confronting the residents of Wyoming County seems stagnant. This does not mean that the Monacans' experiences vis-à-vis colonial forces have been less eventful. Indeed, at various times the Monacans have faced policies of genocide, documentary or otherwise. What it does suggest is that the colonial experiences of these divergent communities within the Appalachian region have been vastly different and have involved different parties at different points in time. What implications do these differences suggest concerning the occurrence or paucity of relations of colonialism and dependency in the region?

As introduced in the first chapter, Michael Hechter posits the following model for determining if a region qualifies as a periphery colony, or an internal colony:

> These three concepts of peripherality may be tentatively sorted out by their relationship to five particular variables: (1) the degree of administrative integration [i.e., the extent to which laws passed for the core apply to the periphery], (2) the extensiveness of citizenship in the periphery [with regard to civil, political, and social rights], (3) the prestige of the peripheral culture, (4) the existence of geographical contiguity, and (5) the length of association between the periphery and core. . . . If each of these variables is assigned a high or low rank, then a *colony* is a region generally ranked low on all five variables; an *internal colony* is given a high rank on (1), (2), and (4), and a medium rank on (5); and a *peripheral region* is ranked highly on all the variables. (Hechter, 1975: p. 349)

Hechter apparently proposed this model with the expectation that it would be embraced for strictly quantitative analysis, as his own work on the Celts was based primarily on statistical data such as voting records. Hechter himself never used the model but only presented it by way of conclusion. Moreover, he did not adequately operationalize his terminology. It is not surprising then, that his model has not been (to my knowledge) put to use. The use of quantitative methodology can, in itself, be problematic when applied to the explication of colonial situations. Descriptive statistics may be useful in revealing how many people died in a given place at the hands of imperial forces, or how much land was lost, but statistical studies of, say, voting records are of limited utility when they do not reveal conditions that cause people to react in certain ways. For example, voting records reveal that West Virginia is a solidly Democratic state, but they do not immediately suggest that many Republicans register as Democrats with the hope of getting elected. Nor does such a trend imply political efficacy among the grassroots citizenry.

As I have illustrated, the people whom West Virginia residents send to the state capital do not necessarily represent their interests but frequently cater to the interests of industry first. Moreover, one must be careful not to fall into the trap of using statistics to rank situations of colonialism or oppression. Such an approach risks the ignoring of some oppressive situations on the grounds that others are more urgent.

Therefore, I suggest a less quantitative application of the Hechter model in order to determine not the degree to which a given region may or may not be colonized, but what conditions must be present in order for specific communities to enjoy meaningful, balanced development and social and political autonomy. This is where Walls's (1976) world-systems application is useful. Employing Wallerstein's (1974) three concepts of peripheral, semiperipheral, and core nation-states, Walls adjusts this model to suggest how certain regions *within* a nation-state become dependent on core areas, and how under certain conditions peripheral regions can become semiperipheral, and semiperipheral areas can move toward equitable integration into the world capitalist system. In other words, rather than dispensing with the colonial model, I am suggesting combining it with dependency analysis and with the insight of world-systems analysts that dependency need not always be irreversible.

I will continue to use Hechter's terminology—colony, internal colony, and periphery—as I have already made the case for instances of internal colonialism in Appalachia. Moreover, the term "colony" still seems applicable when dealing with indigenous peoples in America, especially for federally recognized tribes, since they have not been fully integrated (politically or legally) into the federal system (Deloria, 1988). In previous chapters I assayed in preliminary applications of the Hechter model for the respective communities at different points in time. I will focus on the present, ranking each variable on a scale of 1 to 5—1 being low, 3 being intermediate, and 5 high (see table). Admittedly, this does not represent a clear break from quantification. However, rather than engaging in rigorous statistical analyses that might hide certain unmeasurable factors, I will employ a counterintuitive approach to analyze the data herein. Again, the point is not to make precise measurements of colonialism or dependency, but rather to identify what conditions exist that either perpetuate such situations or allow for their diminishment.

To begin with the Monacans, it is amazing how rapidly the Monacans have emerged from the grasp of a firmly entrenched colonial structure over a period of thirty years or less. Beginning in the 1960s, numerous forces converged to make such a transition possible. The federal courts mandated public school integration and the end of miscegenation laws, mainstream metropolitan values became more sympathetic toward Native Americans, and the county's agriculturally dominated economy gave way to a more diversified economy linked with the nearby metropolis of Lynchburg. Thus, individual Monacans were able to attain a higher degree of education and find better and more equitable employment close to home, rather than leaving the area as had many of their older relatives. These conditions allowed certain tribal members who had moved away long ago to return home. Combined with public sympathy toward

The Monacan Nation and Wyoming County: Variables of Peripheralization

Variable	Monacan Nation	Wyoming County
1. Degree of administrative integration	5	5
2. Extent of citizenship	5	3+/-
3. Prestige	4+/-	1
4. Geographical contiguity	5	3+
5. Length of association between core and periphery	5	5

Natives, such homecomings renewed pride in tribal identity among the Monacans, and reinforced their emergent sense of *Peoplehood,* which had been under constant attack in earlier times. By 1989, the Monacans gained state recognition as an Indian tribe. Moreover, many of those returning home came equipped with new skills they had attained while away—business expertise or the charismatic energy necessary to assert political agendas. Now the Monacan *Nation* is seeking recognition from the federal government as a sovereign indigenous entity. If any one factor stands out as unique among those that have facilitated these positive changes, it is the Monacans' enduring sense of peoplehood. This has been the rallying point for community solidarity and has afforded the Monacans a large measure of political efficacy in recent years.

Although the Monacans are an indigenous people whose lands were invaded and usurped, I would nonetheless assign a rank of 5 for "administrative integration," as most of the Monacans willingly participate in the American political system. By the same token, I would assign a rank of 5 in the category of "citizenship," as the Monacans are now fully franchised voters whose solidarity as a tribe is recognized by state and local politicians. Indeed, candidates for various offices now request special meetings with the tribe at campaign time, realizing that the Monacans are capable of swaying many votes. The category of "prestige," however, is questionable. Although Native Americans currently enjoy a high degree of popularity in the mainstream limelight and in Amherst County, such sympathies are often born of the perception of Indians as "exotic others." Indeed, many non-Indians who had never encountered the Monacans might well be disappointed to find that many of the tangible aspects of aboriginal culture have been lost. Moreover, although tensions between Indians and non-Indians have ameliorated considerably over the past thirty years, racism is not dead in the county. It still lurks in the shadows, whether in the overt form of old ladies referring to Monacans as "Issues," or in more subtle forms, like the hesitance of certain local landowners to sell land to the tribe. Thus, I would assign this variable a fluctuating rank of 4+/-, as it remains an unresolved point. The variable of "geographical contiguity," however, warrants a rank of 5, as it is no longer relevant. Finally, the "length of association between core and periphery" also warrants a rank of 5, although I question this as a consistently determinate variable. As many of the indigenous peoples of Central and South America can testify, time does not necessarily resolve colonial situations.

The current situation in Wyoming County does not seem as positive. The state government of West Virginia has essentially been structured around industrial interests from its inception, making it difficult for anyone to successfully challenge this structure. Although New Deal reforms gave miners a political voice by protecting their legal right to unionize, the coal industry responded by replacing more and more miners with machines. Moreover, these reforms did not address more critical issues such as the absentee ownership of a majority of the land and minerals in southern West Virginia, nor the disproportionately low taxation of these lands. These are still pervading problems in West Virginia, critical factors influencing the current limitations to meaningful and balanced local development. In Wyoming County, nearly 90 percent of the local land base is absentee owned, and corporations consistently challenge local tax assessments and override them by appealing to the state government. Citizens of Wyoming County have occasionally presented a unified political front to bring about reforms, as in the case of the coal reserves tax, but their solidarity is not consistent. They lack a unifying sense of Peoplehood, which has been a critical factor in affording the Monacans political efficacy. Even if such solidarity did exist at the county level, it would be of limited efficacy unless it could be sustained across several West Virginia counties. Unless that happens, Wyoming County will continue to be dominated by a single-industry economy under the current political configuration.

The residents of Wyoming County, unlike the Monacans, have never been in a position—politically or socially—to consider themselves a distinct nation, nor have they ever been treated as such.

Therefore, to the variable of "administrative integration" I would assign a rank of 5. But although they are technically full-fledged citizens of the United States and of West Virginia, this does not mean that their interests are well represented at either level. As I have stated repeatedly, the state government customarily places industry first and people second. Although citizens' groups successfully lobbied for the coal reserves tax in the 1970s, it has not been enforced to its fullest extent by the state government, and local revenues have suffered while citizens have had to bear the brunt of tax burdens. Meanwhile, the federal government has only pursued trickle-down approaches to social and economic development. To the category of "citizenship," then, I would assign a rank of 3+/-, since the political efficacy of Wyoming County residents of is moderately high at times, but inconsistently so. The degree of "prestige," unfortunately, has remained consistently low for the residents of Wyoming County and of West Virginia in general, and warrants only a rank of 1. In mainstream America, West Virginians have come to symbolize the quintessential Appalachian stereotype—that of the "backward hillbilly." To illustrate this point I can draw on personal experience. On more than one occasion, when I mentioned to certain colleagues and acquaintances that part of my research for this study involved West Virginia, their reaction was to hum the theme from the film *Deliverance*. What is more disturbing is the fact that these offensive stereotypes frequently inform and justify development strategies in the region, as evidenced by some of the activities of the ARC. Perhaps there is a mutual relationship between these stereotypes and the variable of geographical contiguity, which I assign a rank of 3+. Although Wyoming County has always been fully integrated into the American federalist system, it remains relatively distant from major metropoles and political centers. The nearest interstate highway is thirty miles from the county line, but because transportation arteries seem to be slowly improving I added the (+) to indicate an ascending rank. Finally, in the case of Wyoming County there is no question that the length of association between core and periphery warrants a rank of 5.

According to my interpretation of this model, the Monacan Nation qualifies as a peripheral region and Wyoming County as an internal colony. The irony is striking. Contrary to the arguments of some colonial theorists that Indian tribes have been the most powerless groups in America (e.g., Thomas, 1966/67; Jorgensen, 1971), here is an instance where certain nonindigenous groups within a single (broadly defined) region appear to be considerably more powerless than an indigenous group within the same region. Three categories stand out: the extent of citizenship, prestige, and geographical contiguity. These categories capsulize the instances where social, economic, and environmental forces have converged to determine how each community has been integrated into the national political economy. It might be argued, then, that if the residents of Wyoming County enjoyed a higher degree of prestige in the mainstream limelight, they might also experience greater political efficacy as citizens, and geographical barriers between the county and metropoles might be breached, which would mean the local economy would become more diversified.

This model, however, leaves some issues unaddressed. Why do the Monacans enjoy a higher degree of prestige? I would venture to say it is because they are less isolated from metropolitan society and especially because of recent mainstream interests in Native Americans as exotic "others." This could be problematic for the Monacans in the long run, as mainstream interests and perceptions of Natives have historically fluctuated between sentiments of preservation, segregation, and assimilation, and have influenced government policy accordingly (Berkhoffer, 1978; Hoxie, 1987). What this means is that any of these variables is likely to fluctuate and could change the entire scheme of power relations. But for the present, perhaps the most important question concerns the distinction between an internal colony and a peripheral region. According to the terminology of this model, the Monacans are still peripheral. What does this mean?

Hechter's meaning for peripheral region was probably more akin to what Wallerstein or Walls would call semiperipheral regions. Thus, I would argue that if a given region or group ranks high in all five variables of the Hechter model, then it can be said that the necessary preconditions exist for the *possibility*, not necessarily the immediate reality, of meaningful and balanced development. These conditions are lacking in Wyoming County for several reasons implicit in the model. First, the residents lack enough sustained internal unity or solidarity with their neighbors in other counties to challenge the existing power structure. Second, they have historically been physically isolated from major centers of government and commerce. This isolation inhibited the capacity of local residents to participate in and influence state politics, especially at the crucial moment when West Virginia was vying for statehood and industrialists leaped at the opportunity to seize control. Likewise, this isolation restricted the availability of capital in the area, especially after Congress standardized American currency during the Civil War. Third, their isolation and contrasting cultural values and lifeways have been the subject of relentless criticism from mainstream society. Although mountaineers are frequently cast in a light of "otherness," they are seldom viewed as exotic, but rather simply as poor whites. With limited political efficacy at the local level, development strategies affecting Wyoming County are most often generated outside the region and are guided by mainstream middle-class biases, which have helped to marginalize local residents over the years.

In short, if one assesses the current situations confronting the Monacan Nation and Wyoming County respectively, it would appear that prospects for meaningful and balanced development are grim in the latter case, while the necessary preconditions are in place for the Monacans. But once again, it must be noted that any of these variables could change at any time, bringing about a reconfiguration of power relations.

And as positive as things may seem for the Monacans, they are actually in a precarious position. They are currently straddling a threshold in which they must decide the degree of political and economic autonomy they wish to exercise as a nation. Will they simply be satisfied with equitable integration into the national political economy as individuals? If they gain federal recognition, then the prospects for collective tribal autonomy look promising; if they do not, they may suffer a severe blow to collective autonomy and morale. On the other hand, in Wyoming County economic prosperity is not as contingent upon local political autonomy. In a sense, then, the people of Wyoming County currently have less at stake than the Monacans.

* * *

My intention in this study has been to explicate the relationship between conditions of economic dependency and colonial processes in two specific communities within the Appalachian region. I have illustrated that in both cases the development of dependency was intimately tied to colonial processes, though certain internal elements likewise contributed to dependency. However, I have also shown that these communities and the colonial situations confronting them have differed in profound ways. Thus, while one might justifiably use this theoretical consolidation to generalize about the relationship between colonialism and dependency in some instances, one must not ignore the detailed nuances revealed through comparative study. Moreover, while my use of more than one theoretical perspective has provided a more holistic understanding of the causes and consequences of underdevelopment in certain parts of the region, I make no claim to a grand theory for understanding political economy in every corner of Appalachia. Just as these two communities and the circumstances confronting them have differed in various ways, other communities are diverse in additional ways. Had I focused on communities within the region that are much more reliant on commercial agriculture, the internal colonial model might have been entirely inappropriate. Instead, I might have found that conditions of dependency hinged instead on major shifts in the national agricultural market and that farmers in such areas experienced economic conditions no different from farmers nationwide. My overall purpose, however, has been to illustrate that in spite of regional diversity, colonial processes have been—and remain—at work in some parts of Appalachia, and that these processes have been accompanied by relationships of dependency.

The tendency to cast Appalachia as a homogeneous region is a social construction, both internal and external. Internally, the founders of Appalachian studies and of regional political movements have posited the notion of regional homogeneity in order to effect a degree of political solidarity. However, I believe that emphasizing the region's diversity may prove more effective in bolstering political efficacy. Why? Because in the long run, skewed power relations within the region and between communities in the region and distant metropoles boil down to a cultural confrontation.

Scholars such as David Whisnant (1994) and Tom Plaut (1979) are on the mark in tracing the sundry social and economic problems of the region to conflicting cultural systems. What they do not emphasize is that several different though overlapping cultural systems exist within the region. From the perspective of mainstream society, however, there is only one generic cultural system—one that is epitomized by chronic poverty. This perception is used to justify uniform "trickle-down" approaches to develop a region so vast and diverse that no single strategy could possibly suit all of its communities. From a mainstream perspective, culturally derived explanations of poverty and strategies to cure it (even where it does not exist) ultimately define the region. As Richard Couto suggests, "These explanations are better understood as power relations expressed, in part, by spatial economic differences rather than as characteristics of residents of different regions. Cultural boundaries are defined by, from, and for the core region" (1995: p. 104).

This is the ongoing dilemma facing every community in the region, regardless of how rich or poor. Even the Monacans face the possibility of becoming "homogenized" Appalachians as long as they espouse values that clash with the larger discursive field of mainstream society, in which capitalism, law, and science—perhaps the three most powerful human forces in the world—mutually reinforce each other. On the other hand, the peculiar forms of colonial oppres-

sion the Monacans had to deal with—especially Walter Plecker's eugenic assault on their identity—had the ironic effect of providing
them with a unique shared experience that strengthened their solidarity in the long run. Paradoxically then, if externally generated
static images and definitions of Appalachia endure long enough,
communities throughout the region will discover a unifying rallying
point through which to advance their own agendas.

NOTES

1. The Seeds of Colonialism

1. This is based on detailed archaeological surveys of twelve Siouan burial mound complexes constructed in the Late Woodland Period (ca. AD 800–AD 1607). Hantman and his colleagues note several commonalties at all of these, including size, peculiar methods of construction, and physiographic location.

2. Hale (1883) recorded the Tutelo delineation for themselves as Yesah, meaning "the People." Mooney (1894) made the correlation between this and many of the recorded names of Siouan tribes (e.g., Nahyssan). Quite possibly, most of the Siouan settlements referred to themselves as Yesah, but may have added appellatives to distinguish residence.

3. Lederer wrote of the Virginia Siouans, "the Indians now seated here, are distinguished into the several nations of Mahoc, Nuntaneuck, alias Nuntaly, Nahyssan, Sapon, Managog, Mangoak, Akenatzy, Monakin, and so forth. One language is common to them all though they differ in dialects" (Alvord and Bidgood, 1912: p. 141).

4. This is based particularly on prolific archaeological recoveries of maize and on the analysis of human bone found at the Rapidan Mound Site dating to the Late Woodland Period (Holland, Spieden, and Van Roijen, 1983), which reveals a diet highly dependent on corn.

5. According to Lederer, "Every nation gives his particular ensigne or arms . . . the Nahysannes three arrows" (Alvord and Bidgood, 1912: p. 143). Bev-

285

erly noted variations in the arrow patterns for each "nation" as later adopted by the General Assembly to identify "friendly" nations (1722: p. 157). As will be discussed later, the appropriation of these cultural symbols by the Virginia government was incorporated into the 1677 treaty between Virginia and the Indians.

6. In fact, a letter dated 27 February 1677 from the Commissioners for Suppressing Bacon's Rebellion stated such motives, "we must confess they [the Virginia Indians] are our best guards to secure us on our frontieres from the incursion and suddaine assaults of those other Barbarous Indians of the Continent" (Stanard, 1970a: p. 277).

2. Tobacco Row

1. Speck continued to correspond with Mr. Johns, and he apparently planned a trip to the area to investigate the claim, but no record exists of such a visit.

2. These were the Pamunkey and Mataponi Reservations in King William County, the Gingaskin in Northampton County, and the Nottoway in Southampton County. The latter two were dissolved (Rountree, 1977: pp. 29–36).

3. Vest suggests a possible link between certain Monacan surnames and those of settlers adjacent to Fort Christanna—notably that of Hix (or Hicks), which may derive from a planter named George Hix, who lived near the fort (1992: pp. 26–27).

4. The campaign to induce the removal of Indians to lands across the Mississippi River was fueled by various motives, both benign and malevolent. Thomas Jefferson had been an early proponent of removal on the grounds that it would shelter Indians from the corruptive influences of white society while preparing them for civilization (Prucha, 1990: pp. 22–23). Andrew Jackson claimed similar motives, though his actions in forcing the issue while advocating states' rights over tribal sovereignty suggest a racially charged desire to free land for white settlement (Prucha, 1990: pp. 71–72). Removal became an official federal policy in 1830 (4 St. 411), though it did not affect the Monacans, as they were not federally recognized as a tribe.

5. Dr. Tom Holm proposed this idea to me. Frantz Fanon (1963) wrote of the "colonizer's guilt," which prompted colonizers to sometimes "justify" their actions through doctrines of ethnocentrism and European progress. Perhaps the proposed institutionalization of interethnic marriages was another form of justification.

6. In the purest sense of the term, a *People* and a *Nation* are one and the

same. As Spicer defines it, "A nation . . . consists of people who have in common a historical experience that they symbolize in ways giving them a common image of themselves" (1994: p. 30).

7. Daniel Gear, a member of the Monacan Nation, has suggested that the reason for the persistence of the term *Issue* in reference to the Monacans may have stemmed from a phonetic similarity between the word *Issue* and what Tutelo-Saponi speaking peoples called themselves in their native language: *Ye-sah* (roughly pronounced ee-saw)— the People.

8. I am indebted to Diane Johns Shields for bringing this contract and others to my attention. This contract and others were folded in the pages of old general store ledgers now in Mrs. Shields's possession.

3. Racism, Resistance, and Resurgence

1. Berkhoffer (1978) covers in detail the development of non-Indian images of Native Americans, including a good discussion on the "Vanishing American" stereotype. Hoxie (1987) and Holm (1978) analyze in detail the federal policies toward Natives during the assimilation era with regard to social perceptions and trends that motivated their formulation and implementation. Holm argues that the early twentieth century marked a watershed in federal Indian policy, as fledgling preservationist sentiments among non-Indians were gradually gaining ground over assimilationist sentiments.

2. J. David Smith provides an excellent and detailed account of Plecker's influence on Virginia miscegenation laws and his maniacal campaign to prevent what he perceived as the further degradation of the white race in Virginia in *The Eugenic Assault on America* (1993). Smith quotes extensively from numerous letters and primary documents authored by Plecker and fellow eugenicists.

3. Several of these letters on which this segment is based are in the Beale Papers, on file at the Monacan Tribal Museum, Bear Mountain, Virginia, including letters written by Indians to the Census Bureau inquiring why the enumerator had not asked them for their race.

4. Several of their letters to the census office can be found in the Beale Papers, Monacan Tribal Museum. Ambler and other businessmen served as the prime "investigators" in Plecker's efforts to prove the 1920 census enumerations inaccurate.

5. This section is based largely on my fieldnotes (Cook, 1996a) except where otherwise specified.

6. George Whitewolf, a Monacan man, was a devoted member of the American Indian Movement throughout the 1970s.

7. Although members of the St. Paul's Vestry did not sit on Tribal Council, they have always had an informal connection with the council in matters of welfare. On one occasion, when it was brought to the attention of the council and people at a tribal meeting that a tribal member had recently been laid off, the same announcement was made in church the next day, and an additional collection was taken for the cause, supplemented by rectory funds.

4. A Frontier Island

1. Ironically, the 1779 law was drafted by such liberals as Thomas Jefferson, James Madison, and Richard Henry Lee, who intended it for the protection of yeoman farmers. Nonetheless, absentee speculators took full advantage of deficiencies in the law, and by 1805, land records revealed in the area of what is now West Virginia 250 grants to absentees ranging from ten thousand to over one hundred thousand acres—five of them in excess of five hundred thousand acres (Rice, 1970: p. 136).

2. Mary Bowman's *Reference Book to Wyoming County History* is used extensively here, as it contains an impressive compilation of primary documents (1965: p. 80).

3. Between 1876 and 1900, the Republican electorate in Wyoming County reached a low of 44 percent in 1880, and a high of 56 percent in 1888 (Williams, 1972: p. 115).

5. Opening the Guyandotte Valley

1. The Glen Rogers mine was technically owned by the Raleigh-Wyoming Mining Company, and although its financial ties with the Pocahontas Field were clear, the mine was geographically situated in the Winding Gulf Field.

2. In Lincoln and Logan Counties, the courthouses conveniently caught on fire and original land records were burned.

3. Dix (1977) provides an excellent detailed description of the miner's work in the hand-loading days, for which there is little space for elaboration here.

4. In 1914, for example, a congressional investigation found that Judge Alston G. Dayton, who had issued a controversial injunction against the UMWA in 1907, held controlling interest in certain coal companies (Lunt, 1992: p. 51).

5. There is a considerable corpus of literature on the mine wars. The information in this section is derived from the following: Lane (1921), Corbin (1990), Savage (1990), and Lee (1969), in which the author, a former attorney general of the state of West Virginia gives a first-hand account of political corruption and the oppression of miners. Lunt (1992) provides a critical analysis of how coal operators shaped state and often national laws to stifle labor opposition.

6. Initially, the majority of employees at Glen Rogers, one of the largest mining communities in the county, were foreign-born (Bowman, 1965: p. 258).

6. The Epoch of Perpetual Dependency

1. In 1925, Wyoming County coal production peaked at 3,183,414 tons, dropping to 2,858,739 tons the following year, and 1,460,186 tons in 1932. It did not exceed 2 million tons again until 1936, or 3 million tons until 1940.

2. Marland served as governor from 1953 to 1957. His staunch adversarial relationship with a state legislature that was still dominated by coal operators accompanied his own personal battle with alcoholism, and he disappeared from public life at the end of his term. He was found driving a taxicab in Chicago in 1965 and died shortly thereafter of cancer (*Independent Herald*, 2 Dec. 1965).

3. The 1996 gubernatorial campaign occurred during my fieldwork in the area, and I was able to follow the race closely. As a Republican, Underwood won the race by a narrow margin because his Democratic opponent, Charlotte Pritt, had challenged incumbent candidate Gaston Caperton in the previous race as an independent, and many people in the state regarded her as a traitor to the Democratic party.

4. Jay Rockefeller, great-grandson of oil magnate John D. Rockefeller, actually came to West Virginia as a VISTA worker in the mid-1960s. When he moved to the state in the late 1970s with the intention of running for governor, he initially used his experience as a VISTA worker to gain political support, but soon abandoned this tactic on the advice of his staff. Apparently, the VISTAS left very few positive memories in the state, whether among county officials or people at the grassroots (Cook, 1996c).

BIBLIOGRAPHY

Adkins, Howard G. 1977. Functional areas in West Virginia. In Howard G. Adkins, Steve Ewing, and Chester E. Zimolzak, eds., *West Virginia and Appalachia*. Dubuque IA: Kendall/Hunt, 185–99.

Alavi, Hamza. 1980. India: Transition from feudalism to colonial capitalism. *Journal of Contemporary Asia* 10: 359–99.

Albers, Patricia C. 1996. Changing patterns of ethnicity in the Northern Plains, 1780–1870. In Jonathon D. Hill, ed., *History, Power, and Identity: Ethnogenesis in the Americas, 1492–1992*. Iowa City: University of Iowa Press, 90–118.

Alexander, Edward Porter, ed. 1972. *The Journal of John Fontaine: An Irish Huguenot Son in Spain and Virginia, 1710–1719*. Charlottesville: The University Press of Virginia.

Althusser, Louis, and Etienne Balibar. 1971. *Reading Capital*. London: New Left Books.

Alvord, C. W., and Lee Bidgood, eds. 1912. *The First Explorations of the Trans-Allegheny Region by the Virginians, 1650–1674*. Cleveland: Arthur H. Clark.

Ambler, James J., IV. 1956. Letter to Florence Cowan (Dec. 28). Bear Mountain VA, on file at Monacan Ancestral Museum.

Anders, Gary. 1979. The internal colonization of Cherokee Native Americans. *Development and Change* 10 (1): 41–55.

Anglin, Mary K. 1992. A question of loyalty: National and regional identity in narratives of Appalachia. *Anthropological Quarterly* 65: 105–16.

——. 1993. Strategic differences: Gendered labor in southern Appalachia. *Frontiers* 14 (1):68–86.

Appalachian Land Ownership Task Force (ALOTF). 1980. *Land Ownership and Property Taxation in West Virginia.* Report submitted to the Appalachian Regional Commission.

——. 1981. *Land Ownership Patterns and Their Impacts on Appalachian Communities: A Survey of 80 Counties.* Report submitted to the Appalachian Regional Commission.

Appalachian Regional Commission (ARC). 1967–96. *Annual Report.* Washington DC: Appalachian Regional Commission.

——. 1968. *State and Regional Plans in Appalachia, 1968.* Washington DC: Appalachian Regional Commission.

——. 1974. The New Appalachian subregions and their development strategies. *Appalachia* 8: 10–27.

——. 1995. History of ARC. *Appalachia* 28 (1–2): 59–68.

Appalachian Research and Defense Fund (ARDF). 1978. Coal government in Appalachia. In Helen M. Lewis, Linda Johnson, and Don Askins, eds., *Colonialism in Modern America: The Appalachian Case.* Boone NC: Appalachian Consortium Press, 277–82.

Atack, Jeremy, and Peter Passell. 1994. *A New Economic View of American History.* 2nd ed. New York: W. W. Norton.

Bailey, Kenneth R. 1973. A judicious mixture: Negroes and immigrants in the West Virginia Mines, 1880–1917. *West Virginia History* 34: 141–61.

Baran, Paul A. 1957. *The Political Economy of Growth.* New York: Monthly Review Press.

Barbour, Phillip L. 1968. Captain Newport meets Opacanough. *Virginia Cavalcade* 17 (3): 12–47.

Barnum, Donald T. 1970. *The Negro in the Bituminous Coal Industry.* Philadelphia: University of Pennsylvania Press.

Barth, Fredrik, ed. 1969. *Ethnic Groups and Boundaries: The Social Organization of Cultural Difference.* Boston: Little, Brown, and Co.

Batteau, Allen, ed. 1983a. *Appalachia and America: Autonomy and Regional Dependence.* Lexington: University Press of Kentucky.

——. 1983b. Rituals of dependence in Appalachian Kentucky. In Allen Batteau, ed., *Appalachia and America.* Lexington: University Press of Kentucky.

——. 1990. *The Invention of Appalachia.* Tucson: University of Arizona Press.

Beaver, Patricia D. 1986. *Rural Community in the Appalachian South.* Lexington: University Press of Kentucky.

Berkhoffer, Robert F., Jr. 1978. *The White Man's Indian: Images of the American Indian from Columbus to the Present.* New York: Alfred A. Knopf.

Bernard, H. Russell. 1994. *Research Methods in Anthropology: Qualitative and Quantitative Approaches.* 2nd ed. Thousand Oaks CA: Sage Publications.

Berry, Brewton. 1963. *Almost White: A Study of Certain Racial Hybrids in Eastern United States.* New York: Macmillian.

Bethell, Thomas N., and Davitt McAteer. 1978. The Pittston mentality: Manslaughter on Buffalo Creek. In Helen M. Lewis, Linda Johnson, and Don Askins, eds., *Colonialism in Modern America: The Appalachian Case.* Boone NC: Appalachian Consortium Press, 259–75.

Beverly, Robert. 1705. *The History of the Present State of Virginia.* Book 3. London.

Bilby, Kenneth. 1996. Ethnogesis in the Guianas and Jamaica: Two Maroon cases. In Jonathon D. Hill, ed., *History, Power, and Identity: Ethnogenesis in the Americas, 1492–1992.* Iowa City: University of Iowa Press, 119–41.

Billings, Dwight. 1974. Culture and poverty in Appalachia: A theoretical discussion and empirical analysis. *Social Forces* 53: 315–23.

Blauner, Robert. 1969. Internal colonialism and ghetto revolt. *Social Problems* 16 (4): 393–408.

Blaut, J. M. 1989. Colonialism and the rise of capitalism. *Science and Society* 53 (3): 260–96.

Bowman, Mary K. 1965. *Reference Book of Wyoming County History.* Parsons WV: McClain Printing.

Bozzoli, Belinda. 1983. Marxism, Feminism, and South African studies. *Journal of South African Studies* 9 (2): 139–71.

Bradshaw, Michael. 1992. *The Appalachian Regional Commission: Twenty-Five Years of Government Policy.* Lexington: University Press of Kentucky.

Branscome, Jim. 1978. The federal government in Appalachia—TVA. In Helen M. Lewis, Linda Johnson, and Don Askins, eds., *Colonialism in Modern America: The Appalachian Case.* Boone NC: Appalachian Consortium Press, 288–93.

———. 1983. What the New Frontier and Great Society brought. In Bruce Ergood and Bruce E. Kuhre, eds., *Appalachia: Social Context Past and Present.* 2nd ed. Dubuque IA: Kendall/Hunt, 247–56.

Brown v. Board of Education. 1954. 347 U.S. 483.

Bryant, Sharon, ed. 1997. *The Monacan Indian Nation: Reclaiming Our Heritage* (Documentary Video). Bear Mountain, VA: Monacan Indian Nation.

Bushnell, David I. 1914. The Indian grave: A Monacan site in Albermarle County, Virginia. *William and Mary Quarterly* 23 (2): 106–12.

———. 1930. The five Monacan towns in Virginia. *Smithsonian Miscellaneous Collections* 82 (12).

Byrd, William II. 1866. *History of the Dividing Line between Virginia and North Carolina as Seen in 1728–29.* Raleigh: Publication of the North Carolina Historical Commission.

Cabbell, Edward J. 1980. Black invisibility and racism in Appalachia: An informal survey. *Appalachian Journal* 8 (1): 48–54.

Campbell, John C. 1921. *The Southern Highlander and His Homeland.* New York: Russell Sage Foundation.

Caporaso, James. 1980. Dependency theory: Continuities and discontinuities in development studies. *International Organization* 34 (4): 605–28.

Casanova, Pablo. 1965. Internal colonialism and national development. *Comparative International Development* 1: 27–37.

Caudill, Harry M. 1963. *Night Comes to the Cumberlands: A Biography of a Depressed Area.* Boston: Atlantic Monthly Press.

Church to give land to Monacan tribe. 1995. *Roanoke Times and World News* (March 8).

Clarkson, Roy B. 1964. *Tumult on the Mountain: Lumbering in West Virginia, 1770–1920.* Parsons WV: McClain Printing.

Clifford, James. 1988. *The Predicament of Culture: Twentieth-Century Ethnography, Literature, and Art.* Cambridge MA: Harvard University Press.

Cohen, Felix S. 1949. Indian self-government. In Lucy Cohen, ed., *The Legal Conscience: Selected Papers of Felix S. Cohen* (1960). New Haven CT: Yale University Press, 305–14.

Cook, Samuel R. 1995. Fieldnotes, Wyoming County WV (July 10–August 5, pilot study).

———. 1996a. Fieldnotes on Monacan Indian Nation (June–December).

———. 1996b. Field Interviews with Monacan tribal members (June–July).

———. 1996c. Fieldnotes on Wyoming County WV (August–December).

———. 1996d. Field Interviews with Wyoming County WV residents (August–September).

———. 1998. The Great Depression, subsistence, and views of poverty in Wyoming County, West Virginia. *Journal of Appalachian Studies* 4 (2): 271–83.

Corbin, David Alan, ed. 1990. *The West Virginia Mine Wars: An Anthology.* Charleston wv: Appalachian Editions.

Cornell, Stephen. 1988. *The Return of the Native: American Indian Political Resurgence.* New York: Oxford University Press.

Couto, Richard A. 1994. *An American Challenge: A Report on Economic Trends and Social Issues in Appalachia.* Dubuque ia: Kendall/Hunt.

———. 1995. Spatial distribution of wealth and poverty in Appalachia. *Journal of Appalachian Studies* 1 (1): 99–120.

Cowan, Florence. 1956. St. Paul's Mission. *The Southwestern Episcopalian* (November): 6.

———. 1963. Letter to the *Amherst New Era Progress* (July 4).

Cubby, Edwin Albert. 1962. The Transformation of the Tug and Guyandotte Valleys: Economic development and social change in West Virginia, 1888–1921. Ph.D. diss., Syracuse University.

Cunningham, Rodger. 1987. *Apples on the Flood: The Southern Mountain Experience.* Knoxville: University of Tennessee Press.

Davis, Robert. 1977. Urbanization in Appalachia: Spatial patterns and social impact. In Howard G. Adkins, Steve Ewing, and Chester E. Zimolzak, eds., *West Virginia and Appalachia.* Dubuque ia: Kendall/Hunt, 49–55.

Day, Graham. 1994. The reconstruction of Wales and Appalachia: Development and regional identity. In Phillip J. Obermiller, and William W. Philliber, eds., *Appalachia in an International Context: Cross-National Comparisons of Developing Regions.* Westport ct: Praeger, 45–66.

Deloria, Vine, Jr. 1988. Beyond the pale: American Indians and the Constitution. In Jules Lobel, ed., *A Less Than Perfect Union.* New York: Monthly Review Press, 249–67.

Deloria, Vine, Jr., and Clifford M. Lytle. 1983. *American Indians, American Justice.* Austin: University of Texas Press.

Dewar, Helen. 1963. Nobody wants the Amherst Indians. *The Washington Post* (May 26): sec. B.

Dix, Keith. 1977. *Work Relations in the Coal Industry: The Hand Loading Era, 1880–1930.* Morgantown wv: Institute for Labor Studies.

———. 1988. *What's a Miner to Do? The Mechanization of Coal Mining.* Pittsburgh: University of Pittsburgh Press.

Dixon, Richard D., and Ram N. Singh. 1977. Changing characteristics of the West Virginia population: 1940–1970. In Howard G. Adkins, Steve Ewing, and Chester E. Zimolzak, eds., *West Virginia and Appalachia.* Dubuque ia: Kendall/Hunt, 69–81.

Dogan, Mattei, and Dominique Pelassy. 1984. *How to Compare Nations: Strategies in Comparative Politics.* Chatham NJ: Chatham House.

Dos Santos, Theodoro. 1970. The structure of dependence. *American Economic Review* 60: 231–36.

Dubofsky, Melvyn, and Warren Van Tine. 1977. *John L. Lewis.* New York: Quadrangle.

Duff, Ernest R. 1931. Letter to W. M. Stewart, Director of the Census (February 4). Bear Mountain VA, Beale Papers, on file at Monacan Ancestral Museum.

Dunaway, Wilma A. 1996. *The First American Frontier: Transition to Capitalism in Southern Appalachia, 1700–1860.* Chapel Hill: University of North Carolina Press.

————. 1997. Rethinking Cherokee acculturation: Agrarian capitalism and women's resistance to the cult of domesticity, 1800–1838. *American Indian Culture and Research Journal* 21 (1): 155–92.

Durkheim, Emile. 1964. *The Division of Labor in Society.* New York: Free Press.

Editorial Staff of Labor Relations Reporter. 1967. *The New Wage and Hour Law: Revised Edition—1967.* Washington DC: Bureau of National Affairs.

Egerton, John. 1983. Appalachia: A view from the hills. In Bruce Ergood and Bruce E. Kuhre, eds., *Appalachia: Social Context Past and Present.* 2nd ed. Dubuque IA: Kendall/Hunt, 238–42.

Eller, Ronald D. 1982. *Miners, Millhands, and Mountaineers: Industrialization of the Appalachian South, 1880–1930.* Knoxville: University of Tennessee Press.

Ergood, Bruce. 1983. Toward a definition of Appalachia. In Bruce Ergood and Bruce E. Kuhre, eds., *Appalachia: Social Context Past and Present.* 2nd ed. Dubuque IA: Kendall/Hunt, 31–41.

Escobar, Arturo. 1994. *Encountering Development: The Making and Unmaking of the Third World.* Princeton NJ: Princeton University Press.

Estabrook, Arthur H. and Ivan E. McDougle. 1926. *Mongrel Virginians.* Baltimore: Williams and Wilkins Co.

Evans, E. Estyn. 1969. The Scotch-Irish: Their cultural adaptation and heritage in the American Old West. In E. R. R. Green, ed., *Essays in Scotch-Irish History.* London: Routledge and Kegan Paul.

Evans, Lewis. 1755. *General Map of the Middle British Colonies and the Country of the Confederate Indian.* Philadelphia: B. Franklin and D. Hall.

Evans-Pritchard, E. E. 1940. *The Nuer: A Description of the Modes of Liveli-hood and Political Institutions of a Nilotic People.* Oxford: Oxford University Press.

Faiman-Silva, Sandra. 1996. *Choctaws at the Crossroads: The Political Economy of Class and Culture In the Oklahoma Timber Region.* Lincoln: University of Nebraska Press.

Feest, Christian F. 1973. Notes on Saponi settlements in Virginia prior to 1714. *Quarterly Bulletin of the Archaeological Society of Virginia* 28 (3): 152–55.

Feller, John W. n.d. Unpublished manuscript on the history of Mullens wv, 1930–1997.

Finger, John R. 1984. *The Eastern Band of Cherokee Indians.* Knoxville: University of Tennessee Press.

———. 1991. *Cherokee Americans: The Eastern Band of Cherokees in the Twentieth Century.* Lincoln: University of Nebraska Press.

Finley, Joseph E. 1972. *The Corrupt Kingdom: The Rise and Fall of the United Mine Workers.* New York: Simon and Schuster.

Fisher, Steve. 1983. Victim blaming in Appalachia: Cultural theories and the southern mountaineer. In Bruce Ergood and Bruce E. Kuhre, eds. *Appalachia: Social Context Past and Present.* 2nd ed. Dubuque IA: Kendall/Hunt, 154–63.

Fixico, Donald L. 1986. *Termination and Relocation: Federal Indian Policy 1945–1960.* Albuquerque: University of New Mexico Press.

Foster, Jim, Steve Robinson, and Steve Fisher. 1978. Class, political consciousness, and destructive power: A strategy for change in Appalachia. *Appalachian Journal* 5 (3): 290–311.

Foucault, Michel. 1980. *Power/Knowledge.* New York: Pantheon.

Frank, Andre Gunder. 1966. The development of underdevelopment. *Monthly Review* 16: 17–31.

Freire, Paulo. 1970. *Pedagogy of the Oppressed.* New York: Continuum.

Gaventa, John. 1978. Property, coal, and theft. In Helen M. Lewis, Linda Johnson, and Don Askins, eds., *Colonialism in Modern America: The Appalachian Case.* Boone NC: Appalachian Consortium Press, 141–59.

———. 1980. *Power and Powerlessness: Quiescence and Rebellion in an Appalachian Valley.* Urbana: University of Illinois Press.

———. 1994. From the mountains to the Maquiladoras: A case study of capitalist flight and its impact on workers. In Phillip J. Obermiller and

William W. Philliber, eds., *Appalachia in an International Context: Cross-National Comparisons of Developing Regions.* Westport CT: Praeger, 165–76.

Geertz, Clifford. 1973. *The Interpretation of Cultures.* New York: Basic Books.

Gidez, Robert M. 1978. Natural hazards in Appalachia. *Appalachia* 11 (2): 1–19.

Gillenwater, Mack M. 1977. Mining settlements of southern West Virginia. In Howard G. Adkins, Steve Ewing, and Chester E. Zimolzak, eds.. *West Virginia and Appalachia.* Dubuque IA: Kendall/Hunt, 132–57.

Ginsburg, Faye, and Rayna Rapp, eds. 1995. *Conceiving the New World Order: The Global Politics of Reproduction.* Berkeley: University of California Press.

Gledhill, John. 1994. *Power and Its Disguises.* London: Pluto Press.

Glen Rogers is coming town of Wyoming County—1921. 1921. *Raleigh Register* (December 21), 1.

Gray, Arthur. 1908. A Virginia tribe of Indians. *The Southern Churchman* (January 4): 1–2.

Green, Barbara. 1987. Monacans rebound from hard times. *Richmond News Leader* (August 27): 26–28.

Griffin, James B. 1942. On the historic location of the Tutelo and Mohetan in the Ohio Valley. *American Anthropologist* 44 (2): 275–80.

Guyot, Arnold. 1861. On the Appalachian Mountain system. *American Journal of Science and Arts* 31: 157–87.

Hale, Horatio. 1883. The Tutelo tribe and language. *Proceedings of the American Philosophical Society* 21 (114): 1–49.

Hall, Helen. 1933. Miners must eat. *Atlantic Monthly* 152: 153–62.

Hansen, Karen Tranberg. 1984. Negotiating sex and gender in urban Zambia. *Journal of South African Studies* 10 (2): 218–36.

Hantman, Jeffrey. 1990. Between Powhatan and Quirank: Reconstructing Monacan culture and history in the context of Jamestown. *American Anthropologist* 92 (3): 676–90.

———. 1994. Powhatan's relations with the Piedmont Monacans. In Helen M. Rountree, ed., *Powhatan's Foreign Relations.* Charlottesville: University Press of Virginia, 94–111.

———. 1998. "Ancestral Monacan Society": Cultural and temporal boundedness in Indian history in Virginia. Paper presented at the Society for American Archaeology 63rd Annual Meeting (Washington DC, March).

Harrison, Fairfax. 1922. Western explorations of Virginia between Lederer and Spotswood. *Virginia Magazine of History and Biography* 30: 323–40.

Hart, John Fraser. 1977. Land rotation in Appalachia. *Geographical Review* 67: 148–66.

Hechter, Michael. 1975. *Internal Colonialism: The Celtic Fringe in British National Development, 1536–1966.* Berkeley: University of California Press.

Henning, William Walter, ed. 1823. *Statutes at Large: Being a Collection of All the Laws of Virginia.* Philadelphia: DeSilver.

Hibbert, Meg. 1995. Monacans celebrate return of land. *Amherst New Era Progress* (October 12): 1.

Hicks, George L. 1970. *Appalachian Valley.* New York: Holt, Reinhart and Winston.

Hill, Jonathon D., ed. 1996. *History, Power, and Identity: Ethnogenesis in the Americas, 1492–1992.* Iowa City: University of Iowa Press

Hitchman Coal and Coke Co. v. Mitchell, et al. 1917. 245 U.S. 229

Holland, C. G., Sandra Spieden, and David Van Roijen. 1983. The Rapidan Mound revisited: A test excavation of a prehistoric burial mound. *Quarterly Bulletin of the Archaeological Society of Virginia* 38: 1–42.

Horvath, Ronald J. 1972. A definition of colonialism. *Current Anthropology* 13: 45–57.

Houck, Peter W. 1984. *Indian Island in Amherst County.* Lynchburg VA: Lynchburg Historical Research Co.

Houck, Peter W., and Mintcy D. Maxham. 1993. *Indian Island in Amherst County.* Rev. ed. Lynchburg VA: Warwick House.

Hoxie, Frederick E. 1987. *A Final Promise: The Campaign to Assimilate the Indians, 1880–1920.* Cambridge: Cambridge University Press.

Hudson, Charles. 1976. *The Southeastern Indians.* Knoxville: University of Tennessee Press.

Hunt, Edward, Frederick G. Tryon, and Joseph H. Willitts. 1925. *What the Coal Commission Found.* Baltimore: Williams and Wilkins.

Independent Herald. 1965–1997. Pineville wv.

Jacobson, Cardell K. 1984. Internal colonialism and Native Americans. *Social Science Quarterly* 65 (1): 158–71.

Jefferson, Thomas. 1982 [1787]. *Notes on the State of Virginia.* New York: W. W. Norton.

Johns, Samuel. 1934. Letter to Frank G. Speck (September 4). Bear Mountain VA, Monacan Ancestral Museum.

Jorgensen, Joseph G. 1971. Indians and the metropolis. In Jack O. Waddell and O. Michael Watson, eds., *The American Indian in Urban Society.* Boston: Little, Brown and Co., 67–113.

———. 1978. *Native Americans and Energy Development.* Cambridge MA: Anthropology Resource Center.

Joshi, Tulasi R. 1977. Human resource development: West Virginia's future. In Howard G. Adkins, Steve Ewing, and Chester E. Zimolzak, eds., *West Virginia and Appalachia.* Dubuque IA: Kendall/Hunt, 93–98.

Kahn, Si. 1978. The Forest Service in Appalachia. In Helen M. Lewis, Linda Johnson, and Don Askins, eds., *Colonialism in Modern America: The Appalachian Case.* Boone NC: Appalachian Consortium Press, 85–109.

Kantor, Shawn Everett. 1998. *Politics and Property Rights: The Closing of the Open Range in the Postbellum South.* Chicago: University of Chicago Press.

Kaplan, Sidney. 1990. Historical efforts to encourage white-Indian intermarriage in the United States and Canada. *International Social Science Review* 65 (3): 126–32.

Kearney, M. 1995. The local and the global: The anthropology of globalization and transnationalism. *Annual Review of Anthropology* 24: 547–65.

Kennedy, N. Brent. 1994. *The Mellungeons: The Resurrection of a Proud People.* Macon GA: Mercer University Press.

Knipe, Edward E. and Helen M. Lewis. 1971. The impact of coal mining on the traditional mountain subculture. In J. Kenneth Moreland, ed., *The Not So Solid South: Anthropological Studies in a Regional Subculture.* Athens: University of Georgia Press, 25–37.

Kurath, Gertrude P. 1954. The Tutelo fourth night spirit release singing. *Midwest Folklore* 4: 87–105.

LaDuke, Winona, and Churchill, Ward. 1985. Native America: The political economy of radioactive colonialism. *Journal of Ethnic Studies* 13 (3): 117–32.

Laing, Joseph T. 1936. The Negro miner in West Virginia. *Social Forces* 14: 416–22.

LaLone, Mary B. 1996. Economic survival strategies in Appalachia's coal camps. *Journal of Appalachian Studies* 2 (1): 53–68.

Lambie, Joseph T. 1954. *From Mine to Market: The History of Coal Transportation on the Norfolk and Western Railway.* New York: New York University Press.

Lamphere, Louise. 1976. The internal colonization of the Navajo People. *Southwest Economy and Society* 1 (1): 6–14.

Lane, Winthrop D. 1921. *Civil War in West Virginia: A Story of the Industrial Conflict in the Coal Mines.* New York: B. W. Huebsch.

Lawson, John. 1860. *History of Carolina.* Raleigh NC: Strother and Marcum.

Lee, Howard B. 1969. *Bloodletting in Appalachia: A Story of West Virginia's Four Major Mine Wars and Other Thrilling Incidents of the Coal Fields.* Morgantown: West Virginia University Press.

Lewellen, Ted C. 1992. *Political Anthropology: An Introduction.* Westport CT: Bergin and Garvey.

Lewis, Helen M. 1983. Fatalism or the coal industry? In Bruce Ergood and Bruce E Kuhre, eds., *Appalachia: Social Context Past and Present.* 2nd ed. Dubuque IA: Kendall/Hunt, 180–89.

Lewis, Helen M., and John Gaventa. 1991. Participatory education and grassroots development: The case of rural Appalachia. New Market TN: Highlander Research and Education Center.

Lewis, Helen M., Linda Johnson, and Donald Askins, eds. 1978. *Colonialism in Modern America: The Appalachian Case.* Boone NC: Appalachian Consortium Press.

Lewis, Helen M., Sue Kobak, and Linda Johnson. 1978. Family, religion, and colonialism in Central Appalachia. In Helen M. Lewis, Linda Johnson, and Donald Askins, eds., *Colonialism in Modern America: The Appalachian Case.* Boone NC: Appalachian Consortium Press, 113–39.

Lewis, Ronald L. 1998. *Transforming the Appalachian Countryside: Railroads, Deforestation, and Social Change in West Virginia, 1880–1920.* Chapel Hill: University of North Carolina Press.

Leyburn, James G. 1962. *The Scotch-Irish: A Social History.* Chapel Hill: University of North Carolina Press.

Lieble, Charles L. 1977. The Appalachian region—myth or reality. In Howard G. Adkins, Steve Ewing, and Chester E. Zimolzak, eds., *West Virginia and Appalachia.* Dubuque IA: Kendall/Hunt, 1–8.

Loeb, Penny. 1997. Shear Madness. *U.S. News & World Report: Special Report* (August 11).

Love, Joseph L. 1990. The origins of dependency analysis. *Journal of Latin American Studies* 22 (1): 143–68.

Loving v. United States. 1967. 385 U.S. 1.

Lunt, Richard D. 1992. *Law and Order v. the Miners: West Virginia, 1907–1933.* Charleston WV: Appalachian Editions.

Malinowski, Bronislaw. 1922. *Argonauts of the Western Pacific.* New York: Dutton.

Mance v. Brown, Warden. 1913. 71 WV 519.

Marcus, George E. 1994. After the critique of ethnography: Faith, hope, and charity, and the greatest of these is charity. In Robert Borofsky, ed., *Assessing Cultural Anthropology.* New York: McGraw-Hill, 40–54.

McCoy, Clyde B. and Virgina McCoy Watkins. 1981. Stereotypes of Appalachian migrants. In William W. Philliber and Clyde B. McCoy, eds., *The Invisible Minority: Urban Appalachians.* Lexington: University Press of Kentucky, 20–31.

McIlwane, H. R., and Wilmer Hall, eds. 1925–45. *The Executive Journals of the Colonial Council of Virginia.* 5 vols. Richmond: Virginia State Library.

McKelway, Bill. 1995. Return of the Monacans. *Richmond Times-Dispatch* (April 23): G1–G3.

McLeRoy, Sherrie S., and William R. McLeRoy. 1993. *Strangers in Their Midst: The Free Black Population of Amherst County, Virginia.* Bowie MD: Heritage Books.

McLoughlin, William G. 1984. *Cherokees and Missionaries.* New Haven CT: Yale University Press.

Medicine, Bea. 1998. American Indians and anthropologists: Issues of history, empowerment, and application. *Human Organization* 57 (3): 253–57.

Merrell, James. 1984. The Indians' New World: The Catawba experience. *William and Mary Quarterly* 41: 537–65.

Mitchell, Robert D. 1977. *Commercialism and Frontier: Perspectives on the Early Shenandoah Valley.* Charlottesville: University Press of Virginia.

Mitchell v. Hitchman Coal and Coke Co., et al. 1914. 214 Fed. 685.

Monmonier, Mark S. 1977. Spatial aspects of West Virginia's physician shortage. In Howard G. Adkins, Steve Ewing, and Chester E. Zimolzak, eds., *West Virginia and Appalachia.* Dubuque IA: Kendall/Hunt, 81–91.

Mooney, James. 1894. Siouan tribes of the east. *Bureau of American Ethnology Bulletin 22.* Washington DC: Government Printing Office.

Mouer, L. Daniel. 1981. Powhatan and Monacan regional settlement hierarchies: A model of relationship between social and environmental structures. *Quarterly Bulletin of the Archaeological Society of Virginia* 36 (1): 1–21.

———. 1983. A review of the archaeology and ethnohistory of the Monacans. In J. Mark Wittkofski and Lyle E. Browning, eds., *Piedmont Archaeology* (Publication no. 10). Richmond: Archaeological Society of Virginia, 21–39.

Murray, Paul T. 1987. Who is an Indian? Who is a Negro? Virginia Indians in the World War II Draft. *Virginia Magazine of History and Biography* 95 (2): 215–31.

Neely, Sharlotte. 1984. The Snowbird Cherokees: Ethnic preservation in the southern mountains. In Patricia D. Beavers and Burton L. Purrington, eds., *Cultural Adaptations to Mountain Environments*. Athens: University of Georgia Press, 107–21.

————. 1991. *Snowbird Cherokees: People of Persistence*. Athens: University of Georgia Press.

Neill, E. D. 1886. *Virginia Crolorum: The Colony Under the Rule of Charles the First and Second, 1625–1685, Based Upon Manuscripts and Documents of the Period*. Albany NY: J. Munsell's Sons.

New mining town going up in Wyoming County. 1914. *Raleigh Register* (August 27), 1.

News From Monacan Country. 1996. (September/October).

North, E. Lee. 1985. *The 55 West Virginias: A Guide to the State's Counties*. Morgantown: West Virginia University Press.

Nyden, Paul J. 1979. An internal colony: Labor conflict and capitalism in Appalachian coal. *Insurgent Sociologist* 8: 33–43.

O'Neill, William J. 1969. The Amherst County Cherokee, Virginia's Lost Tribe. *The Washington Post* (June 15, Potomac section).

Palmer, William P., ed. 1875. *Calendar of Virginia State Papers and Other Manuscripts, 1652–1781*. Richmond: Virginia State Library.

Pascoe, Peggy. 1989. Race, gender, and interracial relations: The case of interracial marriage. *Frontiers* 12 (1): 5–18.

Patterson, Palmer. 1971. The colonial parallel: A view of Indian history. *Ethnohistory* 18 (1): 1–17.

Perdue, Theda. 1998. *Cherokee Women: Gender and Culture Change, 1700–1835*. Lincoln: University of Nebraska Press.

Perry, Huey. 1972. *"They'll Cut Off Your Project": A Mingo County Chronicle*. New York: Praeger.

Plaut, Tom. 1979. Appalachia and social change: A cultural systems approach. *Appalachian Journal* 6 (4): 250–63.

Plecker, Walter A. 1924. Letter to Irish Creek Resident (July 29). Bear Mountain VA, Monacan Ancestral Museum.

————. 1925a. *The New Family and Race Improvement*. Richmond VA: Bureau of Vital Statistics.

————. 1925b. Letter to W. M. Stewart, Director of the Census (January 14). Bear Mountain VA, Beale Papers, on file at Monacan Ancestral Museum.

————. 1926a. Letter to R. F. St. James (September 1). Bear Mountain VA, Monacan Ancestral Museum.

————1926b. Letter to Charles Davenport (September 1). Bear Mountain VA, Monacan Ancestral Museum.

————. 1940. Letter to Clerk of Rockbridge County Circuit Court (October 4). Bear Mountain VA, Monacan Ancestral Museum.

————. 1947. *Virginia's Vanished Race.* Richmond: Virginia Bureau of Vital Statistics.

Polanyi, Karl. 1944. *The Great Transformation.* New York: Holt, Reinhart and Winston.

Pommersheim, Frank. 1995. *Braid of Feathers: American Indian Law and Contemporary Tribal Life.* Berkeley: University of California Press.

Porter, Frank W., ed. 1986. *Strategies for Survival: American Indians in the Eastern United States.* Westport CT: Greenwood Press.

Pratt, Raymond B. 1979. Tribal sovereignty and resource exploitation. *Southwest Economy and Society* 4 (3): 38–74.

Precourt, Walter. 1983. The image of Appalachian poverty. In Allen Batteau, ed., *Appalachia/America: Autonomy and Regional Dependence.* Lexington: University Press of Kentucky, 86–111.

Prucha, Francis P. 1962. *American Indian Policy in the Formative Years: The Indian Trade and Intercourse Acts, 1790–1834.* Lincoln: University of Nebraska Press.

————. 1976. *American Indian Policy in Crisis: Christian Reformers and the Indian, 1865–1900.* Lincoln: University of Nebraska Press.

————. ed. 1990. *Documents of United States Indian Policy.* 2nd ed. Lincoln: University of Nebraska Press.

Raltz, Karl B. and Richard Ulack. 1984. *Appalachia, a Regional Geography: Land, People, and Development.* Boulder CO: Westview Press.

Rasmussen, Barbara. 1996. The politics of the property tax in West Virginia. *Journal of Appalachian Studies* 2 (1): 141–47.

Rice, Horace R. 1991. *The Buffalo Ridge Cherokee: The Color and Culture of a Virginia Indian Community.* Madison Heights VA: BRC Books.

Rice, Otis K. 1970. *The Allegheny Frontier: West Virginia Beginnings, 1730–1830.* Lexington: University Press of Kentucky.

Rothberg, Diane. 1980. The mothers of the nation: Seneca resistance to Quaker influence. In Mona Etiene and Eleanor Leacock, eds., *Women and Colonization: Anthropological Perspectives*. New York: Praeger, 63–86.

Rountree, Helen C. 1977. The Indians of Virginia. In Walter A. Williams, ed. *Southeastern Indians Since the Removal Era*. Athens: University of Georgia Press, 27–48.

Ryan, Joan, and Robinson, Michael. 1996. Community participatory research: Two views from Arctic Institute practitioners. *Practicing Anthropology* 18 (4): 7–11.

Sahlins, Marshall. 1965. On the sociology of primitive exchange. In M. Brenton, ed., *The Relevance of Models for Social Anthropology*. London: Tavistack.

Saks, Eva. 1988. Representing miscegenation law. *Raritan* 8: 39–69.

Salstrom, Paul. 1994. *Appalachia's Path to Dependency: Rethinking a Region's Economic History, 1730–1940*. Lexington: University Press of Kentucky.

———. 1996. Appalachia's informal economy and the transition to capitalism. *Journal of Appalachian Studies* 2 (2): 213–33.

Salstrom, Paul and Hollenhorst, Steve. 1994. Increasing dependency and the touristization rag. *Appalachian Journal* 21 (4): 410–20.

Savage, Lon. 1990. *Thunder in the Mountains: The West Virginia Mine War, 1920–21*. Pittsburgh: University of Pittsburgh Press.

Schaeffer, Claude E. 1942. The Tutelo Indians in Pennsylvania history. In Frank G. Speck, and George Herzog, *The Tutelo Spirit Adoption Ceremony: Reclothing the Living in the Name of the Dead*. Harrisburg: Pennsylvania Historical Commission, v–xvii.

Schneider, Harold K. 1989. *Economic Man: The Anthropology of Economics*. Salem wi: Sheffield Publishing Co.

Schutz, Alfred. 1970. *On Phenomenology and Social Relations* (Helmut R. Wagner, ed.). Chicago: University of Chicago Press.

Scott, Catherine V. 1995. *Gender and Development: Rethinking Modernization and Dependency Theory*. Boulder co: Lynne Rienner Publishers.

Shifflett, Crandall A. 1982. *Patronage and Poverty in the Tobacco South: Louisa County, Virginia, 1860–1900*. Knoxville: University of Tennessee Press.

Sider, Gerald. 1993. *Lumbee Indian Histories: Race, Ethnicity, and Indian Identity in the Southern United States*. New York: Cambridge University Press.

———. 1994. Identity as history: Ethnohistory, ethnogenesis, and ethnocide in the southeastern United States. *Identities* 1 (1): 109–22.

Simon, Michael Paul Patrick. 1986. Indigenous Peoples in developed frag-
ment societies: A comparative analysis of internal colonialism in the
United States, Canada, and Northern Ireland. Ph.D. diss., University of
Arizona.

Simon, Richard M. 1980. The labor force and uneven development: The Appalachian coalfields, 1880–1930. *International Journal of Urban and Regional Research* 4: 46–71.

———. 1981. Uneven development and the case of West Virginia: Going
beyond the colonialism model. *Appalachian Journal* 8 (3): 165–86.

Smith, J. David. 1992. Dr. Plecker's assault on the Monacan Indians: Legal
racism and documentary genocide. *Lynch's Ferry: A Journal of Local History* 5 (1): 22–25.

———. 1993. *The Eugenic Assault on America: Scenes in Red, White, and Black.*
Fairfax VA: George Mason University Press.

Smith, John. 1819 [1629]. *The True Travels, Adventures, and Observations of
Captain John Smith, etc.* 2 vols. Richmond VA: Franklin Press.

Speck, Frank G. 1935. Siouan tribes of the Carolinas as known from Catawba,
Tutelo, and documentary sources. *American Anthropologist* 37: 201–25.

Speck, Frank G., and George Herzog. 1942. *The Tutelo Spirit Adoption Ceremony: Reclothing the Living in the Name of the Dead.* Harrisburg: Pennsylvania Historical Commission.

Spicer, Edward H. 1962. *Cycles of Conquest: The Impact of Spain, Mexico, and
the United States on the Indians of the Southwest, 1533–1960.* Tucson: University of Arizona Press.

———. 1971. Persistent cultural systems: A comparative study of identity
systems that can adapt to contrasting environments. *Science* 174 (46):
795–800.

———. 1980. *The Yaquis: A Cultural History.* Tucson: University of Arizona
Press.

———. 1994. The nations of a state. In Karl Kroeber, ed., *American Indian
Persistence and Resurgence.* Durham NC: Duke University Press, 27–49.

Stanard, William G., ed. 1907a. Letter from the Commissioners for Suppressing Bacon's Rebellion to the Governor and Assembly of Virginia,
February 27, 1676–77. *Virginia Magazine of History and Biography* 14 (3):
271–77.

———. 1907b. Treaty Between Virginia and the Indians, 1677. *Virginia
Magazine of History and Biography* 14 (3): 289–97.

Stavenhagen, R. 1965. Class, colonialism, and acculturation. *Studies in Comparative International Development* 1 (7): 53–77.

Stewart, Kathleen. 1996. *A Space on the Side of the Road: Cultural Poetics in an "Other" America.* Princeton NJ: Princeton University Press.

Stoler, Ann L. 1989. Making empire respectable: The politics of race and morality in Twentieth-century colonial cultures. *American Ethnologist* 16 (4): 634–60.

Strachey, William. 1849. *The Historie of Travile into Virginia Britania.* London: Hakluyt.

Striplin, E. F. Pat. 1981. *The Norfolk and Western: A History.* Roanoke VA: The Norfolk and Western Railway Co.

Stull, Donald, and Jean J. Schensol, eds. 1987. *Collaborative Research and Social Change: Applied Anthropology in Action.* Boulder CO: Westview Press.

Sturtevant, William. 1971. Cree into Seminole: North American Indians. In Eleanor Leacock and Nancy Lurie, eds., *Historical Perspective.* New York: Random House, 92–128.

Swanton, John R. 1936. Early history of the eastern Siouan tribes. In *Essays in Anthropology Presented to A. L. Kroeber.* Berkeley: University of California Press, 371–81.

———. 1943. Siouan tribes and the Ohio Valley. *American Anthropologist* 45: 49–66.

Tams, William Purviance, Jr. 1963. *The Smokeless Coal Fields of West Virginia: A Brief History.* Morgantown: West Virginia University Library.

Thomas, Robert K. 1966/67a. Colonialism: Classic and internal. *New University Thought* 4 (4): 37–44.

———. 1966/67b. Powerless politics. *New University Thought* 4 (4): 44–53.

———. 1990. The taproots of peoplehood. In Daphne J. Anderson, ed., *Getting to the Heart of the Matter: Papers and Letters of Cherokee Anthropologist Robert K. Thomas.* Vancouver: Native Ministries Consortium.

Tooker, William Wallace. 1895. The Algonquian appellatives of Siouan tribes in Virginia. *The American Anthropologist* 8: 376–92.

Turner, Victor. 1969. *The Ritual Process.* Chicago: Aldine.

United Mine Workers v. Red Jacket Coal and Coke Co. 1927. 18 F2d 839.

United States, American Indian Policy Review Commission. 1977. *Final Report, May 17, 1977.* Washington DC: Government Printing Office.

United States, Bureau of Mines. 1950. *Report of the Health and Safety Division, Fiscal Year 1949* (IC 7562). Washington DC: Government Printing Office.

United States, Bureau of the Census. 1811–1991. *Census of the United States.* Washington DC: Government Printing Office.

———. 1841. *Compendium of Enumeration of Inhabitants and Statistics: The Population, Wealth, and Resources of the Country.* Washington DC: Government Printing Office.

———. 1864. *The Eighth Census of the United States: Agriculture.* Washington DC: Government Printing Office.

———. 1883. *Report on the Products of Agriculture as Returned at the Tenth Census.* Washington DC: Government Printing Office.

———. 1895. *Report on Statistics of Agriculture at the Eleventh Census, 1890.* Washington DC: Government Printing Office.

———. 1902. *Twelfth Census of the United States: Agriculture.* Vol. 5. Washington DC: Government Printing Office.

———. 1913. *Thirteenth Census of the United States: Agriculture.* Vol. 7. Washington DC: Government Printing Office.

———. 1925. *United States Census of Agriculture, 1925.* Washington DC: Government Printing Office.

———. 1974. *Statistical Abstract of the United States, 1974.* Washington DC: Government Printing Office.

United States, Department of Agriculture. 1935. *Economic and Social Problems and Conditions of the Southern Appalachians.* Miscellaneous Publication No. 205. Washington DC: Government Printing Office.

United States, Office of the Federal Register. 1978. Federal Acknowledgement of Indian Tribes. *Federal Register* 43 (September 5): 39362–64.

United States Senate. 1922. *West Virginia Coal Fields: Personal Views of Senator Kenyon, and Views of Senators Sterling, Phipps, and Warren* (Sen. Rep. 450, 67th Cong., 2nd Sess.). Washington DC: Government Printing Office.

———. 1925. *Report of the United States Coal Commission.* (Sen. Doc. 195, 68th Cong., 2nd Sess.). Washington DC: Government Printing Office.

van den Bergne, Pierre. 1978. Education, class, and ethnicity in southern Peru: Revolutionary colonialism. In Phillip G. Altbach and Gail P. Kelley, eds., *Education and Colonialism:Comparative Perspectives.* New York: McKay.

Vest, Jay Hansford. 1992. The Buzzard Rocks: Saponi-Monacan traditions from Hico, Virginia. *Lynch's Ferry: A Journal of Local History* 5 (1): 26–31.

Virginia Assembly. 1924. The Virginia Racial Integrity Law, 1924. *Acts and Resolutions of the General Assembly of the State of Virginia* No. 5. Richmond: Superintendent of Public Archives.

———. 1944. *Acts and Resolutions of the General Assembly of the State of Virginia* ch. 52. Richmond: Superintendent of Public Archives.

Virginia Department of Labor and Industry. 1988. *The Child Labor Laws of Virginia*. Richmond: Virginia Department of Labor and Industry, Division of State Labor Law Administration.

Virginia Historical Society. 1883–91. *Collections of the Virginia Historical Society* n.s. 3–10.

Wailes, Bertha. 1928. Backwards Virginians: A further study of the Win Tribe. Master's thesis, University of Virginia.

Wallerstein, Immanuel. 1974. Dependence in an independent world: The limited possibilities for transformation within the capitalist world economy. *African Studies Review* 17: 1–26.

———. 1975. Class formation in the capitalist world-economy. *Politics and Society* 5: 367–75.

———. 1983. *Historical Capitalism*. London: Verso.

Walls, David S. 1976. Central Appalachia: A peripheral region within an advanced capitalist society. *Journal of Sociology and Social Welfare* 4: 232–47.

———. 1977. On the naming of Appalachia. In J. W. Williamson, ed., *An Appalachian Symposium: Essays Written in Honor of Cratis D. Williams*. Boone NC: Appalachian Consortium Press.

Washburn, Wilcomb E. 1957. *The Governor and the Rebel: A History of Bacon's Rebellion in Virginia*. Chapel Hill: The University of North Carolina Press.

Watts, Ann DeWitt. 1983. Does the Appalachian Regional Commission really represent a region? In Bruce Ergood and Bruce E. Kuhre, eds., *Appalachia: Social Context Past and Present*. 2nd ed. Dubuque IA: Kendall/Hunt, 225–33.

Wells, C. D. 1889. *Something About Wyoming County, West Virginia*. Oceana WV (privately published promotional pamphlet).

West Virginia Department of Transportation. n.d. Official State Highway Map. Charleston.

West Virginia Geological Survey. 1915. *Report, 1915: Wyoming and McDowell Counties*. Charleston: West Virginia Geological Survey.

West Virginia State Department of Mines. 1886. *Fourth Annual Report*. Charleston: West Virginia Dept. of Mines.

———. 1910. *Annual Report, 1910*. Charleston: West Virginia Dept. of Mines.

Whisnant, David E. 1994. *Modernizing the Mountaineer: People, Power, and Planning in Appalachia.* Knoxville: University of Tennessee Press.

White, Richard. 1983. *The Roots of Dependency: Subsistence, Environment, and Social Change Among the Choctaws, Pawnees, and Navajos.* Lincoln: University of Nebraska Press.

Whitehead, Captain Edgar. 1896. Amherst County Indians. *Richmond Times Dispatch* (April 19).

Wilkins, David E. 1993. Modernization, colonialism, dependency: How appropriate are these models for providing an explanation of North American Indian underdevelopment? *Ethnic and Racial Studies* 16 (3): 390–419.

Williams, Cratis D. 1983. Who are the southern mountaineers? In Bruce Ergood and Bruce E. Kuhre, eds., *Appalachia: Social Context Past and Present.* 2nd ed. Dubuque IA: Kendall/Hunt, 54–58.

Williams, John A. 1972. The New Dominion and the old: Antebellum and statehood politics as the background of West Virginia's 'Bourbon Democracy.' *West Virginia History* 33: 317–407.

———. 1976. *West Virginia and the Captains of Industry.* Morgantown: West Virginia University Press.

Winfree, R. Westwood. 1975. Monacan farm, Powhatan County, Virginia. *Quarterly Bulletin of the Archaeological Society of Virginia* 29 (2): 65–93.

Wolf, Eric R. 1997. *Europe and the People Without History.* 2nd ed. Berkeley: University of California Press.

Woods, Edgar. 1901. *Albemarle County.* Charlottesville VA: Mitchie Co.

Wyoming County Chamber of Commerce. n.d. *Wyoming County, West Virginia: Points of Interest* (promotional pamphlet).

Yancey, Robert F. 1935. *Lynchburg and Its Neighbors.* Richmond VA: J. W. Fergeson and Sons.

Zimolzak, Chester E. 1977. Changing ownership patterns in the West Virginia coal industry: Oligopoly and its geographic impact. In Howard G. Adkins, Steve Ewing, and Chester E. Zimolzak, eds., *West Virginia and Appalachia.* Dubuque IA: Kendall/Hunt, 158–86.

Branham v. Burton, 113
British. *See* Great Britain
Brown v. Board of Education, 114,
    117, 270
buffalo, 32
Buffalo Creek, 245
Bum Chums, 95
Bushnell, David, 33, 50
Byrd, Robert C., 252
Byrd, William, 44, 52

CAG. *See* Council of Appalachian
    Governors
Camden, Johnson N., 155–56
Caperton, Gaston W., 245, 289 n.3
capital, 158, 172
capitalism, 13, 123, 176–77, 180,
    258; colonial, 67, 147; and cul-
    ture, 2, 22–23; and dependency,
    82–83; poverty and, 237–38
CAPS. *See* Community Action Pro-
    grams
Captains of the Episcopal Army, 90
captive mines, 231
cash: reliance on, 223, 234, 236,
    260
cash crops, 149
caste system, 69, 262
Catawbas, 40
cattle, 79, 80, 142
Cayuga Nation, 45
ccc, 226
census, 68; of Amherst County,
    54–56, 107, 109–10; farming, 69,
    70; of Wyoming County, 141,
    148–49
Central Competitive Coal Field,
    206

Chafin, Don, 203
Charleston (wv), 174
Cherokees, 37, 89, 136
Chesapeake and Ohio (C&O) Rail-
    road, 163, 172, 173
Chicago Lumber Company, 168
children, 98–99, 209
churches: community role of,
    145–46, 235
Civil Rights movement, 7, 117
Civil War, 144, 152, 153–54, 161,
    162
Clark and Company, E. W., 165
class structure: and coal industry,
    219–20
Clear Fork, 137, 143
coal camps. *See* company
    towns/camps
Coal Codes, 227
coal industry, 6, 36, 250; absentee
    ownership of, 241–42; Appala-
    chian, 9, 72–73; class structure
    and, 219–20; company towns/
    camps and, 191–98; dependency
    and, 267–68; division of labor
    and, 220–21; employment in,
    177–78, 180, 184–89, 190–91,
    204–5, 232–33; environmental
    damage of, 236–37, 245; federal
    investigation of, 207–8; federal
    regulation of, 214–15; Great De-
    pression and, 213, 216–22; labor
    costs and, 230–31; labor reform
    and, 215–16; land speculation
    and, 163, 165; and local econ-
    omies, 238, 239–40; mechaniza-
    tion in, 227–29; mine safety and,
    189–80; politics and, 198–201,

elections: coal companies and,
194–95
elites: coal industry and, 194,
219–20
Elkins, Stephen B., 156
Ellis, A. J., 168
employment, 82, 94, 182; in Amherst County, 122, 123, 266–67,
268; in coal industry, 177–78,
180, 184–89, 190–91, 192,
194–95, 196–97, 204–5, 206–7,
213, 232–33; during Depression,
216–17; of Monacans, 75–76,
123–24; unions and, 201–3, 208;
of women, 220–21; in Wyoming
County, 180, 239, 252–53
energy crisis, 240
English, 140
environment, 170–71, 196, 236–37,
245, 273
Episcopal Church, 85, 126; mission
of, 89–97; social action by,
119–20; and tribal business,
120–21
erosion, 170, 236
Escobar, Arturo, 13, 23
Estabrook, Arthur A., 94, 107–8
ethnicity, 7, 64, 128–29
ethnogenesis, 63–64; Monacan,
87–88, 128
eugenics, 94, 104–5, 110, 116–17,
131–32, 264
Eugenics Records Office, 94
Euro-Americans: in Amherst
County, 52–54, 262, 266; subsistence strategies of, 144–45; in
Wyoming County, 137, 138–39,
140
Eurocentrism, 24, 95, 286 n.5

Europe and the People without History
(Wolf), 24
Europeans, 177; colonial laws of,
37–38; contact with, 34–35, 39;
exploration by, 35–36; on upper
James River, 51–53; warfare and,
36–37
Evans, Lewis, 50
exchange: interhousehold, 99, 233,
234–35
exploration: European, 35–36,
38–39

Fairchild Corporation, 241
Fair Labor Standards Act, 78, 79
families, 143, 146, 153, 193, 255,
258; land ownership and, 183–84,
217, 272; land title and, 141–42;
subsistence gardens of, 97–98
Fanon, Frantz: *The Wretched of the
Earth*, 110
farmers, farms, 142, 225; in Amherst County, 55, 69–70; and coal
industry, 185–86; land speculators and, 158–59, 181–82; subsistence, 8, 72, 73, 97–99, 144–45,
223–24, 234, 236, 260; in Wyoming County, 148–49. *See also*
agriculture
Farmers Home Administration, 240
Fayette County, 172
federal government, 127–28, 240,
251–52; development programs
of, 246–51; race issues and, 114,
116, 117, 269–70; relief programs of, 222–26
Ferguson, James, 152–53
feudalism, 141; in Amherst County,
66–67, 260, 264

integration, 97, 267; public schools, 114–16

intermarriage, 61, 64, 68, 104; Indian-white, 52, 57–58, 61; land speculation and, 163, 165; "white integrity" and, 105–6

Irish Creek, 52

Iroquoian tribes, 35, 39, 40, 41, 44, 45, 47

Iroquois, 124, 137–38

Iroquois Confederacy, 50, 56, 64

Iroquois League, 44, 48

Irwin, Jesse, 166

Island Creek Coal Company, 202, 241, 245

Issue, 68–69, 110, 134, 287 n.7

Italians, 177

Itman, 196, *plate 5*

Itman Mine, 176, 219, *plate 6*

James, James Elwood, 214

James River, 37, 50; Euro-Americans on, 51–53, 55, 261

Jefferson, Thomas, 50, 58, 286 n.4

Jim Crow laws, 85

job training program (JTPA), 120

Johns, Dorothy, 106, 107

Johns, Robert, 52, 61

Johns, Samuel, 50–51

Johns, Thomas, 61

Johns, William, 52, 61

Johns, William "Will," 61

Johns family, 61–62

Johnson, Lyndon B., 247, 249

Johns Settlement, 61–62, 100, 126

JTPA. *See* job training program

Kanawha and James Turnpike, 150–51

Kanawha Canal, 55, 150

Kanawha County, 172, 203

Kanawha Field, 174, 202–3

Kanawha Ring, 155

Kanawha Valley, 151, 152

Kennedy, John F., 247

Kimball, Frederick, 165

kinship: in Wyoming County, 143, 254–55. *See also* families

Kopperston, 196

labor, 87, 124, 182, 209, 260; in coal industry, 72–73, 172, 184–89, 190–91, 192, 194–95, 196–97, 204–5, 228, 230–31; cooperative, 99, 235; minimum wages and, 78–79; Monacan, 7, 22, 67, 262, 264, 267, 272; orchard industry and, 70–72, 266, 272; organization of, 200–207, 215; tenant farmers as, 66–67; unions and, 201–3, 208; wage, 75–76, 211; women and, 220–21

labor reform, 204, 205, 206, 213; New Deal and, 214–16, 227, 268, 270–71, 278

LaLone, Mary B., 233, 234, 235

land: agricultural, 54, 225, 261–62; control of, 213, 236, 241–42; and identity, 129–30; livestock and, 79–80; sales of, 179, 217; speculation in, 163, 165, 181–82, 288 n.1; taxation of, 143, 224; timber industry and, 168, 169; titles to, 138, 140–42, 158–59

land grants, 139, 163, 166, 169, 288 n.1

land ownership, 20, 21, 95, 211–12, 217, 288 n.2; absentee, 8, 20,

trucking, 252
truck mines, 231
Tucker, John Randolph, 108
Turner, Nat, 60
Turner, Victor, 131
Tuscaroras, 35, 42
Tutelo Confederacy, 26, 30
Tutelos, 26, 27, 28, 34, 37, 38, 39,
46, 47, 48, 50, 51, 64, 100, 285
n.2; at Fort Christanna, 42, 43,
44, 45
Twin Falls State Park, 246–47

Ulster, 140–41
UMWA. *See* United Mine Workers of
America
Underwood, Cecil, 245, 289 n.2
unemployment, 214, 228, 239, 269
unions, 268; coal industry and, 187,
201–3, 205, 206–7, 215, 227,
228–29, 266; Wyoming County
and, 208–10, 231–32
United Mine Workers of America
(UMWA), 200, 228; dependency
and, 229–30; federal politics and,
206–7; leadership of, 229–30;
strikes and, 202–3; West Virginia
and, 201–2, 205, 214, 288 n.4;
Wyoming County and, 231–32,
266
U.S. Bureau of Indian Affairs, 270
U.S. Bureau of Mines, 190
U.S. Circuit Court of Appeals, 206,
207
U.S. Coal Commission, 173–74, 192,
193, 207–8
U.S. Department of Agriculture, 225
U.S. Steel Corporation, 173, 208,
231, 252–53

U.S. Supreme Court: on desegregation, 114, 117, 270; on yellow
dog contracts, 206, 207
urbanization: in Amherst County,
80, 82

values, 19, 238
Virginia, 3, 4, 114, 138; colonial
laws of, 58–59; colonization of,
260–61; copper trade in, 33–34;
discrimination in, 85–88; education in, 151–52; genocidal laws
of, 37–38, 46–47, 262; miscegenation laws in, 22, 105–7, 108–9;
and mixed-race people, 84–85;
and Monacans, 7, 15, 50– 51,
263–64, 269; Native Americans
in, 35, 38–39, 56, 286 n.6;
Siouan-speaking tribes in, 26–28,
30–32; transportation in, 150–
51; treaties and, 41, 42; warfare
in, 36–37, 40; and West Virginia,
150, 151–52; and Wyoming
County, 160–61. *See also* Amherst
County
Virginia Company, 260
Virginia Council of Indians, 121–22
Virginia Indian Company, 43
Virginian Railway, 167, 175, 176,
180
Virginia Ordinance of Secession,
153
Virginia's Vanished Race (Plecker),
104
Volunteers in Service to America
(VISTA), 248, 289 n.4
voting rights, 86, 262

wages, 71, 94, 223; agricultural,

WPA. *See* Work Progress Administration
The Wretched of the Earth (Fanon),
110
Wyco, 195
Wyoming Coal Company, 176, 195
Wyoming County, 4, 6, 7–8, 22, 135,
146, 151, 237, 239, 257, 272, 273,
map 4; Civil War and, 152–53;
class structure in, 219–20; coal
industry in, 171, 174, 175, 176,
177–78, 186–87, 190–91, 210–11,
213, 216–22, 227–29, 262–63,
264, 289 n.1; colonialism and,
259, 261, 276, 278–79, 280, 281;
community in, 19, 260; company
towns in, 194, 195–97; dependency in, 214, 226–27, 267–68; division of labor in, 143–44; economy in, 20, 149–50, 179–80, 240,
252–55, 268–69, 282; environment of, 136–37; Euro-Americans
in, 138–39; farming in, 147–49;

federal programs and, 248, 250;
formation of, 146, 152; Great
Depression and, 223–27; infrastructure of, 240–41; interhousehold exchange in, 234–35; investment in, 166–67; isolation of,
160–61, 162–63; and kinship,
254–55; land ownership in, 181–
82; land titles in, 141–42; New
Deal and, 225–26; nonmarket
economy of, 233–34; politics
and, 152–53, 160, 198–200, 251–
52, 265–66, 270–71, 288 n.3; remoteness of, 146–47; Scotch-
Irish in, 9, 142–43; as suburb,
253–54; taxation in, 143, 242–
43; timber industry in, 167, 168–
69; tourism in, 246–47; unions
in, 208–10, 231–32
Wyoming Land Company, 176
Wyoming News, 166

Yablonski, Joseph (Jock), 230

Printed in the USA
CPSIA information can be obtained
at www.ICGtesting.com
CBHW051255181024
16057CB00005B/647